CARIBOU
and the North

A Shared Future

MONTE HUMMEL ~ JUSTINA C. RAY

Forewords by Robert Redford and Stephen Kakfwi
Sketches by Robert Bateman

DUNDURN PRESS
TORONTO

Library and Archives Canada Cataloguing in Publication

Hummel, Monte, 1946-
   Caribou and the north : a shared future / by Monte Hummel and Justina C. Ray ;
forewords by Robert Redford and Stephen Kakfwi ; sketches by Robert Bateman.

Includes index.
ISBN 978-1-55002-839-3

   1. Caribou. 2. Caribou--Conservation. 3. Endangered species. 4. Wildlife conservation.
I. Bateman, Robert, 1930- II. Ray, Justina C. III. Title.

QL737.U55H82 2008   599.65'8   C2008-903944-0

1   2   3   4   5   12   11   10   09   08

Conseil des Arts du Canada Canada Council for the Arts Canadä ONTARIO ARTS COUNCIL CONSEIL DES ARTS DE L'ONTARIO

We acknowledge the support of the **Canada Council for the Arts** and the **Ontario Arts Council** for our publishing program. We also acknowledge the financial support of the **Government of Canada** through the **Book Publishing Industry Development Program** and **The Association for the Export of Canadian Books**, and the **Government of Ontario** through the **Ontario Book Publishers Tax Credit program**, and the **Ontario Media Development Corporation**.

Care has been taken to trace the ownership of copyright material used in this book. The authors and the publisher welcome any information enabling them to rectify any references or credits in subsequent editions.

J. Kirk Howard, President

Editor: Barry Jowett
Copy-editor: Andrea Waters
Text design: Jennifer Scott
Jacket design: Erin Mallory
Printer: Friesens

Front jacket image: Caribou from the Beverly herd in the early fall crossing the Thelon River, Northwest Territories. © Steven Barger
Back jacket image: Caribou near Cape Henrietta Maria on Hudson Bay in northern Ontario. © Ken Abraham, Ontario Ministry of Natural Resources
Monte Hummel's author photo by Sherry Pettigrew
Justina C. Ray's author photo by Jay Malcolm

Printed and bound in Canada.
www.dundurn.com

Mixed Sources

Product group from well-managed forests and other controlled sources
www.fsc.org Cert no. SW-COC-1271
© 1996 Forest Stewardship Council

FSC

Dundurn Press
3 Church Street, Suite 500
Toronto, Ontario, Canada
M5E 1M2

Gazelle Book Services Limited
White Cross Mills
High Town, Lancaster, England
LA1 4XS

Dundurn Press
2250 Military Road
Tonawanda, NY
U.S.A. 14150

TABLE OF CONTENTS

SECTION ONE:
THE IMPORTANCE OF CARIBOU

SECTION TWO:
PRESSURES ON CARIBOU: PAST, PRESENT, AND FUTURE

SECTION THREE:
KEY STEPS FOR CONSERVING CARIBOU

SECTION FOUR:
EXPERT PROFILES OF DIFFERENT KINDS OF CARIBOU

LIST OF MAPS

TO GLEN DAVIS, who was cruelly and inexplicably taken from us in Toronto on May 18, 2007. This book was Glen's idea and, as he did for so many other conservation projects, he generously donated funds to make it possible.

Glen was a friend and fellow traveller. He loved wild country and everything associated with it, especially bears, wolves … and caribou.

We hope our book contributes to Glen's unforgettable conservation legacy, not just looking back, but as Glen would have wanted it — making a difference for the future.

Tyler Garnham

Above: Glen Davis on the Firth River, Northwest Territories, 2006.

Below: Glen Davis in the Arctic National Wildlife Refuge, Alaska, 2005.

Monte Hummel

FOREWORD

THE POWER OF NATURE has inspired me in a profound fashion throughout my life. It is the essence of beautiful wild lands, teeming with extraordinary wildlife, which has always been natural perfection for me; I can never imagine why anyone would do anything to alter it, to endanger it. Sadly, that is not the case with caribou. In the Arctic National Wildlife Refuge in Alaska, the coastal calving grounds of the Porcupine caribou herd are at extremely high risk from industrial development.

A diligent coalition of organizations and individuals has so far prevailed in its protection, but it is only a temporary victory, as these important calving grounds are still not permanently safeguarded. Until we make oil and gas drilling impossible, this most sensitive of wildlife habitats, and thus the caribou, will remain profoundly vulnerable.

The Porcupine herd is made up of barren-ground caribou, shared by both Canada and the United States, but these represent only one of the many kinds of caribou that used to move over half the area of North America.

Now, as this book's title suggests, *all* caribou — barren-ground, mountain, and woodland — are confined to "the North," specifically northern Canada and Alaska. So important are caribou to this North that it would be hard to find a wildlife species more central to northern ecosystems and human cultures.

This is the shared future that constitutes the theme of this book. Caribou and the North form a fateful bond. In fact, it could be said that "So go the caribou, so goes the North; and so goes the North, so go the caribou."

The authors and many contributors remind us that, although most of us live in the relatively settled and crowded southern parts of North America, we are now making decisions regarding the fate of some of the last remaining wild parts. We are making decisions regarding some of the last great places on Earth and some of the mightily great species on Earth, like the amazing caribou.

Some of us will never live there, or even visit, but it is still part of being an American or Canadian to know that big parts of our continent thrive in a natural state.

And not to be overlooked are those folks who still *do* live in caribou country. Time and again, they have spoken up, and never more eloquently than when they feel the caribou are threatened. Consequently, caribou have helped modern conservationists find common cause with local residents, supporting a concern that is championed and led by the people who live there.

It is my sincere hope that this book will serve to raise awareness of the importance of caribou wherever they are found; to fairly present the past and present threats to these crucial animals; and to inspire new actions to ensure that their shared future with the northern land is one we can all be proud of.

ROBERT REDFORD—
SUNDANCE, UTAH

FOREWORD

NORTH AMERICAN DENE peoples represent one of the oldest civilizations on Earth. Yet the rest of our country and the world haven't really known or understood much about us! Over the past fifty years, dramatic changes have brought my people from isolated seasonal hunting and fishing camps to permanent communities, such as my hometown on the Arctic Circle. But mainstream urban life is still a very faraway reality. Thousands of miles of wide-open spaces are much closer to home. In our culture it is still common to hear people say, "Our land is our life."

One of our elders expressed his own version of this simply and powerfully to Mr. Justice Thomas Berger in the 1970s inquiry into a Mackenzie Valley gas pipeline: "If you take care of the land, it will take care of you. If you destroy the land, it will destroy you." I was raised on that message. It helped define both me and my life's work as I moved from young community activist to president of our Aboriginal Dene Nation to premier of the Northwest Territories.

There were others in those rooms when our people spoke to Berger. They heard and understood as few southerners have. They understood that the northern reaches of our planet are more than just one of the Earth's last great wildernesses; so much more than a collection of isolated world heritage sites and national parklands. They understood the fundamental, interdependent relationship between northern lands, northern Aboriginal peoples, and the caribou that roam those lands and sustain those peoples. If the caribou are destroyed, we are destroyed as a people.

Our caribou know no boundaries. They claim the entire North, moving freely from one state, province, territory, or country to another. As national and international neighbours, we share our caribou and must work together to take care of them. We also share in our understanding that the things that threaten caribou know no boundaries. We *all* need to understand that.

We get to work with many people over our careers. We get to work with few people throughout our careers. I have had that good fortune with Monte Hummel. He was one of those other people in the room during the Berger inquiry. His World Wildlife Fund work has been so compatible with the vision northern peoples have of themselves and their natural resources. From the south, he has come north often, to more parts of the North than most northerners. His mission has been to teach others what he has seen and learned, and to act. It has been an excellent collaboration of ideas, passion, and purpose.

The wealth of scientific knowledge that the Wildlife Conservation Society brings to the table is also important, especially through Justina Ray's work on wildlife (including wolverines and caribou) with boreal forest communities.

This book bears witness to the respectful intelligence and deep concern the authors bring to their understanding of the North, its peoples, and its majestic caribou herds. I am honoured to encourage people all over the continent and the world to roam our homelands alongside the caribou though these beautiful and important pages.

Stephen Kakfwi, former premier, Northwest Territories
Denendeh, Canada

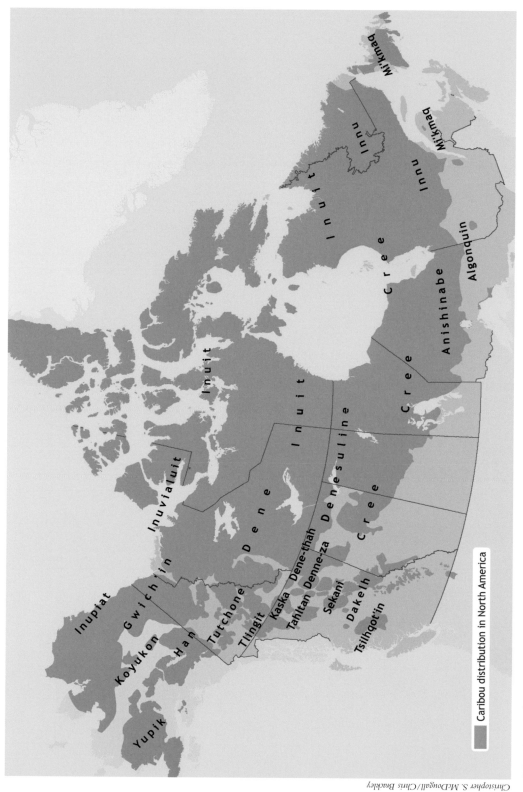

Map 0.1. *Aboriginal peoples and caribou distribution in North America.*

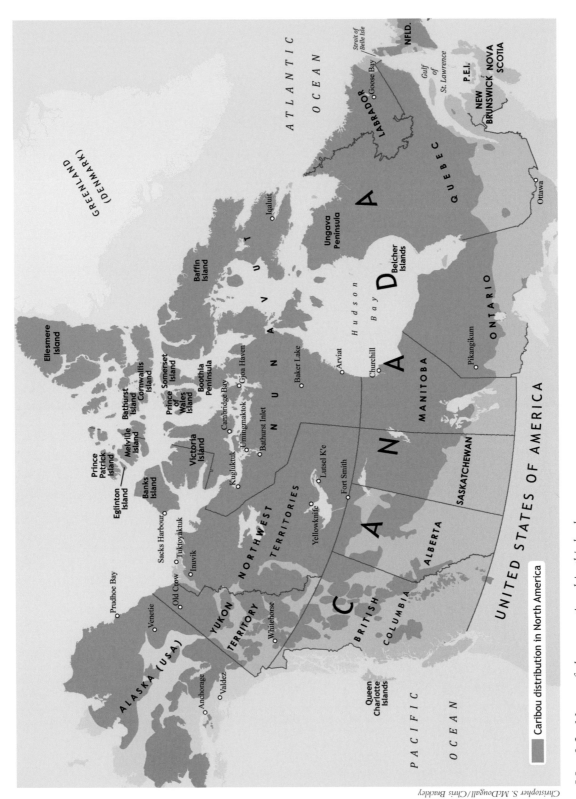

Map 0.2. *Names of places mentioned in this book.*

Caribou distribution in North America

INTRODUCTION

Why Caribou, Why the North,
Why a Shared Future?

A BOOK SHOULD begin with a story …

A university-based ecologist has been invited by a Dene community to speak to them about different kinds of protected areas, because they are concerned about what's happening around them.

The professor has arrived with a PowerPoint presentation and laser pointer. He speaks too quickly, causing the Chipewyan translator to struggle to keep up with him. But the community and band council members patiently let him go on without interruption — a courtesy traditionally extended to whomever has the floor.

He's in full flight now, explaining various science-based criteria for establishing protected areas, including "representativeness," which is based on "identifying and capturing enduring features of the landscape." These features are derived from "topographic relief and the origin of parent materials," followed by "physiographic and pedological characteristics" — all essential to different aspects of "reserve design." Any questions so far?

Silence.

Undeterred, the lecturer now swings into "biota" that should also be considered, their "floristic and faunal attributes," and "related areas critical for wildlife, such as key habitats for caribou."

The audience perks up. The Chief, who has been biding her time, then asks on behalf of everyone, "Caribou? Did you say something about areas important for caribou?"

"Yes."

"Why didn't you just say so? We're definitely interested in protecting *them*!"

Different versions of this story have been repeated in one form or another right across the North, illustrating how important caribou are to the people who live there. That's because this animal's comings and goings have meant the difference between life and death for certain Aboriginal peoples, such as the inland Inuit who faced a tragic die-off as recently as the 1950s, as well as for non-Aboriginal visitors, such as Englishman John Hornby and his two companions, who died of starvation in the spring of 1927 when they couldn't find caribou along the Thelon River. Caribou are fundamental to many cultures across the circumpolar North, going back thousands of years. They sustain people, but they are revered for even more than the essentials of life, such as food and clothing. Caribou weave their way through stories of creation, values, and respect for the land itself. In these pages, you'll find moving testimony such as, "If the caribou die, then we die," "Caribou blood runs through my blood," and "Without caribou, we wouldn't have made it through."

If the Arctic wolf could speak, its sentiments would be much the same, as would those of many more living things. Because caribou animate tundra, forest, and mountain landscapes. They are positioned at the very centre of the food web in northern ecosystems. To regenerate, the great migratory herds flood over the Barren Lands in an unforgettable tide of life to bring thousands of calves into the world; mountain caribou seek the safety of higher elevations; solitary boreal forest caribou give birth unseen and alone on secluded islands. If the caribou are still there, chances are the land is still healthy. If they aren't, chances are there's trouble.

And trouble is what caribou are now experiencing. They've lost about a third of their original distribution in the boreal forests. They're showing up on species-at-risk lists as "endangered," "threatened," or "of special concern." Many of the normally abundant far northern herds are in widespread and dramatic decline. Those declines may or may not be part of the caribou's natural cycle. The problem is that we just do not know — but given widespread climate change and many other modern pressures on this species, we do know that the past may not be a secure guide to its future. More and more communities are reporting that they didn't see any caribou this year. Harvest quotas and reductions are not only proposed, but also generally accepted as necessary, even by those with a constitutionally entrenched right to hunt.

Trouble is also what's on the horizon in northern North America as its residents enter a new — some would say long overdue — economic era. There are plans for the largest energy projects the North has ever seen, with tens of billions of dollars already invested in gas fields, conventional oil reserves, pipelines, coal gasification, and oil sands. There is also the largest mineral rush in our history, including exploration, drilling, sampling, and active mining for diamonds, uranium, gold, and other minerals. All of this is now moving ahead in caribou country. As Robert Redford observes in the first Foreword, "So goes the North; so go the caribou; so go the caribou; so goes the North."

Yes, there's trouble. But this is not the end of the story by any means ...

First, although they are inherently quite vulnerable, caribou have also proven to be an impressively resilient species for some 2 million years, and they probably have some surprises in store for us yet. Therefore, not everyone agrees that caribou are in trouble. They point out that alarm bells have been sounded in the past, only to have caribou numbers rebound. And the North's natural resources have long been coveted and exploited, to at least some extent, over many centuries. Yet vast wilderness areas remain. So ... is what's happening now any different?

Second, even in the face of these new pressures, it's not as if we have no idea of what needs to be done to conserve caribou for the long term. In fact, many suggestions are sketched out in this book. And the resiliency of caribou holds out the promise of a positive response — if we take action while it can still make a difference. So if a caribou death knell is ever tolled, it will not be because we didn't know what to do, but because we chose not to do it.

Finally, it may just be that caribou are *so* culturally and ecologically important that they will serve not as *victims* but rather as *arbiters* of what happens to the North. Certainly no other animal has the same power or is better placed to inspire change. And since caribou above all need space — a lot of it — sorting things out for this species would have formative consequences for a huge expanse of land — everything from the boreal forest to the High Arctic Islands — which constitutes almost half the area of North America.

Improbable? Beyond hope? We don't think so; we don't think we can *afford* to think so. After all, if not caribou, then what other natural element of the North will bring humanity to its senses?

SECTION ONE

THE IMPORTANCE OF CARIBOU

INTRODUCTION

WHAT IS A CARIBOU?

Like all questions that at first sound pretty straightforward, this one can get complicated quickly. That's because, although they are all thought to be one *species*, there are definitely different *types* of caribou in North America and the world. Caribou are in fact known by many different names. So, when someone is referring loosely to "caribou," it is important to clarify exactly which caribou they are talking about. Boreal forest? Migratory tundra? Mountain? Peary? All of these occupy significantly different habitats; some are endangered, some are threatened, some are declining (perhaps within natural rates of population fluctuation, perhaps not); others appear to be stable, maybe even increasing.

It's not quite as simple as "A caribou is a caribou is a caribou," because the behaviour and conservation status of these animals vary greatly across their North American distribution. That said, they also have many things in common — above all, their wonderful adaptation to the North. To witness a caribou's tireless, smooth gait moving across a frozen boreal lake, streaming over the tundra, traversing mountain slopes, or wandering the icy High Arctic Islands is to witness evolution itself — an animal completely at home where few others would even venture, let alone thrive.

CHAPTER ONE

Some Basic Biology

THE DEER FAMILY

IN DRY BIOLOGICAL terms, the caribou is a large-bodied ungulate ("hoofed mammal"). More specifically, it belongs to the group called *Artiodactyla*, or even-toed ("cloven") hoofed animals, like deer, bison, goats, sheep, and swine, so called by virtue of the fact that the two crescent-shaped toes on each foot bear most of their weight, rather than one toe as with *Perrisodactyla*, the horse family.

Caribou are one of several members of the deer family that reside on the North American continent, joining moose, elk, and black-tailed, mule, and white-tailed deer. Caribou are distinguished from moose or deer by many features. For example, the antler shape is different: rather than the large palm that characterizes a moose, male caribou antlers have a distinct brow tine (also called a plough or shovel) over the nose. Smaller than moose or elk, caribou are also separated from most other deer species by their choice of habitat and diet. Caribou readily feed on and digest lichens, allowing them to flourish in high-elevation and tundra environments. They also prefer older coniferous forests and bog expanses where few moose, elk, or deer feel at home. Caribou share their range with moose in upland boreal forests, but it is rare to find both in the same locations. Moose prefer younger, more deciduous forests, especially recently burned areas and along waterways.

For those of us lucky enough to get really close to a caribou, it produces a distinct clicking sound when walking, caused by the tendons slipping over the bones of its feet. With their cloven hooves, caribou leave two-toed prints that are about as wide as they are long, and rounder in shape

Caribou

White-tailed deer

American elk

Moose

than those belonging to other deer species. Caribou have large dewclaws that leave distinct crescent-shaped marks with the hoofprints. In winter, caribou tracks are difficult to miss, especially when small groups walk across lakes, leaving behind braided trail ribbons that weave across the white expanses. There will also be trademark evidence of "cratering," digging for lichen and other food under snow and ice with those specially adapted hooves. Caribou have

Elena Jones

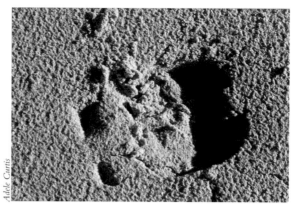

Adele Curtis

Left: Evidence of caribou "cratering" for food through the snow.

Above: Classic two-toed caribou track, with two "dewclaws" trailing behind.

even been known to crater on frozen lakes and ponds, searching for vegetation growing on small islands or muskrat mounds called "push-ups" out on these bodies of water.

REINDEER AND CARIBOU — WHAT'S THE DIFFERENCE?

Most North American and European children are introduced to caribou at an early age through Santa's reindeer, leaving them captivated by the idea that Santa Claus, and therefore Christmas, would be nothing without these magical creatures who guide him to and from the mythical North Pole. (Incidentally, some Aboriginal people regard hitching caribou to a sleigh as abusive and disrespectful, proving that one culture's magic can be another's mistake.)

Although they are referred to by different names, in fact domestic reindeer and wild caribou are considered to be a single species throughout the world — *Rangifer tarandus* — despite the fact that caribou actually encompass a remarkable variety of different forms of the same animal spanning the top of the world. But not even careful genetic scrutiny has provided sufficient evidence to call this animal anything other than one species across its global distribution. Indeed, any caribou can readily interbreed with another anywhere in the world and produce offspring that will be fertile and otherwise viable.

Generally speaking, the monikers "reindeer" and "caribou" are split not just between domestic and wild but also between European and North American members of the same species.

Wild European members of the species are more likely to be called "wild reindeer" than caribou. Reindeer and caribou reside fairly continually in most areas of the world's north, above the 62nd latitude in Eurasia and the 50th in North America. Most domesticated reindeer are found in northern Scandinavia and Russia, with some having been introduced to North America, particularly Alaska, as well as a small herd near Tuktoyuktuk in the Canadian western Arctic and another on the Belcher Islands in southern Hudson Bay. Although wild caribou populations of one kind or another occur throughout most of northern North America, the last remaining wild reindeer in Europe are now only found in portions of southern Norway, Greenland, and Iceland (where they were reintroduced more than two hundred years ago). In Russia, wild reindeer are widely distributed.

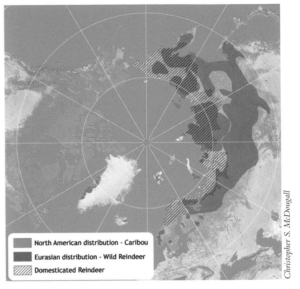

Christopher S. McDougall

Map 1.1. *Polar view of global caribou (Rangifer tarandus) distribution.*

BODY AND COAT — FIT FOR THE NORTH

Most adult caribou have dark brown coats with creamy white manes, necks, bellies, and rumps. The coat colour can, however, be quite variable, according to the season and even where the caribou are found. Most Peary caribou, in the High Arctic Islands, have an almost white winter coat, as do some individual caribou elsewhere in the North during fall and winter.

Adult caribou males, or bulls, have large and massive bodies, while the adult females, or cows, are generally smaller, with a more slender physique. All caribou have relatively short furry ears, a short furry tail, long noses with a keen sense of smell, and well-furred faces. They have long legs and are capable of running at high speeds, individually or as a group, sustained by unusually large hearts for their body size. Young calves can keep up with their mother within hours of being born.

Caribou are supremely adapted to cold and snow, which of course characterize the northern environment, through a robust body form and warm coat. Indeed, staying one step ahead of predators requires caribou to spend most of their lives in some of the most inhospitable terrain imaginable. Their fur is composed of two layers: a dense, woolly undercoat and a longer hair overcoat.

Glen and Rebecca Grambo

Caribou in autumn with white manes and rumps popping out on the tundra near Whitefish Lake, Northwest Territories.

In combination, these layers protect the animal from extreme temperatures. Caribou hairs grow especially long and are hollow inside, keeping caribou buoyant in the water and allowing air to be trapped, thus keeping warmth close to their bodies, even when swimming. These hairs also cover the muzzle, the short tail, and are even found on the bottoms of the feet!

Caribou have many other fascinating adaptations that assist them through the long, cold winters and short summers. After sustaining weight loss in the winter, they have a remarkable ability to regain their body reserves during the brief summer months. During cold, dry winters, they tend to urinate less because of their ability to conserve water by recycling urea within their bodies. Within a caribou's long muzzle there are elaborately scrolled nasal bones, offering a relatively enormous surface area to both warm air that is breathed in and to extract moisture when exhaling.

Caribou are highly selective feeders, taking those plant parts that are most nutritious and digestible — a key to their ability to prosper in Arctic environments. Lichens, which contain easily digestible carbohydrates, are plentiful in all caribou habitats. In winter, caribou mostly seek out mats of lichens on the ground beneath the snow or hanging from tree branches. Once winter wanes, caribou track the timing of the

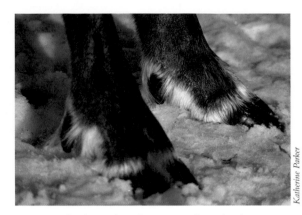

Hair on the legs of caribou extends right down to the feet.

spring burst of plant growth as they carefully pick out available leaf and flower buds. As ruminants, caribou rely on micro-organisms in parts of their compartmentalized stomachs for digestion; they are thereby able to extract maximum nutritional value from their food. With their heads down scanning for the best plant parts, they quickly bite off and swallow their food. They then rest and re-chew the vegetation, grinding the tough plant cell walls with their efficient cheek teeth and re-swallowing, while keeping a wary eye out for predators.

Like people, individual caribou display tremendous variability in appearance and body form, even within the same population. Different members contrast in everything from body size and shape to coat colour and facial characteristics such as snout length or antler form.

Each caribou individual is different. This cow, along the Thelon River, is in transition from her winter to spring coat.

MORE ABOUT CARIBOU FEET

The caribou's broad, concave hooves are yet another fascinating adaptation to the harsh and often treacherous northern environment. A hoof is comprised of two large crescent-shaped toes and two dewclaws. When deep snow covers the ground, caribou walk on all their toes, which spread out and act like snowshoes. Their feet begin to grow harder in the fall, and develop particularly sharp edges that can easily break through ice layers to search for food. Their feet can also act as

34

paddles for swimming or as ice picks when navigating steep, rocky, and icy mountainsides.

The large, flexible feet of caribou are also very useful in non-snow conditions, when the uneven ground can be soft and spongy. Here their feet help by providing a large surface to support the caribou's body. This ability to navigate rough terrain is needed in mountainous, forested, and Arctic environments alike — another northern adaptation held by all caribou.

"Hooves clacked on water-polished stones." — Ken Madsen, from *Under the Midnight Sun: Gwich'in, Caribou & the Arctic National Wildlife Refuge,* Englewood, Colorado: EarthTales Press, 2002.

Serge Couturier

This antlered female caribou from the Rivière George herd uses her specialized hooves to track over a frozen lake, living dangerously on thin ice in late October.

One male, followed by two female caribou, tries to escape the chilly waters of a lake by breaking through the ice. Caribou can break ice in this manner to reach the lakeshore or strongest ice cover, where they can climb to safety.

ANTLERS — WHY?

Caribou are the only deer species where both males and females have antlers: a bony outgrowth of the skull that pushes out in early spring and is shed later every year. No two caribou have the same antler shape and size. The general form of antlers is large, curved, and partly palmate (broad and flat, with finger-like projections).

Male antlers are broader and more massive, while those of females are shorter, more slender, and irregular in shape. Males and females generally shed their antlers at different times of the year. Adult bull antlers are shed in early winter or late fall, after the breeding season, when fighting between bulls is most common. Younger bulls shed their antlers later in winter or spring.

A healthy adult bull displays antlers, complete with distinct brow tine, or "plough."

Glen and Rebecca Grambo

"When they [caribou] fall through the ice in the winter time they have the ability to get out of the water because of the way their hooves are structured. When the moose falls through it will drown, even the deer. But not the caribou, it has the ability to get out. When there is no snow on the ice, the caribou can run on the ice. It will not slip. It is even able to gallop. But not the deer, it will slip and slide all over the place ... The caribou hoof is bent forward and the outside has an edge. On the moose and deer it is not like that, the inside surface comes out more [convex]. The caribou is also a very fast swimmer, the fastest swimmer around. Even the best paddler cannot catch up to a caribou when it is swimming." — George B. Strang, First Nations elder, from *Keeping Woodland Caribou on the Land: Cross-cultural Research in the Whitefeather Forest*. Pikangikum, Ontario: Whitefeather Forest Management Corporation, 2006.

Cows, on the other hand, tend to keep their antlers until they calve in the spring, with non-pregnant individuals usually casting their antlers a few weeks beforehand. Finding a lot of smaller discarded female antlers in a particular area, therefore, can indicate that it was a calving area. It is thought that the antlers are useful for females as they prepare for birth, vie for calving sites, or compete for food in late winter. Where caribou are most gregarious or live in large herds, antlers may therefore be more useful. This may also explain why females that are more widely dispersed (as they are in forest environments) tend to have smaller antlers, with a certain proportion not growing any antlers at all. Although antler regrowth begins for mature bulls in late winter, females begin to regrow their antlers just after giving birth.

CARIBOU IN NORTH AMERICA

Caribou are the most abundant large land-based mammal in the Far North — there is simply no other large mammal in North America that lives in such large social aggregations or embarks on such extensive migrations. Farther south, these characteristics change: caribou groups are smaller, and the migrations between seasonal calving and wintering grounds are shorter.

The climate and vegetation of the North make a gradual transition from tree-covered expanses to those covered by permanent ice, all of which are inhabited by caribou. Moving northward, the biomes (ecosystems with similar climates and plant and animal communities) that characterize the North are: boreal (or coniferous) forest, Arctic tundra, and polar desert. All these biomes have at least two things in common: snow and extreme temperatures, dominated in most seasons by cold and dryness. Nevertheless, all are home to caribou, which are simply not equipped to reside in the south, where other North American ungulates live.

Coniferous forests lie between the tundra to the north and the deciduous forests to the south, with summer temperatures that are warm enough to support at least slow tree growth. Once unsuitable soil conditions take over and summer growth temperatures are too cool, tree cover becomes increasingly sparse, and low-lying bushes and other small plants tend to take over in a transitional zone with scattered trees, known by many as the taiga. The taiga then gives way to

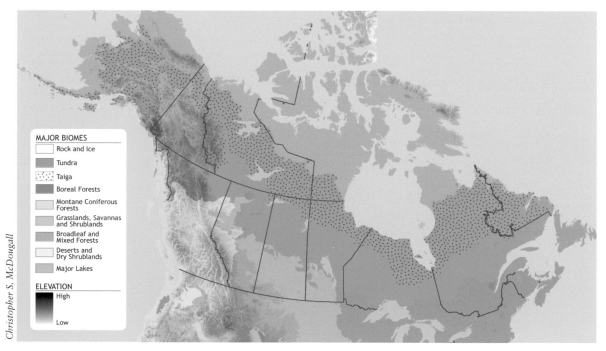

Map 1.2. *Major biomes or ecosystem types across northern North America, with topographical relief.*

the tundra. Tundra habitats are generally devoid of trees, except for dwarf forms of species such as birch and willow. Here, the dominant life forms are shrubs, grasses, mosses, and lichens. The ground remains frozen most of the year, partially melting on the surface only in summer.

In the mountains, there are parallel transitions from the lower elevation forests to a transition zone called the alpine (which undergoes more thorough melting in the summer than the Arctic taiga) to the highest elevation areas of rock and ice, devoid of trees but with some montane mosses and lichens.

Present-day caribou reside in almost every Canadian province, except New Brunswick, Nova Scotia, and Prince Edward Island. In the United States, Alaska is the only state with an abundance of this species, although one critically endangered population makes its way from British Columbia as far south as the mountains of Idaho and Washington State.

Across the North, caribou range from western Alaska to eastern Newfoundland and Labrador. Caribou even persist in the Canadian High Arctic, for example on Queen Elizabeth, Banks, Victoria, and Bathurst Islands.

Although caribou occur right across the continent north of sixty, populations still occur south of this line as far as the 50th latitude, with isolated populations even farther south. The

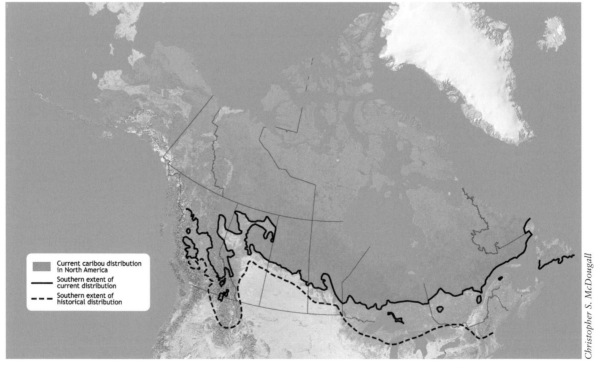

Map 1.3. *Present-day caribou distribution in North America and southern extent of historical occurrence (1880s).*

Gordon's Esker overlooking Whitefish Lake in the Northwest Territories, a region that is well known as a corridor for caribou migration.

southern limit of caribou distribution has been pushed northward over the past century and a half with the loss of viable boreal forest habitat.

Caribou share many characteristics with the Far North itself. During certain times of the year, no trace of them can be found, so that large areas appear dead to the world. Then, suddenly, these same areas can explode with life all around, only to have it quietly disappear again in a few days, weeks, or months. Therefore, the appearance of caribou offers resident predators (including humans) an abundance of meat for a relatively short time, beyond which the land produces nothing comparable for a long time. This is why early travellers called the Barren Lands "the land of feast and famine."

In forested regions of North America, the absence or presence of caribou is even more variable. Like the green needles on the trees, caribou life never completely disappears, but it can be sparse or apparently gone one minute and then reappear the next. Consequently, it is rare for any boreal forest predator to rely solely on caribou as a source of sustenance. But when a caribou does materialize, most predators will try to take advantage of the opportunity. Consequently, caribou spend most of their lives trying to avoid being eaten as well as trying to get enough to eat themselves.

A young tundra wolf along the Hanbury River.

Jay and Carolyn Pritchett

Indeed, there is growing evidence to suggest that in some parts of caribou distribution, predators have evolved to display some of the same behavioural traits as the prey upon which they depend. One such trait is migration. Humans in the Far North, for example, frequently "followed the food" by moving with the caribou or travelling to special places where these migrating animals can be intercepted.

A specialized form of wolf has evolved in the Canadian tundra, where wolves follow caribou migrations. They den on the tundra, then return south along with the caribou toward the end of summer. This is in sharp contrast to wolves that reside exclusively in boreal forests and maintain established territories. Here, where caribou populations do not reach such high densities as farther north, wolves tend to specialize in other prey, such as moose, elk, and deer, although they will certainly take caribou when the opportunity arises.

SUPREMELY ADAPTED

Through everything from their bodies to their seasonal movements across dramatically diverse natural habitats, to the effects they have on other living things, caribou have both shaped and been shaped by the North. The two are inseparable, braided together by the larger forces of nature that have produced both. The inspiring ability of all caribou to adapt is perhaps their greatest strength, and it has caused them to take the shape of their environment, resulting in remarkably different kinds of caribou across the full breadth of their North American distribution.

CHAPTER TWO

What's in a Name? —
Different Types of Caribou

AMONG BIOLOGISTS AND caribou hunters alike, there is no dispute that caribou have different physical appearances and behaviours in different areas. No wonder — during the 2 million or so years since caribou reached North America, they have been through four cycles of continental glaciation. As the ice sheets advanced and retreated, like a flowing tide caribou dispersed and adapted to local conditions. As a result, and as we have already seen, caribou are beautifully suited to the nuances of their various North American environments. However, this remarkable diversity in caribou appearance and behaviour causes headaches when trying to name different kinds of caribou and classify their relationships to each other. It's not the caribou that are the problem, because they have only done what came naturally by adapting to different conditions. Rather, the problem is our human need to classify them.

SO, WHY CLASSIFY?

The test of a good classification system is whether it captures the full diversity of the wildlife species being classified, at a scale that is meaningful for both conservation and management purposes. For any given caribou herd or population, we need to know what behaviours, movements, foods, pressures, and habitats might be unique. Only then can we take relevant steps to make sure caribou are maintained in healthy populations across the different landscapes where they are found. This is central to those who must officially decide not just on what *species* are at risk (for example "endangered" or "threatened"), but which *populations* are at risk as well.

Caribou are particularly elusive in this respect, but that shouldn't stop us from trying to classify them as best we can. There have, in fact, been different ways of classifying caribou — some more useful than others for furthering conservation of the diversity inherent in the species. Although the framework we are using in this book is based on the best knowledge of the species right now, no doubt it too will be refined and modified over time.

ONE SPECIES

As we have already explained, given the chance, all caribou would be capable of interbreeding and producing viable and fertile offspring. Consequently, anything beyond a common species designation, *Rangifer tarandus*, is unmerited. In other words, the Peary caribou in the High Arctic is the same species as the mountain caribou found on the Gaspé Peninsula of Quebec, the George River caribou of Quebec and Labrador, or the famous Porcupine caribou of Alaska and Yukon.

So if they aren't different species, what are we to make of the observable differences between caribou? Read on …

DIFFERENT CLASSIFICATIONS FOR DIFFERENT PURPOSES

Many different ways have been proposed to classify the tremendous diversity evident among caribou. The most traditional means — common to all species — is to classify them on the basis of *morphological differences*, for example, differences in shape, size, skull features, antler forms, or coat colours and patterns. These kinds of physical differences are generally linked to the evolutionary processes that have shaped species over time. Individuals with similar morphological characteristics are usually judged to be closely related, and therefore are traditionally classified as subspecies. This has resulted in some familiar names for different kinds of caribou, such as "woodland" or "barren-ground," which are discussed in more detail further on in the book.

The idea of classifying caribou based on their *behaviour* comes from one of North America's leading caribou biologists, Dr. Tom Bergerud, who distinguished between *migratory* and *sedentary* caribou. This distinction is rooted in how caribou use space, in particular the movement and distribution of females at calving time. In Bergerud's words, migratory caribou "space away," undertaking a trek together to a distant calving area, whereas sedentary caribou "space out," distancing themselves from one another. Both kinds of movement are regarded as strategies to minimize contact with predators, especially wolves, depending on the different habitats where the caribou and wolves are found.

THREE ECOTYPES

While Bergerud's migratory/sedentary classifications are helpful at an overarching level, additional factors, such as terrain or habitat, are useful for distinguishing different caribou ecotypes, namely *migratory tundra*, *boreal forest*, and *mountain* caribou. Most migratory animals use tundra habitats. Most sedentary animals are confined to boreal forest regions. But caribou in the mountains fall under either the migratory or sedentary umbrellas.

While we recognize that different classification systems have different purposes, we feel that the ecotype approach has best clarified our ecological understanding of caribou and is most useful for their conservation.

Migratory tundra caribou are those that travel to and assemble on traditional spring calving grounds in tundra areas of North America. They undertake long-distance migrations, generally in the order of hundreds to thousands of kilometres, back and forth between the tundra and their winter range. Most tundra populations spend their winter under tree cover in the boreal forest, but those residing in the High Arctic, such as Peary caribou, or those on the Alaskan coastal plains or the northeast Canadian mainland tundra can remain on the tundra during all seasons. Migratory

Serge Couturier

A huge post-calving aggregation of migratory tundra caribou, in this case the Rivière George herd, in late July, flows like a living tide over their northern homeland.

"After a few more minutes of indecision, two of the lead animals crept to the edge, nosed the soft ice, and, with all eyes watching, took a skating step in. Water lapped at their hooves as they stood there, then rose to their shins as they slid forward, but in the same moment they tried to back out, the rest of the herd surged from behind and all but pushed them in…. [There was] a critical point where, no matter what the circumstances, a group decision was made and there was no turning back. No sooner were the two lead scouts plunging up to their knees through water than every animal was in motion, individual trepidation switching to group bravery as they charged forward, three abreast." — Karsten Heuer, from *Being Caribou*. Seattle: The Mountaineers Books, 2005.

Boreal forest caribou in Manitoba.

Vince F.J. Crichton

tundra caribou usually occur in large groups, sometimes tens of thousands of individuals, especially during snow-free months. They breed during the fall migration, then disperse into smaller groups during the winter, only to reassemble on their way north to the tundra in spring, as cows head to their calving grounds.

Female boreal forest caribou calve alone, often on islands or within large, wet muskegs, and spend several months alone with their calves during the time when the young are most vulnerable to predation. Individuals tend to congregate in the autumn mating period (rut) and the winter, but in considerably smaller groups than the migratory tundra ecotype. The movements of boreal forest caribou between summer and winter ranges are generally shorter in distance (one hundred kilometres or less) than that of their migratory tundra cousins, and they spend the entire year south of the tree line. In some regions, migratory tundra and boreal forest caribou populations overlap, especially in forest habitats during the winter months, and are difficult to distinguish from one another. Therefore, although the more sedentary boreal forest caribou are generally heralded as symbols of boreal forest conservation, it should not be forgotten that many parts of this forest are home to thousands of migratory tundra caribou as well, especially in winter.

Mountain caribou calve at upper elevations. Those that calve and live in subalpine forests during the summer tend to be sedentary and live in small groups, whereas caribou that calve and summer in open alpine areas form larger groups (hundreds or even

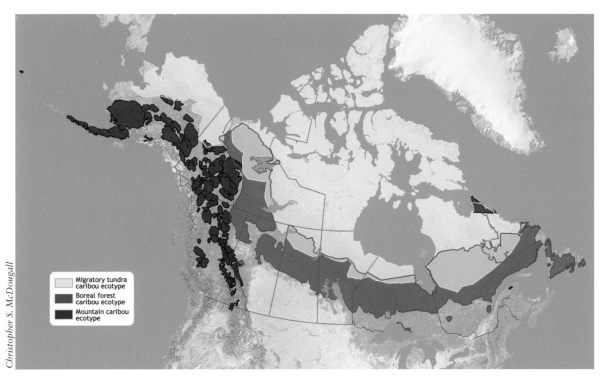

Christopher S. McDougall

Map 1.4. *Three principal ecotypes of North American caribou: migratory tundra, boreal forest, and mountain.*

thousands of animals) and are often migratory, moving moderate distances to their calving areas. Mountain caribou use a variety of winter habitats, including windswept alpine ridges, subalpine forests, and low-elevation forests. Most mountain caribou live in areas with relatively shallow snow, and forage largely on terrestrial lichens during winter. Other mountain caribou live in areas of extremely deep snowpacks (two to five metres) and forage on arboreal lichens during winter from the canopy of old forests. This observed difference in winter diet — terrestrial versus arboreal lichens — has been suggested by authorities such as the Committee on the Status of Endangered Wildlife in Canada as a further way to classify mountain caribou.

Dave Gustine

Lactating cows and their calves rest in a snow patch at high elevation north of the Prophet River, in the Muskwa-Prophet watershed in northcentral British Columbia.

45

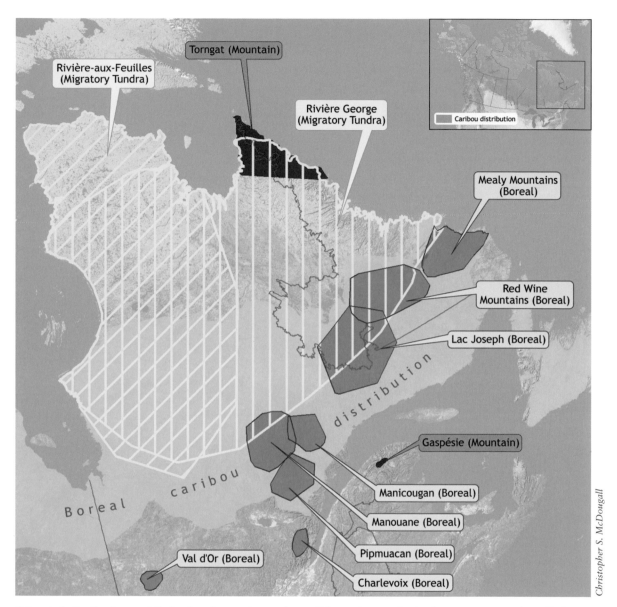

Rivière-aux-Feuilles (Migratory Tundra)

Torngat (Mountain)

Rivière George (Migratory Tundra)

Mealy Mountains (Boreal)

Red Wine Mountains (Boreal)

Lac Joseph (Boreal)

Caribou distribution

Gaspésie (Mountain)

Manicougan (Boreal)

Manouane (Boreal)

Pipmuacan (Boreal)

Val d'Or (Boreal)

Charlevoix (Boreal)

Boreal caribou distribution

Christopher S. McDougall

Map 1.5. *In Quebec and Labrador, the varying ecology of the region results in the circumstance that all three caribou ecotypes co-exist on the same land base. Also striking is the relative level of knowledge and study that has characterized the different populations. Some — like the Rivière George (George River) and Rivière-aux-Feuilles (Leaf River) herds and the boreal forest populations in Labrador — have been subject to decades of radio-telemetry so their ranges are well-delineated, although they have been shifting over time. There are other large areas where boreal caribou occur, but due to lack of study, population boundaries — if they exist — are unknown. Several populations in southern Quebec are isolated from the main caribou distribution.*

46

MANY POPULATIONS AND HERDS

Regardless of ecotype (migratory tundra, boreal forest, or mountain), any group of caribou will use a *range* (an area that circumscribes its movements and activities over the course of a year). Such a range will be particular to each collection of caribou and is generally identifiable from those used by other groups, although some range overlap between groups is common. Caribou belonging to such a group are known as a local *population* or *herd*.

Population boundaries for some caribou are easy to identify, especially with modern technology such as GPS (Global Positioning System) transmitters, and have not changed to any significant extent over several decades. Others shift when caribou abundance changes. For example, winter ranges often expand and contract as caribou numbers increase and decline. At least some neighbouring herds overlap in their winter ranges, but then tend to separate and go their own ways as they return to their calving and summer ranges.

For migratory tundra caribou in particular, where enormous groups return to the same general calving ground year after year, herds are named after a geographic feature associated with that area, such as a lake or a river: the Beverly herd has traditionally calved near Beverly Lake, the Bathurst herd near Bathurst Inlet, etc.

It is important to understand that in the Far North, for migratory tundra caribou in particular, people are really focused both biologically and politically on the main herds. For example, there are four herds that use the Alaskan Northern Slope: the Porcupine caribou herd, migrating into the disputed coastal plain or "1002 lands" to calve in the Arctic National Wildlife Refuge; the smaller but fascinating Central Arctic herd, for which the Refuge is on the periphery of its range, apparently increasing in numbers in spite of extensive development focused on Prudhoe Bay; the Teshekpuk Lake herd, the only one of the four to remain on the coastal plain during the winter, but which bears its calves by the wetland-rich lake; and the sprawling Western Arctic herd, Alaska's largest and of vital importance to the thirteen thousand people that reside within its range, which may be opened to development interests in the near future. The different geographies and histories of each herd bring different pressures and prospects for the future.

For sedentary boreal forest and mountain caribou, populations are more often named for the area in which they live all year round, for example Owl Lake, a boreal forest population in Manitoba, or the Nelchina mountain caribou herd in Alaska. In low-lying boreal forest habitats that can stretch uninterrupted for thousands of kilometres, local population boundaries are often much more difficult to discern, especially if no barriers — such as mountains, some large rivers, or human development — are evident.

Although knowledge of the range boundaries for any population, regardless of ecotype, is important for their management or conservation, often the only way to determine the area in

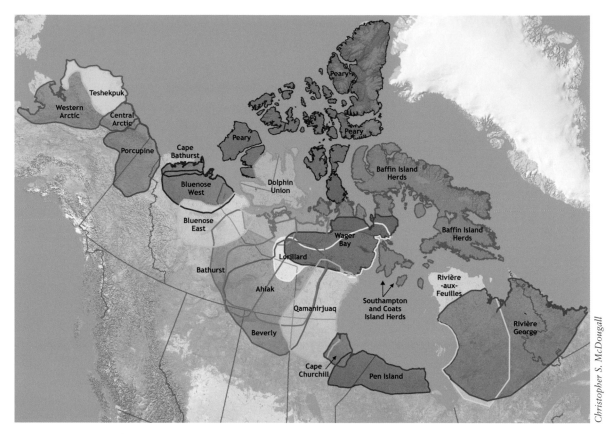

Map 1.6. *Ranges of major migratory tundra caribou herds in North America.*

Christopher S. McDougall

Serge Couturier

Some caribou travel in small groups, making herds or populations difficult to define. This group of adult females begins its spring migration toward the north in late March.

question is to attach radio transmitters to individual caribou, then follow and document their year-round movements. This is an expensive enterprise, and it is more common in some areas within caribou distribution than others. For migratory caribou, this tool has been used often enough for biologists to have reasonable confidence that an animal located at calving time or during the rut does belong to a particular herd. On the other hand, the tendency of sedentary animals to scatter means that it is not always possible to identify an individual caribou as belonging to a particular herd or population based simply on its location.

HOW LOCAL KNOWLEDGE CAN HELP

Caribou defy our desire for crisp, all-or-nothing categories. Like all wildlife, just when you think you've sorted things out, caribou can surprise and humble you. The best way to make sense of this, and to minimize mistakes, is to combine modern scientific approaches with the knowledge of the people who have lived with caribou for centuries.

For example, in the 1960s and 1970s, before radio collars appeared on the scene, biologists needed to mark caribou using ear tags. When they asked Inuit hunters where the best places would be to do this, the Inuit directed the scientists to traditionally known river crossing areas where biologists could get close enough to the animals to attach the tags. Similarly, over the decades, generations of Aboriginal hunters have come to notice minute physical differences in caribou from different herds, even when they may be mixing together on the wintering grounds or during migration. For example, caribou from the north are often lighter or smaller than those from more southerly ranges. Local observers are also excellent sources of information regarding seasonal movements of caribou, both recent and over the long term, indicating where

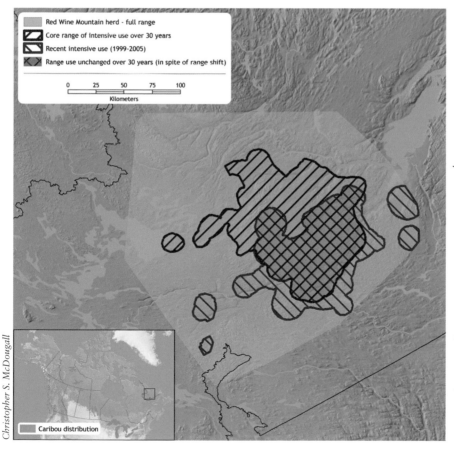

Christopher S. McDougall

Map 1.7 *The boreal forest Red Wine herd in Labrador has been studied using radio-telemetry for close to three decades. This work has demonstrated that while the herd used its full range over this period, there were evidently areas of more intensive use. Further, these areas shifted within the range over time, even though an area of constant (intensive) use was maintained. These findings suggest that range use is dynamic over time.*

the caribou appeared and when, in comparison with previous years. In addition, hunters can provide good information on the condition or health of the animals, especially by the presence of fat under the skin, around internal organs, and even in bone marrow.

These examples underscore the value of working with local people whose ancestors evolved with caribou. The stakes were nothing less than survival, so it stands to reason that these people would become very knowledgeable about subtle morphological and behavioural differences in the animals upon which they depend. This kind of traditional knowledge, combined with scientific techniques such as radio/satellite tracking and DNA analysis, make a powerful combination not just for classifying caribou but for saving them as well.

Map 1.8. In far northern Ontario, opportunistic observations of the migratory Pen Island herd recorded during the early summer for four different periods since 1965 indicate that the principal calving areas appear to have shifted from the western to the eastern part of the range. In later years, most observed aggregations have been smaller in size than in the 1980s. These kinds of changes make it difficult to make definitive statements about the locations and numbers of caribou populations.

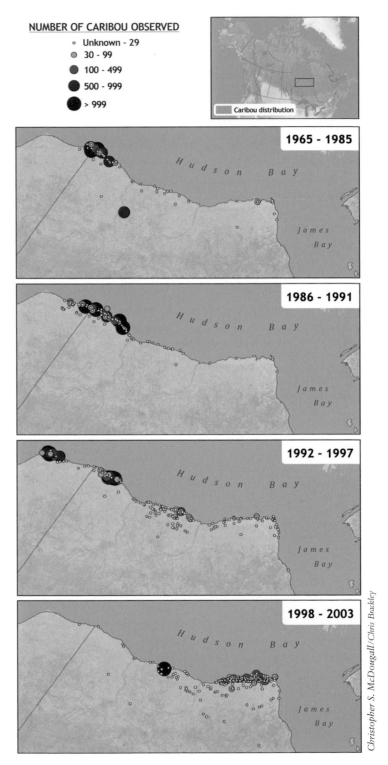

NUMBER OF CARIBOU OBSERVED
- Unknown - 29
- 30 - 99
- 100 - 499
- 500 - 999
- > 999

Caribou distribution

1965 - 1985

1986 - 1991

1992 - 1997

1998 - 2003

Christopher S. McDougall / Chris Brackley

OTHER FAMILIAR NAMES FOR THE DIFFERENT KINDS OF CARIBOU

As previously noted, various caribou subspecies have been proposed and are still commonly used. But where do the commonly used terms "woodland caribou" and "barren-ground caribou" fit into the classification system we have suggested?

Caribou were once thought to belong to more than one species. However, as we have seen, that thinking has since changed. This revision was advocated in the 1960s by noted Canadian mammalogist and author of *The Mammals of Canada* Frank Banfield. Although he amalgamated all reindeer and caribou into one species, Banfield also described five *subspecies*, including the now extinct Dawson caribou (*Rangifer tarandus dawsoni*). These subspecies were based primarily on skull measurements, which are now thought to be too dependent on environmental conditions, and his method has been overtaken by new techniques such as DNA analysis.

But most significantly, Banfield's classification fails to capture some important ecological variation evident even within his proposed subspecies. For example, one of his proposed subspecies, *Rangifer tarandus caribou*, commonly called "woodland caribou," includes some mountain, boreal forest, and migratory tundra caribou. Other proposed subspecies, including *Rangifer tarandus groenlandicus* (found in the Northwest Territories and Nunavut) and *Rangifer tarandus granti* (found in the Yukon and Alaska), both commonly known as "barren-ground caribou," include not just migratory tundra caribou but some mountain caribou as well.

The point is that by relying exclusively on differences in body form, the proposed classifications do not, in our view, sufficiently differentiate the ecological diversity inherent in caribou across their distribution, and hence have less relevance to conservation. Furthermore, the proposed subspecies have been inconsistently used and differently interpreted, which we feel has led to more confusion than clarity. In fact, most caribou biologists agree that a taxonomic revision that makes sense of all this diversity, using modern tools, is sorely needed.

However, there is one important example where one of Banfield's subspecies notion *does* capture the unique ecological pressures of a caribou population's environment, and that is for Peary caribou on the High Arctic Islands (*Rangifer tarandus pearyi*). Although ostensibly falling under the category of migratory tundra caribou, the different

"The land and the caribou are still the first topic of conversation in Lutsel K'e, where binoculars sit on every windowsill. In late July or early August, Lutsel K'e Dene watch for an insect with a long segmented body with yellow-on-black markings. When it appears at the people's bush camps near treeline, they say, 'It's from the caribou. Look, the caribou are coming back.'" — Ellen Bielawski, from *Rogue Diamonds*, Vancouver: Douglas and McIntyre, 2003.

Migratory Pattern	Ecotype	Subspecies	Examples of herds/populations
Migratory	Migratory tundra	Peary (*R.t. pearyi*)	Banks Island (NWT), Melville Island (NU)
		Barren-ground (*R. t. groenlandicus*)	Bathurst (NWT/NU), Bluenose East (NWT/NU)
		Grant's (*R.t. granti*)	Porcupine (AK/YK), Western Arctic (AK)
		Woodland (*R. t. caribou*)	Pen Islands (ON/MB), George River (QC/NF)
	Mountain	Grant's (*R. t. granti*)	Muchatna (AK), Fortymile (AK)
		Woodland (*R. t. caribou*)	Wolverine (BC), Narraway (AB)
Sedentary	Boreal forest	Woodland (*R. t. caribou*)	Owl Lake (MB), Little Smoky (AB)
	Mountain	Grant's (*R. t. granti*)	Chisana (AK)
		Woodland (*R. t. caribou*)	South Selkirks (BC), Narrow Lake (BC)

circumstances of its harsh environment, combined with its endangered status, merit separate attention for this subspecies.

For readers seeking more information, Section Four provides detailed profiles of migratory tundra, boreal forest, mountain, and Peary caribou, based on updated information contributed by leading experts.

CHAPTER THREE

The Ecological Importance of Caribou

SCIENTISTS AND OTHERS are just beginning to appreciate how large mammals (both predator and prey species) shape the environment of which they form a part. Unfortunately, these roles are often understood only by observing changes after the species in question have disappeared. By that time, their habitats are usually converted, degraded, or even destroyed.

In cases where large mammal numbers have diminished, scientific scrutiny of the ecological conditions before and after their decline seldom takes place, although the people who live there can often describe such changes because they experience them directly. Where these relationships *have* been studied, they are complex and difficult to disentangle, because predators can influence the number, distribution, and even behaviour of their prey. But prey species, such as ungulates, can in turn play a critical role in determining the number, distribution, and behaviour of their predators. Ungulates, of course, depend on vegetation for food, so their numbers can be subject to the quality and availability of plants, which in turn are tied to nutrient supply, weather, and climate. Even their parasites can influence caribou behaviour and health. So there are many ecological circles within circles to consider.

CARIBOU IN THE FOOD CHAIN

By virtue of their enormous numbers at high latitudes and their wide-ranging capabilities, it is not difficult to imagine that caribou must be fundamental elements of northern ecosystems. Often they are the sole ungulate in such places, so their physical footprint is impossible to miss, lingering for many years after they have passed through an area. Caribou and muskoxen are the only ungulates that have evolved to graze tundra habitats, and caribou alone exploit lichens in boreal forest environments.

Fundamental, however, is the fact that predators of various sizes rely on the regular bounty of caribou. Some species, such as wolves, follow caribou movements. Others, such as grizzly and black bears, specialize in vulnerable caribou calves during May and June. Wolverines, foxes, and ravens wait their turn to exploit caribou meat through scavenging the carcasses of caribou killed by something else, although wolverines are also known to kill caribou on occasion.

"What drives the cycles in barren-ground abundance? The answers lie in a complex dance between caribou having enough to eat and being able to avoid being eaten. And that dance is set to the rhythm of climate. Weather interacts with just about every aspect of caribou ecology, and weather has its own patterns over decades." — Anne Gunn, from "What Price the Caribou?", *Northern Perspectives*. Ottawa: Canadian Arctic Resources Committee, Volume 31, Number 1, Spring 2007.

Paul Zakora

Steven Barger

C. Long / The Wolverine Foundation, Inc.

Above left: This fox snacks on a cow caribou killed earlier by wolves.

Above right: Grizzlies often rest or sleep right on a carcass, with a good chance that nothing else is going to try to take it away. Denali National Park, Alaska.

Right: Although wolverines have been known to kill live caribou, usually they scavenge animals already killed by some other means.

Aside from being a food source to other animals, caribou play an active role in other ecosystem processes, such as nutrient cycling. In nutrient-poor tundra soils where plant decomposition rates are slow due to cold ground temperatures, caribou fecal pellets offer a rare source of nutrients. Some twenty to twenty-five times a day, one caribou will drop about 30 grams of pellets, an accumulation of about 220 kilograms per year. In the case of a herd numbering several hundred thousand animals, this can add up to a considerable amount of fertilizer. Caribou also play an important role in nutrient cycles of aquatic systems, although indirectly, through the clouds of mosquitoes that feed upon them. A blood meal permits the mosquitoes to produce eggs. Once the larvae hatch, they feed voraciously on minute food particles suspended in the water column and in turn serve as food for fish and birds.

Human predators also rely heavily on caribou, except that we can locate caribou at great distances (for example using radio telemetry or airplanes) and we can travel quickly by land, water, or air to intercept them. We can also disrupt caribou habitat, for example, through industrial development. Consequently, humans have the capacity to overwhelm other predators and prey alike.

While the ecological importance of caribou likely diminishes as they become less abundant north and south of their geographic stronghold, caribou appear in the diet of virtually all large predators wherever they occur. Therefore, as a component of the food chain, when caribou disappear from or decline in a given area, they certainly have the potential to fundamentally alter predator ecology. These changes for predators often depend on the number of alternative large prey species available, such as moose, deer, elk, and beaver, as well as other smaller herbivores, such as hares and ground squirrels.

MASS MIGRATIONS

Beyond shaping the ecology of northern ecosystems, there are other aspects of caribou ecology that elevate them as symbols for the conservation of wild places. First, they are one of the last best examples on Earth of long-distance migration. Mass migration of ungulates is truly an inspiring natural spectacle — a once common phenomenon that is becoming increasingly rare in the world. While bird migrations can continue by flying above the fray, so to speak, few large ungulates can make their way across landscapes unimpeded, due to the pervasive and expanding human footprint.

The natural phenomenon of mass migrations transcends individual animals. While the species may not have disappeared altogether, their organized wanderings over hundreds or thousands of kilometres have been all but lost for pronghorn antelope and bison in North

America; for Saiga antelope in Kazakhstan, Russia, and Mongolia; for wildebeest in Africa; and for elephants in both Africa and Asia.

Protected areas are almost never established at a scale that preserves these migratory phenomena. As a result, the only places they remain are untrammelled areas where long-distance travel is still possible. Such areas define the North — a symbol of restraint, where the complete life history of a migratory animal such as the caribou still has the space to play out to its fullest. This means that when we tinker with the vast ranges used by a caribou herd, modifying the environments through which they wander, we risk compromising their very way of life and, ultimately, their survival.

"When the buffalo went from the plains, the people of the plains, the Cree, the Dakota — their culture died, their spirit died. Here, we have a chance to save it." — Fred Sangris, Chief, Yellowknives Dene, quoted from his address to the NWT Barrenground Caribou Summit. Inuvik, Northwest Territories, January 2007.

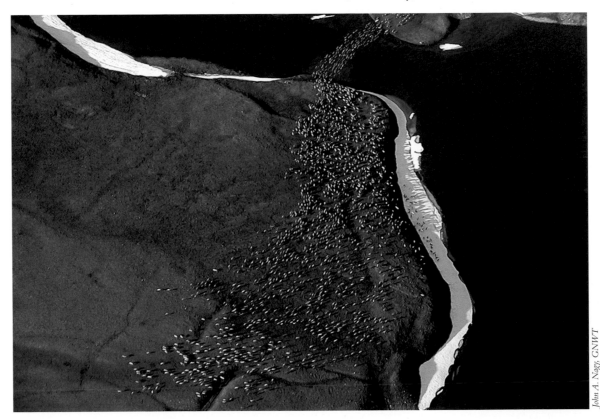

John A. Nagy, GNWT

A magnificent aerial photo of migratory tundra caribou migrating in a steady stream over land and water.

CARIBOU AS SYMBOLS OF ECOSYSTEM HEALTH

By virtue of their sensitivity to changes in the condition of their range, caribou can be the first among the obvious components to disappear from a natural ecosystem. How well caribou are thriving in a given landscape, therefore, is often an indication of how secure it is overall as a natural system. The collapse or disappearance of a caribou population can be a harbinger of the fate of other less visible, but equally sensitive, elements of the same ecosystem. On the other hand, when humans begin to modify a landscape, if the continued survival of caribou is *not* compromised, then we have a good chance of conserving the rest of the natural puzzle pieces as well.

Just over 20 percent of the planet still has intact large mammal fauna. Large portions of the North American caribou distribution constitute one such area — a big chunk of the world's total. This remains true despite the fact that caribou are among the twenty species of the world's large mammals that have experienced the greatest documented range retraction in the past several centuries. The disappearance of any large mammal is generally representative of human impact on the full spectrum of wildlife species in a given natural system. Therefore, maintaining the full extent of caribou occurrence represents one of the best opportunities in the world to safeguard the benefits we all derive from functioning ecosystems (otherwise known as "ecosystem services") and to conserve biodiversity itself. It is particularly important that we grasp this opportunity now, because caribou occur in one of the world's regions with the

"Caribou are not sensitive and delicate creatures that will vanish at the first stress imposed by northern development. They have proved themselves remarkably resilient and adaptable animals. They have endured and prospered during the climatic and geological turmoil of the ice age, evolving to live in environments too severe for all other deer. Caribou still migrate past human settlements, despite heavy hunting and harassment. Sometimes they have to be chased off village airstrips so that planes can land. They cross roads and railways and even travel along them. The great herds will continue to flow like a river of life across the barren-lands … if we give them a chance.

"But if men continue to hunt without regard for the productive capacity of the herds; if the last of the North becomes criss-crossed by highways, railroads, pipelines, and high-tension lines; if petro-chemical plants spew out sulphur dioxide that kills lichens; if the boreal forest is cut for pulpwood and fence posts; if the last wild rivers are dammed and diverted, then the caribou will disappear. There is a limit to the adaptability of even the most resourceful species." — George Calef, from *Caribou and the barren-lands*. Ottawa: Canadian Arctic Resources Committee, Firefly Books, 1981.

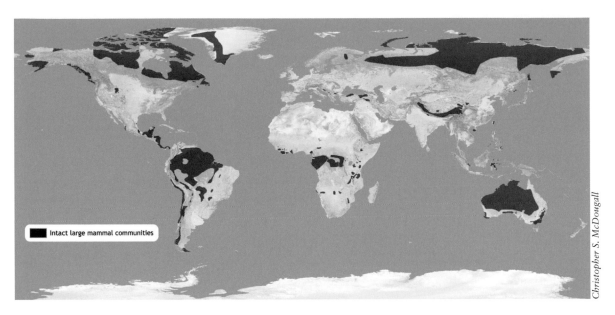

Map 1.9. *Northern Canada is one of the few remaining areas in the world that still contain the full complement of large mammals (body mass of over twenty kilograms) that occurred there five hundred years ago, known as "intact" communities.*

highest likelihood of future species loss, and the traits of wildlife there render them particularly sensitive to human impact.

Our collective challenge, therefore, is not to "manage wildlife" but to manage *ourselves* in such a way that caribou will continue to be a remarkable part of northern landscapes.

CHAPTER FOUR

The Importance of Caribou to People

"If the caribou die, then we die."
— *Michael Van Leewen, Lutsel K'e, Northwest Territories.*

THESE FEW WORDS speak eloquently to the importance of caribou to many northern peoples. They were spoken not by a hereditary chief in the 1800s during treaty making, not by an Inuit victim of the tragic starvation in the 1950s when the caribou didn't come, and not even by a contemporary elder. Instead, the statement comes from a thirteen-year-old Dene youth in 2007, during a regulatory board hearing regarding proposed uranium exploration in important caribou habitat.

Caribou have been, and continue to be, particularly crucial for First Peoples of the taiga and tundra. The great migratory herds there even today are valued at over $100 million per year in meat value alone, and it would be impossible to place a dollar value on their broader cultural significance. Perhaps seals play a similar role for northern marine peoples, such as Inuit. But Inuit too have traditionally supplemented their diet, shelter, clothing, and tools using caribou, especially when the animals venture coastward or when the hunters venture inland. Farther south, in the boreal region, caribou become less plentiful, and other large mammals, especially moose, are found in increasingly large numbers, so these alternatives gradually play a more and more important role.

However, so important are caribou to far northern Aboriginal cultures that it is very difficult to convey a real sense of this relationship to a southern audience. This is because urban North Americans are so distant from caribou country and from the animal itself. Ironically, it

"If we take steps now, we'll hear the thunder again." — Danny Beaulieu, Resource Officer, Northwest Territories Environment and Natural Resources, quoted from his address to the Northwest Territories Barren-ground Caribou Summit. Inuvik, 2007.

Miranda Cassawy of Lutsel K'e, NWT, helps her grandmother make dried meat for her extended family.

is also difficult to convey the significance of caribou to a northern audience. But in this case, it is because people are so embedded in caribou country and so close to the animal itself. After all, when something is literally in your bloodstream, how do you stand back far enough to put its importance into words?

Perhaps the answer in both cases is to simply let northerners speak for themselves. That has been our approach here, based mostly on written contributions and interviews provided especially for this book, in addition to other published literature. Our objective is not to provide another third-person, anthropological inventory of various uses northern cultures have made of caribou. Rather, we have assembled fresh, first-person accounts of something that is difficult to put into words, especially into the words of a second language like English. We're trying to get at a deeply held experience or feeling, without which people wouldn't be who they are.

We will also briefly explore how caribou have worked their way into the broader North American consciousness; if we lose that, we are in danger of losing this crucial element of northern life.

"I've been working with the elders on our history for the past ten years, and most of the history brings people back to the caribou, the trails, the history, how our people depended on it. Without the caribou, we wouldn't have made it through. The caribou provided everything, tools, food, clothing. The caribou are central to Dene culture. Even today, when people harvest it, they have so much respect for caribou." — Fred Sangris, Chief, Yellowknives Dene, from "What Price the Caribou?" *Northern Perspectives*. Ottawa: Canadian Arctic Resources Committee, Volume 31, Number 1, Spring 2007.

"HOW WILL OUR PEOPLE SURVIVE WITHOUT CARIBOU?"

Norma Kassi is a well-known spokesperson for the Gwich'in, specifically the Vuntut Gwitchin in the northern Yukon. The Gwich'in people of both Alaska and Canada are best known for their long-standing opposition to oil drilling in the calving grounds for the Porcupine caribou herd, especially on the coastal plain of the Arctic National Wildlife Refuge in Alaska. Norma has been involved with this issue for more than twenty years. The Vuntut Gwitchin have also been key to establishing protected areas, including Vuntut National Park on the Canadian side, to help protect caribou habitat. Norma is originally from Old Crow in the Yukon, where she was raised on the land, and she has served on the boards and committees of many Aboriginal and non-Aboriginal organizations. She was twice elected a member of the Yukon Legislative Assembly, and is currently facilitating community-based health research in the Yukon through the Arctic Health Research Network-Yukon, a non-profit society she co-founded in 2007.

Norma told us of a "very powerful truce" that came about through a legend whereby caribou and the Gwich'in always carry a part of one another's hearts deep within them. This truce is meant to be sacred, and moving away from it will result in serious consequences for both parties. In Norma's words, "Caribou blood runs through my blood and all Arctic peoples'."

Norma speaks emotionally of living on the land in tents with her grandfather, mother, aunts, and uncles every spring and fall when the Porcupine caribou came by. The caribou were what sustained her family and community through the summers and winters. "Our mattresses, blankets, and clothing were all made of caribou skins; our whole lives were connected to caribou.

"I once asked a representative of an Alaskan conservation organization how she felt after wining one these votes [in Washington to protect the calving grounds of the Arctic National Wildlife Refuge)] She was surprisingly glum: 'We never win,' she said. 'We just put off losing.'"
— Clive Tesar, from "What Price the Caribou?", *Northern Perspectives*. Ottawa: Canadian Arctic Resources Committee, Volume 31, Number 1, Spring 2007.

"I continually remember my mother getting up at four o'clock in the morning during continuous daylight to watch for the caribou. In the Gwich'in language she asks the raven to 'Watch for the caribou's eye,' since that is the raven's favourite part. My grandfather does prayer ceremonies for the caribou to come, and I look up at their faces to see if there is any sign of them. A little bird sits on our tent pole at five o'clock and sings a song reminding us to give thanks and to be forever grateful. So I do that from under my blankets on spruce boughs in the tent."

Norma speaks haltingly now, through tears, as she relives those moments …

"Finally, the raven talks to my grandmother, then we see the caribou coming over the mountain. Everyone is excited, and my grandfather hitches up the dogs to go across the lake (my brothers do all this now). On his return, I run to greet him. He gives me a mixture of caribou blood and nutrients first to restore my strength, then we eat the fat, brisket, and other favourite parts the next day, and everyone is alive and happy again.

"The cows sleep on the lake, and we must be quiet, respectful, and send prayers that they make it safely to the calving grounds to have their little ones."

When Norma actually visited the calving area in June 2005, she had to ask her Gwich'in elders for permission, assuring them we would be in the foothills only, not walking on the coastal plain — the birthing place itself. This was the first time Norma had ever seen newborn calves, in a place held so sacred by the Gwich'in that they do not go there, even in times of famine.

Today, Old Crow remains an isolated community, highly dependent on caribou. In fact, according to Norma, if anything, caribou are now more important than ever, "because the Porcupine and Crow rivers, which the hunters travel to get moose and other traditional foods, are drying up more and more, and the salmon are decreasing each year. The caribou are fewer

Monte Hummel

The Porcupine herd (cows, calves, and bulls) struggles to cross the Firth River in spring flood.

and less accessible, but there are still enough that if we came together now, we could talk about saving them and ensuring fair conservation measures."

Norma spoke of visiting the oldest person in Venetie, Alaska, a few years ago. This Gwich'in elder was ready to go to the spirit world. He told her, "We're going to make it, but there will be trouble for the caribou."

She feels that is what's happening now. The caribou are in trouble from industrial activity, over-harvesting, and climate change, as well as because "people are moving away from that sacred truce, no longer holding respect for caribou in their hearts.

"But how will our people survive without caribou, without traditional food, and without conservation of the very fundamental things that sustain us?"

"WHERE CARIBOU WERE OF OPTIMAL IMPORTANCE RATHER THAN MONEY"

For twenty-eight years, Ray Griffith lived and worked in Lutsel K'e, a small community of about 350 people on the East Arm of Great Slave Lake, Northwest Territories, in the territory of the Akaitcho Dene. During this time, he undertook many jobs, including band manager, but mainly he lived and travelled on the land with hunters and elders who have traditionally depended primarily on the Beverly caribou herd, but also on Qamanirjuaq, Bathurst, and Ahiak animals. Today, he continues to work on caribou-related concerns from WWF-Canada's Yellowknife office.

Ray told us of a particularly memorable fall caribou hunting trip in 1974.

It all began with a summer of "talking, making plans, and poring over maps in preparation." He notes that late spring and summer are the only seasons with no caribou, but with an abundance of other edible species: "evidence, they tell me, of the Great Spirit looking after us," he says.

During that summer, in preparation for the fall and winter, Pierre Catholique, now a respected elder, made Ray a beautiful pair of birch and caribou snowshoes. But Ray also needed a parka and pants made of caribou hide with the hair left on, which could only be harvested in the fall when the caribou don't have warble flies and the hair stays on the hide better.

Now, feel the zest in Ray's own words:

"Great anticipation and excitement accompany this fall caribou hunt. It is a community/family affair, and in some years provides the first fresh meat and break from a steady diet of fish. Whole families, most of Lutsel K'e, travel by boat to the end of the [Great Slave] lake, and from there make the arduous three-mile Pike's Portage climb to a rolling plateau about one thousand feet above the lake, carrying canoes, tents, and everything needed to sustain large families for a couple of weeks.

"The elevation change brings us suddenly to the tree line and the beginnings of the great treeless plain, the Barrens, stretching hundreds of miles north and east all the way to the Arctic Ocean and Hudson Bay. The Barrens are spectacularly beautiful in brilliant red fall colours of the low shrubs, lichens, and mosses, mostly bug-free and usually heavily populated with fat caribou.

"The heavy packing, canoeing, setting camps, and long, fast hikes while hunting and butchering caribou was a muscle-aching workout even for my twenty-three-year-old, quite fit body. Even the kids and dogs were packing. The fall caribou hunt was a special time for everyone, and I relished the strong feeling of participating in an unbroken tradition from ancient times, using trails and campsites thousands of years old, and using them in very much the same way."

And now, Ray's caribou parka and pants take shape.

"Judith prepared the caribou hides for me by softening them and cutting them into shapes to be sewn into a parka and pants. She showed me how to sew them, and I did the rest except for the finishing, for which she added fasteners, trims, etc. She also tanned hides for other items we needed for the winter … with an enormous amount of work, she cut the hair off, scraped, soaked in caribou brains, then dried, worked, and smoked hides to make soft but tough tanned hides, both moose and caribou. The tougher moose hides were used for moccasins, and caribou hide was used for everything else, mitts, gloves, hats, and bags of all types. The caribou back sinews were dried and used for thread. The largest caribou hides were reserved to be used for mattresses laid over the spruce branches with which we covered the floor of our winter tents. Shopping was the easy part; we bought only shells, traps, wool socks and underwear, candles, matches, and a shockingly small amount of food meant to last until Christmas."

Chipweyan students and elders of Lutsel K'e Dene School gather around a big smoky spring campfire to roast meat after a successful caribou hunt.

Ray describes his first encounter with a Barren Lands legend, in whose name WWF has established a scholarship for Lutsel K'e youth:

"Here at the end of the lake is where I first met Noel Drybones and his family, camped next to Gus D'Aoust — the old Barrens trapper who still operated his trading post. They were the only permanent residents of this place they called Fort Reliance.

"Fort Reliance, as Gus said, is a 'gem on the face of the Earth.' Set on the cold clear lake among high, steep-sided hills close to tumultuous streams and rivers that tumble in falls down to the lake. Noel and Gus loved this place. Noel never forgave his fellow band members for be-

ing lured by the school in Lutsel K'e and family allow-
ance payments to abandon the paradise of their ances-
tral home at the end of the lake near the tree line where
caribou are plentiful most of the year. Alone among the
band families, Noel refused to move into the community. For over fifty years he stubbornly maintained his
traditional livelihood, staying year-round 'in the bush'
on or near the Barrens. He was very proud of his independence and refused to become dependent on government money, while at the same time extolling the
virtues and wealth of his traditional home among the
caribou on the Barrens and at the end of the lake at
Fort Reliance."

"Akaitcho elder Albert Boucher from Lutsel K'e talked of the difficulties of finding caribou now, and the need to support and help each other to work together. He recalled a prophecy that says that when the caribou go, there will be tears in your eyes as you see only old trails made by the caribou." — *Northwest Territories Barren-ground Caribou Summit*. Inuvik: Northwest Territories Environment and Natural Resources. August 2007.

On this trip, Ray learned how to set traps on caribou remains on lakes, in the forest, and out
on the tundra. He heard caribou legends, wrapped caribou around him, put caribou inside him,
and got to know caribou people. He summed it all up as follows:

"This was the North of the caribou and the fur trade. I felt I had actually succeeded in
escaping the clutches of the western industrial complex, here where caribou were of optimal
importance rather than money. We had left town two and a half months before with a small box
of grub, and it wasn't finished … We had followed the caribou to keep ourselves and our dogs
well supplied for the winter. It was now Christmas, and time to return to town for the festivities
of the season and the end of my planned life in the North. But the experience had been too
overwhelming, too much to leave behind. It changed my life. I never did return south."

"WE RETURNED TO THE IGLU FOR A SMALL FEAST"

David Pelly is a well-known northern author who has spent many years living with Inuit in
Nunavut, especially at Cambridge Bay on the Arctic Ocean and at Baker Lake. The latter is now
the only permanent community of inland Inuit, people who depend on caribou, especially the
Beverly and Qamanirjuaq herds, whose calving areas are not far away. They also harvest animals
from the Ahiak herd, which calves in the Queen Maud Gulf Migratory Bird Sanctuary. Note
that the Lutsel K'e Dene First Nation in the Northwest Territories, as described by Ray Griffith,
uses these same herds. Over the years, David has travelled extensively with Inuit and conducted
more than a hundred interviews with hunters and elders, producing documented transcripts that
tell us so much about how Inuit have used and continue to use the land.

David describes a winter caribou hunt out of Baker Lake with an elder, Mannik, in 1983:

"We travelled north from town by the light of the full moon. Old Mannik made our iglu somewhere near Amarook Lake. On that otherwise memorable evening, the surroundings looked like everywhere else to me: white and more or less flat. I had yet to learn much; the signposts of the tundra landscape were hidden from my inexperienced eyes.

"During the next day's daylight, we went looking for caribou. In mid-winter, there aren't many, but there were, Mannik assured, usually some around here. We found a few. He picked out the one he wanted, and after carefully approaching, as an old hunter would, he shot a single bullet. The animal dropped. We drove over slowly on our machine. The bull caribou was still alive, just. Mannik took out his knife and deftly inserted it into the back of the caribou's neck, then, with a strong, swift movement of his wrist, dispatched the caribou for good by severing its spinal column. I was initially somewhat horrified. He explained: it was quick and it saved a bullet. In days gone by, a bullet meant a lot of food. Mannik continued with this knife, and in no time at all, the caribou was gutted, skinned, quartered, and packed into our *qamutik* [sled]. We returned to the iglu for a small feast."

On another trip with Pirjuaq, two days out from Baker Lake, the two peered out over what seemed like thousands of square kilometres of tundra. "For me, with my southern perspective, it was awe-inspiring and intimidating. For Pirjuaq, it was home. His eyes penetrated the unending whiteness in search of caribou."

Eventually, hours later, amidst the rocks on the slope of a gently rising hill two kilometres off, there were several caribou, "no bigger than specks of dirt," on David's camera lens. Pirjuaq's unaided eyes told him that none of the eight caribou were worth taking, considering their age, sex, and general health.

Meat is above all what caribou mean to Inuit, not just in ancient times but today as well. Recent studies indicate that the two principal herds hunted by Baker Lake (Beverly and Qamanirjuaq) are worth at least $20 million per year for all the Dene and Inuit communities that depend on them. Multiply that by all the barren-ground caribou herds in the North American Arctic and a conservative estimate would be a total food value of $100 million per year. Alternative protein would not be nearly as nutritious, tasty, or affordable.

Among traditional uses of caribou by Inuit, Dr. Andrew Stewart cites the following:

"Caribou skins were made into clothing, tent and kayak coverings, sleeping robes, containers for carrying water, rope (by braiding strips of skin), and communal drums; whole sets of antlers were employed as tools (shovels, dog team anchors), and antler as a raw material was used for making arrowheads, bows, and handles for implements, among other things; leg bones were particularly valuable for making tools; sinew from the back and legs of caribou provided string for backing and threading bows, for lashing and repairing broken tools, as well as for fish lines and thread for sewing; and fat could be burned in lamps during winter in addition to being an essential food in winter to supplement lean meat."

David Pelly also points out the centrality of caribou for Inuit cultural and artistic expression. For example, from Baker Lake, we have Oonark's "Flight of the Shaman," with a caribou positioned right inside the shaman's body, "suggesting it as the object of the shaman's quest for food to feed his hungry people."

But it is the Inuit starvations, most famously in the 1920s and 1950s when the caribou didn't come, that most poignantly demonstrate the supreme importance of caribou to northern peoples — literally the margin between life and death. It is difficult to listen first-hand to the stories still told by grieving survivors of those days. One can only imagine what it must be like to tell them. Hundreds of Inuit of all ages perished on the frozen tundra, some awaiting rescue and transfer into more permanent communities. Several of these tragedies were captured in the haunting black and white images of famous photographer Richard Harrington.

However, we must resist the temptation to consign the uses and importance of caribou to the past. As David Pelly points out, "For the people of the Barren Lands, the so-called Caribou Inuit, the one thing that has, until now, remained constant, as a matter of preference rather

Library and Archives Canada /Richard Harrington PA-112086.

Many inland Inuit families starved in the 1950s when the caribou did not return, a tragedy starkly captured by Richard Harrington in now-archived photographs.

Sheila Spence, The Winnipeg Art Gallery.

Jessie Oonark
Baker Lake, 1906–1985
Printmakers: Michael Amarook,
b. 1941, and Martha Noah, b. 1943
Flight of the Shaman, 1970
stencil, stonecut on paper, A/P 50
52.3 x 67.0 cm
Collection of The Winnipeg Art Gallery
The Swinton Collection
Accession #: G-76-846

than absolute necessity, is the role of caribou in their diet. One wonders how long it will, or can, remain that way, in the face of changing cultural realities, of changing wage-employment patterns, and of changing priorities in the use of the land."

Monte Hummel

Caribou hides stretched out in Baker Lake indicate the ongoing importance of caribou to Inuit.

"THE CARIBOU ARE THE DRUM, THE SONG, AND THE HEARTBEAT OF THE PEOPLE"

Larry Innes is the executive director of the Canadian Boreal Initiative, headquartered in Ottawa. However, Larry lives in Goose Bay, Labrador, among the Innu (also known as the Montagnais or Naskapi), Algonquin-speaking people closely related to the Cree. Since the early 1990s, Larry has lived, worked, and travelled with the Innu, advocated for them in their many legal fights, and assisted in their successful and precedent-setting land use planning efforts. Among other things, this work has focused on conserving the caribou upon which Innu culture depends, principally the George River and Leaf River herds.

Larry reminds us, "The centre of the Innu world is not a place, but rather revolved around the caribou migration. As one of the last nomadic hunting people on the planet — moving only recently and reluctantly to permanent communities in the late 1950s and 1960s — Innu have followed the vast caribou herds of the Quebec-Labrador Peninsula on their timeless march for millennia."

Today, however, the Innu "have largely traded snowshoes for snowmobiles, and canoes for power boats and bush planes. They no longer travel with the caribou, but many families still make extended forays into the country in the spring and the fall, maintaining their connections to the places and the practices which characterized their once nomadic way of life."

Such places include crossing sites where caribou concentrate or funnel through narrow valleys or rivers, especially during migration. These places are well known and held dear by all caribou hunting peoples.

Larry explains, "*Nutshimit* is a place where traditional Innu culture can be lived, and where the impositions of the dominant culture are less intrusive. It is a place of healing, where families

Serge Couturier

"Caribou concentrate or funnel through narrow valleys or rivers, especially during migration." A post-calving aggregation in late July, Rivière George herd.

69

are able to reconnect, away from village life. And more fundamentally, *nutshimit* is rich with meaning, where the Innu language comes alive, where the stories that connect people to the places can be told in their full context, and where even dreams are part of the reality."

Central to all this are caribou. The hunter does not "take" or kill an animal against its will, but with its consent. Therefore, caribou are "given" and must be treated with respect and handled properly — something understood even by the younger generation raised in the villages — so the ritual caribou feast, or *mukushan,* is still practised after successful hunts.

Larry also provided the following account, drawn from his travel on the land with Innu hunters:

"The hunters' return transformed the whole camp. Young children, never ones to miss a moment, were caught up in the excitement that rippled through the camp like a current. They chased between the tents, peering furtively at the hunters as they assembled a tripod from young trees.

"The women are selecting a few choice cuts for the feast that will surely follow, and threading twine through sinews to hang the meat. Some will be made into *pasteu-uiash,* a dry meat delicacy, but most will be carefully packed and stored on a scaffold until it can be sent back to the community on the next bush plane. The hides will be scraped and smoke-tanned, a laborious task that will keep several of the women busy for the next several days.

"The elder has taken the long leg bones to his tent and, kneeling on the boughs that carpet the floor, carefully cracks the bones and extracts the marrow. This he mixes in a small fire-blacked pot with the fat carefully scraped from the caribou rump and sets it on the tin tent stove. Once it has cooked, he will let it cool. It will form the centrepiece of the *mukushan,* the ritual feast.

"The whole camp gathers together that night, kneeling together in the large canvas tent around a white blanket spread out between them over the boughs. The meal is simple — freshly baked bannock, boiled caribou meat, and the elder's bone marrow cake. All eat together, and nothing is wasted. Stories are told, often ribald and amusing ones, about the day and the days before.

"At the end, as the children begin to doze in the heat radiating from the cherry red stove, the elder unwraps his drum. He holds the skin above the stove for a moment, adjusts the snares, and then hangs it in front of him, suspended on a thin cord from the ridgepole. He was already an old man when he made this drum, after he dreamed the song. The song is his own, but it is as ancient and as unchanging as this place, where his ancestors have camped, hunted, and sung since the time before time.

"The caribou are the drum, the song, and the heartbeat of the people."

"FOR AS FAR AS WE COULD SEE, THE COUNTRY WAS COVERED WITH CARIBOU"

Alex Hall is nothing short of a legend among wilderness canoe trippers. University educated as a wildlife biologist, he now lives in Fort Smith, Northwest Territories, and for nearly forty years has earned his full-time living by guiding Arctic canoe trips for clients from all over the world. In his award-winning book, *Discovering Eden: A Lifetime of Paddling Arctic Rivers*, Alex has recorded many experiences with both Arctic landscapes and wildlife — especially the Barren Lands, and especially caribou. For this book, in addition to emphasizing the

Alex Hall

Alex Hall's own photo of caribou "scattered over the distant green meadows and treeless hills."

role caribou play in North American First People's culture, we wanted to include some non-Aboriginal perspectives. Who better than someone who is sought out by adventurers whose lifetime wish is to capture these animals on film, in their trip journals, and for "off-season" memories?

Alex describes one of the greatest days in his life, July 21, 1978, which began to unfold at four in the morning on the Hanbury River in the Thelon Wildlife Sanctuary. He was awakened by voices — the din of untold thousands of guttural sounds that warned him something formidable was approaching. He scrambled out of his tent, rounded up his clients, and they all hiked up a high hill overlooking the tundra on the other side of the river. Here is Alex Hall's description of what they saw:

"For as far as we could see, the country was covered with caribou. There were tens of thousands of wild animals in sight! With many of them still in their white winter coats, they seemed like countless tiny snowflakes scattered over the distant green meadows and treeless hills.

"We had discovered a richness on the tundra that couldn't compare to money, a wealth that has nothing to do with material goods or high wages. While we'd been caught up in the swirl of blizzards, bears, and migrating animals, the only economy and freedom that had meant anything were the economy of movement and the freedom of thought. Guided by forces and knowledge we'd never known existed, we had stumbled into a dimension that neither university education, religious teachings, nor anything else in our Western upbringing had taught. It had taken a while, but for a few brief weeks we'd become caribou: content in our suffering, secure in our insecurity, fully exercising the wildness that had been buried within us all along." — Karsten Heuer, from *Being Caribou*. Seattle: The Mountaineers Books, 2005.

"Caribou are not beautiful in July. The bulls and cows are a skinny, moth-eaten looking bunch in that month, still shedding their ragged winter hair. These animals on the Hanbury ranged in colour from almost white to dark brown, with most sporting some gradation or patchwork combination of those shades in between. Bulls were relatively scarce, but their antlers were now two-thirds grown, covered in velvet. The calves, already impressive runners at six weeks of age, were there by the thousands in a variety of hues from creamy white to cinnamon to chocolate brown.

"It was the cows and calves that were making all the noise. In the confusion of travelling in these incredible numbers, the cows seemed to be grunting almost continuously at their wayward calves to keep track of them, while the calves, in a higher pitch, honked back. Over the course of that day, a mounting swell of these low, primitive sounds announced the arrival of each new wave of animals that swept into sight. In addition to the cacophony, our senses were bombarded by the sweet aroma of fresh caribou manure, which floated on the breeze all day, and even throughout the next one after the land lay empty again."

Alex goes on to describe massive waves and columns of caribou flowing into valleys, pooling up, feeding, and moving on, only to be replaced by another large aggregation. In the process, the tundra was being cut up into hundreds of new caribou trails. He even stood still among them, engulfed by thousands of caribou that were feeding, resting, and nursing. "We felt immensely privileged to be accepted into the midst of so many wild creatures, and to witness a day in their lives at such close quarters."

That one herd took over twenty-four hours to pass, and based on experience, Alex estimated their number at two hundred thousand!

"With the sun now low on the northwestern horizon, and the murmur from the great herd still riding on the wind, my clients and I retired to our tents for the night after an extremely long but inspiring day. For me, the experience had felt like the stuff of legends, as if we had been allowed a glimpse of a primordial world teeming with life. Just before I drifted off to sleep, I wrote in my journal that I had never been so proud to be a Canadian."

This kind of experience is life changing, and unfortunately reserved for the very few who chance to witness it first-hand. In fact, even after thirty-seven summers of canoeing remote rivers, Alex reports that he himself has happened on large caribou herds of tens of thousands of animals no more than fifteen times. "The Barren Lands comprise one-eighth of the land mass of Canada, and herds of even hundreds of thousands of animals are swallowed up in this vastness, like grains of sand in the desert."

Still, even in their absence, caribou make their presence known: through billions of trails, tracks on eskers and beaches, cast-off antlers, whitened bones from wolf kills, hair caught in shrubs and along riverbanks, and always pellets of caribou dung everywhere. And then there are exciting sightings and traces of all the other wildlife species that depend on caribou — wolves, wolverines, grizzlies, foxes, ravens, and eagles.

Caribou sign and movement enliven the tundra. Just knowing they are still out there animates the land. In Alex's words, "You are always aware of the possibility that out of this emptiness a mass of caribou could suddenly materialize. Indeed, let the silhouette of just one caribou appear on a distant ridgeline and this land becomes alive — totally transformed. As long as there are great herds of caribou, this gigantic tundra wilderness will always be, to my mind, the most vibrant place left on Earth. But without caribou, it would be little more than a desolate waste, and certainly not a place that many of us would want to spend time in."

"I AM ALWAYS HAPPY TO SEE TRACKS OF CARIBOU"

Pikangikum is a remote First Nations community in the boreal forest of northwestern Ontario, home to the Anishinabe (Ojibwa) people, who traditionally harvested woodland caribou. In fact, the Pikangikum First Nation's territory includes a provincial wilderness park called Woodland Caribou, as well as the Whitefeather Forest, for which a management plan is being developed that considers industrial forestry, but in such a way that the land continues to be protected. The elders' quotes in this section are taken directly from a draft 2006 report by the Whitefeather Forest Management Corporation titled *Keeping Woodland Caribou on the Land: Cross-Cultural Research in the Whitefeather Forest* (see complete citation under References).

Roy Owen and Solomon Turtle explained that in the past, Pikangikum people used caribou for smoked and dried meat, moccasins, shoes, mittens, hide mats, mattresses, fur cutters, and scrapers. Even the toenails were used as part of a shake rattle for dances in a long building called a *wabanoo*, held up by poles in the middle. "People would dance around those poles [clockwise]. This rattle showed the significance of the caribou to people at that time. They used everything and didn't throw anything away," said Elder Whitehead Moose.

As with the Dene, Inuit, and Innu, caribou hide with the fur still on it was always best for bedding and other items used to keep warm.

Unlike Aboriginal cultures farther north, however, the Pikangikum people no longer hunt caribou very much. There are a number of reasons for this, but most interviewees cited a preference today for moose meat. That in turn has raised the issue of whether the caribou are declining, at least in part, *because* they are no longer being harvested. That's because using wildlife is one way of showing respect for it. In the words of Solomon Turtle, "Why should the Creator give us more when we don't harvest so much anymore?"

There is also concern about so much attention being paid to the caribou, especially by southern conservationists, almost as if there is nothing *else* of significance in the forest.

"Is the caribou the only animal recognized on the land? I don't hear any other animals being discussed. For instance, the squirrel makes its home in the trees but nobody ever fights for the squirrel; nobody ever protects

Caribou move through the boreal forest of northern Ontario.

Justina C. Ray

the land for the squirrel. Why not? It amazes me. Is the caribou the only animal alive today?" said Gideon Peters.

So caribou are seen as part of something bigger, something called *cheemahnahcheetohwin*, which is like taking care of the land in such a way that it will continue to take care of you:

"*Cheemahnahcheetohwin* is a traditional process based on how long something will sustain you, it would have to be for a long period of time, even indefinitely. It is as if you have food in your box, and it will be there for a long time, it will preserve you. It is the same with animals; if you take what you need, then they will be there to preserve you. Same with the trees: take only what you need. This doesn't mean you are protecting those things just so they can be around," said Whitehead Moose.

In this way, caribou continue to play a role in Anishinabe culture as part of a broader world view and land ethic. There are also modern caribou clans or totems, to protect family genetics and indicate a person's lineage. This is still intensely felt: "I feel that the caribou is close to me; that I am close to it. That is why I was given the caribou as a totem. I am always happy to see tracks of caribou. I can kill one but I cannot desecrate my relationship with the caribou. They didn't kill that caribou for just any reason but for survival, such as for food and clothing," said Jake Keijick.

CARIBOU AND THE NORTH AMERICAN PSYCHE

To be sure, caribou are central to both the ecology and the cultures of the North. There are some who would like Aboriginal culture in particular to be thought of as something more resilient, adaptable, and modern than a way of life dependent on wildlife in general, let alone on one species. However, even they concede that a future that maintains the option to embrace the best of both worlds, a wage economy *and* life on the land, would be preferable.

But what about the 99 percent of North Americans who live elsewhere? Why should they become interested in caribou?

First, the fact that caribou equate with the North raises the question of how the North itself figures into the larger North American psyche. This is a daunting subject, about which much has already been written.

Certainly Canadians think of themselves as a northern people, even though 80 percent of them, a larger percentage than Americans, live in what Statistics Canada has classified as urban centres. The theme of the North explicitly figures into the national anthem; it haunts Canadian art, literature, and music (the Group of Seven, Robert Bateman, Farley Mowat, Glenn Gould); and iconic northern wildlife species such as polar bears — indeed, any mention of the Arctic — literally shouts "Canadian!" to the rest of the world.

Map: Christopher S. McDougall / Photo: Julie Yamaguchi

Map 1.10. As an illustration of the importance of caribou to people, many hundreds of towns, lakes, rivers, and other places bear the name "caribou" in North America.

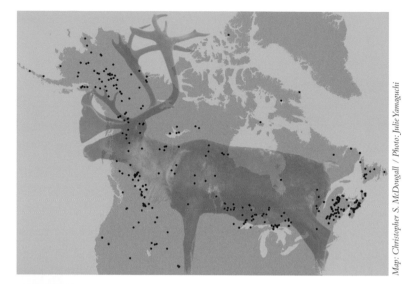

Below: The backlit form of caribou antlers, a shape that has come to symbolize the North for many Americans and Canadians alike.

Andrew Leith Macrae

Beyond the myth and the "brand," however, if you include the boreal region — which alone occupies over half the area of Canada (580 million of 1 billion hectares) — the vast majority of the country *is* in fact northern. And the Aboriginal cultures that long predate European contact and settlement have come to stand for Canada — arguably more compellingly than large urban centres. Whether you're among those who are frustrated or moved by such images, there's no denying them.

For the United States, Alaska seems to serve much the same function, fulfilling a northern myth in the national consciousness. As a relatively recent addition to the country, the state is considered to be both geographically and psychologically distinct from the "lower forty-eight." Alaska continues to be stereotyped (mostly positively) as a pristine last frontier where a person can still be unfettered and self-reliant in business, or go big game hunting, or escape civilization by homesteading in the wilderness. And where would coffee-table books or television nature specials be without Alaska?

But in fact, some of America's (and the world's) greatest proactive conservation achievements have been accomplished in Alaska. These date back to President Eisenhower, who established the Arctic National Wildlife Refuge in 1960, and President Carter, who in 1980 signed the Alaska National Interests Lands Conservation Act, which protected more than 100 million acres of national parks, refuges, and forests. This stands today as one of the most impressive wilderness complexes on Earth. Therefore, the notion that Alaska is still a wild and beautiful part of the planet is a reality, not just a myth.

So what role do caribou play in the powerful impression the North has made on North Americans, and on others who stand in envy of our natural birthright?

Since 1937, a caribou has appeared on the Canadian quarter, and during a national CBC contest, the great migratory herds were repeatedly nominated as one of Canada's unique "wonders of the world." Who among us is not moved by Alex Hall's description, and who doesn't yearn to experience the breathtaking tide of life he witnessed flowing across the tundra on that day? Caribou have come to represent a wilderness phenomenon that many North Americans would love to experience at least once in their lifetimes.

Certainly for the United States, one of the best-known national conservation issues is the long-standing struggle over proposals to drill in the caribou calving area of the Arctic National Wildlife Refuge. In fact, it is one of the highest profile American conservation issues for other nationalities as well, especially Europeans. This concern has made its way onto the agenda for high-level meetings between virtually every American president and Canadian prime minister over the last twenty-five years. Incidentally, the majority of Americans and Canadians alike do *not* support drilling in the Refuge. So caribou have periodically come to the fore in both nations' consciousnesses, when this issue makes its rounds every few years.

As oil and gas development proliferates in Alaska on the North Slope, along with new pipeline proposals, and as oil and gas development and diamond and uranium mining do the same in Arctic Canada, there is every likelihood that caribou will become more, rather than less, of a catalyst for public debate.

Similarly, boreal forest caribou have become the popular symbol — some might less charitably say "poster children" — for conservation of the forests they inhabit. High-profile market campaigners are pressuring large corporate consumers of wood products from the boreal forest to improve their purchasing policies and to avoid products from endangered forests, using threatened caribou as the lightning rod for their campaigns. The suppliers in turn are being asked to improve their management practices, including leaving room for caribou. These environmental expectations are intensifying, and they are spilling over into

Steven Barger

Caribou have come to stand for big, wild areas that are becoming globally scarce. This is a bull caribou from the Denali herd in early fall, Denali National Park, Alaska.

purchasing preferences for all of us. So again, it is reasonable to speculate that caribou are on the ascendancy when it comes to North Americans' collective radar screen. Already there are co-operating Canadian-American advocacy organizations in both countries heightening awareness of the link between the boreal forest and caribou.

Although it may not have reached national or international awareness yet, certainly the plight of southern mountain caribou is a high-profile concern in the British Columbia press. And rightly so, because these animals are genuinely endangered, on the brink of extinction. British Columbia conservation issues, such as saving old-growth temperate rainforests, have had

"The results of the [Caribou] Summit clearly demonstrate pan-northern agreement that action must be taken to reduce harvesting and focus on recovery. A very real sense of responsibility and concern was demonstrated and was evident by the actions identified that were aimed at both Aboriginal and public governments as well as the various stakeholders and management agencies in the North. It was particularly poignant to hear Aboriginal leaders talk about their willingness to forgo exercising harvesting rights for the sake of recovery of the caribou populations." — Executive Summary, *Northwest Territories Barren-ground Caribou Summit*. Inuvik: Northwest Territories Environment and Natural Resources, August 2007.

a habit of moving quickly beyond that province in terms of public consciousness — another potential growth front for caribou.

Most northerners would be mildly amused, and sometimes irritated, by what it takes to interest everyone else in caribou. Certainly *they* need no convincing. In light of widespread declines in many western Arctic herds, in January 2007 the government of the Northwest Territories decided to host a Caribou Summit in the small western Arctic community of Inuvik. The organizers originally planned for fifty to sixty participants, but nearly two hundred showed up, bursting the seams of the town. They came from Alaska and all affected Canadian political jurisdictions — elders, hunters, grand chiefs, ministers, members of the legislative assembly, former premiers, co-management boards, biologists, industry representatives, guide outfitters, non-government organizations, and the media. Overnight, because of caribou, Inuvik became the place to be. As one participant put it, "Let's face it, if you're not going to protect caribou, you're not going to protect anything."

CONCLUSION

THERE IS JUST no question about the overwhelming ecological and cultural importance of caribou, first and foremost for northerners, and increasingly for North Americans at large. This animal stands at the very centre of things in the North. It has come to symbolize the future of inspiring landscapes and a way of life that has much to teach us.

In his essay *Wilderness*, under the sub-heading "The Remnants," the great American conservationist Aldo Leopold wrote, " In Canada and Alaska there are still large expanses of virgin country ... to what extent Canada and Alaska will be able to see and grasp their opportunities is anybody's guess."

More than fifty years later, Leopold's challenge to see and grasp our opportunities remains before us all — Canadians and Americans alike. But now the opportunities are fewer; the options are being foreclosed. In many ways, the future of caribou will be the measure for whether we saw and grasped our opportunities while we still had the chance.

Steven Barger

SECTION TWO

PRESSURES ON CARIBOU:
PAST, PRESENT, AND FUTURE

INTRODUCTION

VISITORS AND RESIDENTS alike are swayed by the vast, untrammelled landscapes that still characterize most of the North. It may all have been flown over many times, huge areas may have been at least lightly traversed on the ground, and certainly humans have been present there for millennia. But the North still harbours some of the last truly wild areas on our planet.

Yet a tire track in the tundra can persist for years. And over the past thirty or forty years, those tire tracks, and much more, have been impacting caribou country throughout the North as it experiences increasing pressure on its ecological and cultural systems. We are at a crossroads: there's so much on the drawing board, so much new development being contemplated and beginning to show itself, that we now face irreversible decisions about how all of this, or which parts of it, will actually proceed, and under what conditions. Such decisions are rarely made all at once. Rather, they are made one at a time, incrementally whittling away almost unnoticeably at natural values, in what has been described as the "salami effect." Each slice doesn't seem like much at the time, but the salami is gradually getting smaller nevertheless, and eventually — sometimes surprisingly if you haven't been watching what's going on — it is gone. This is the larger context in which a viable future for caribou must be fashioned.

History has shown us repeatedly that seemingly limitless resources have an underlying vulnerability. Our technology has made hitherto inaccessible areas increasingly easy to reach, and our ability to view the world from space has given us a keen sense of the nature and extent of the human footprint. Look at a satellite image of the Earth's polar region at night. Using artificial light to indicate human impact, northern North America, which happens to coincide with caribou distribution, emerges as one of those globally rare, still-natural locations from which a person can see the stars in an unpolluted, dark night sky. But it also shows human pressures hugging the southern rim. And there are existing pockets of light in the North itself — the territorial capitals, scattered communities, and a few large diamond mines. What's unseen is the equivalent of the electrical current driving all this, namely plans to move southern pressures northward and existing northern activities outward.

Caribou are often regarded as "resilient" because they are so supremely adapted to all manner of environments. They certainly deserve this reputation, having weathered great changes over thousands of years. But they have not yet witnessed the kinds of fast-paced, fundamental shifts that are already here, with more on the horizon. The extent to which caribou can adapt to such changes in the long run remains an open question. But in our view the early signals are not encouraging: they deserve our attention and actions now, while they can still make a difference.

Since Europeans first began to describe North American wildlife in written form, the word *crisis* has been invoked to describe the situation facing caribou on numerous occasions. But, as most Aboriginal residents of the

NASA-AVHRR, NDVI, Seawifs, MODIS, NCEP, DMSP and Sky2000 star catalog; AVHRR and Seawifs texture: Reto Stockli Visualization: Marit Jentoft-Nilsen

Satellite photo: A nighttime satellite photo over Earth's northern polar region shows how dark and natural this area remains at the moment.

North often remark, declines have happened before and have been experienced as a part of life. "The story of caribou in North America is a story of constant change," says caribou scientist Tom Bergerud. If anything, caribou populations have demonstrated a marvellous propensity to rebound from lows, even when such lows were caused by humans. It is also not uncommon for populations to plunge for entirely natural reasons, only to rebound to previous levels and beyond. And there are occasions when populations have increased at the same time that they faced development pressures in their range, contrary to both intuition and predictions. However, relying on that capacity for regrowth, while at the same time applying still more pressure, is not a formula for success.

By better understanding what makes caribou not just resilient but also inherently vulnerable, by learning from the past, and by looking realistically at the pressures that caribou currently face, we will be best equipped to strike a future path in the face of profound change. Such an approach should also cause us to ask which changes are acceptable, and which we must avoid if at all possible. Ultimately, saving caribou will involve mustering the courage to say yes to the things we value, and no to the forces that threaten them. In so doing, however, we will be increasingly forced to confront the trade-offs this will entail, and to curb our appetite for northern natural resources as we are faced with the reality that we cannot necessarily have both all the time.

David J. Tilley

A mid-summer group of Newfoundland caribou.

CHAPTER FIVE

What Makes Caribou Vulnerable?

NATURAL CYCLES

NATURAL EBBS AND flows, so characteristic of northern environments, cycle during the course of a year and over decades. Many scientists and northern residents alike say that for caribou these cycles occur on the order of every forty years, but it may not be as neat and tidy as that. There are definitely natural dips in numbers of the great herds, followed by resurgences, both relatively synchronized across many migratory tundra populations in the Far North. Some specific populations may rise and fall at a slower pace, but the same overall rhythm is evident. During this past century, many populations experienced downturns in the 1930s, then again in the 1970s. The latest surge was in the 1990s. But starting in this century, most migratory tundra herds have declined — some by as much as 85 percent. Is this latest downturn yet another part of natural cycles that make snapshot views and judgments about caribou status such a challenge? Or is it the front end of a longer term decline that should generate bona fide alarm regarding the ultimate fate of the species?

The George River herd, in Quebec and Labrador, is one population that has been documented continually since the 1950s. During this time, herd numbers have fluctuated from as many as 650,000 animals to as few as 5,000. This has led to everything from proposals to set up an abattoir on the tundra to commercially process these caribou at their population highs, to doom and gloom hand-wringing over the future of the herd when 10,000 caribou drowned in one episode during migration. Similarly in Alaska, the western Arctic herd, which currently numbers about 500,000 animals, crashed to as low as 75,000 in the mid-1970s.

Serge Couturier

The mighty Rivière George migratory tundra herd of northern Quebec and Labrador has numbered as high as over half a million animals, and has been counted at fewer than ten thousand.

So, dramatic changes in caribou numbers can generate confusion and alarm bells, complete with premature announcements regarding the disappearance of entire herds. Some herds have "gone missing," only to reappear out of nowhere after a few years. This has happened with the Qamanirjuaq population at different times in the past, and with the Beverly herd as recently as 2007. Such anecdotal assessments are not hard to understand, given the vastness of the terrain. But with the rising sophistication of research tools, combined with increasingly focused attention on this animal, biologists and managers are getting better at locating and counting caribou. The direct observations of the people who live there are also being incorporated with more frequency into pronouncements about the state of a given caribou population.

More than anything, the population cycles witnessed over the past few hundred years speak to the potential of caribou to rebound from past pressures if *the opportunity to do so still exists.* Generally speaking, that means that there must be adequate time and space for the pressures of habitat change, disturbance from human land use activities, climate change, natural predation, and hunting to be alleviated. Of increasing concern is the role that new human-induced pressures can play in reducing opportunities for caribou recovery, thereby compounding the lows in natural population cycles.

NATURAL DISTURBANCE

As with population cycling, climate patterns and natural disturbances are a historical and ongoing fact of life for caribou, to which they have adapted over time. At large scales, these include forest fires, which have always been an integral component of caribou range, especially in the boreal forest. Fires can affect the availability of critical food lichens literally overnight. Therefore, they have the potential to alter substantial parts of caribou range by rendering them unusable from one day to the next. Over time, caribou compensate for this loss of range by shifting to more suitable swaths of older forest; generally they do not reside

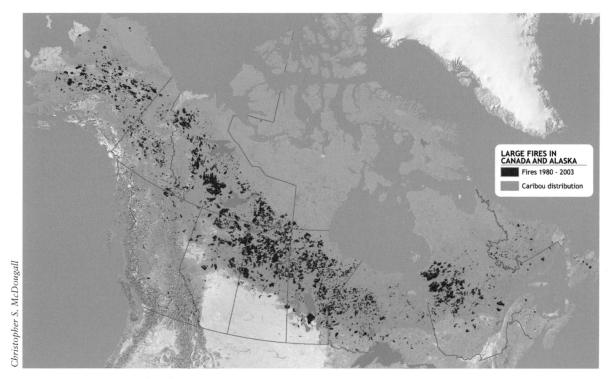

Christopher S. McDougall

Map 2.1. *Large forest fires (more than two hundred hectares in size) across Canada and Alaska during the years 1980–2003.*

in burned areas until those areas are at least fifty years old — the time it takes most lichens to regrow. Therefore, having large available ranges in a disturbance-prone landscape, so that caribou always have an unburned area to turn to, appears to be a key mechanism for them to withstand these natural events.

Another ongoing natural disturbance for caribou habitats has been insects. Waves of mountain pine beetle, spruce budworm, and other pests passing through on a periodic basis can alter the boreal forest in ways similar to fire, causing individual trees, or pockets and swaths of forest, to die. However, such outbreaks in the past have generally served to alter structure in the forest and not necessarily to kill all the food sources for caribou. What's different in the modern age is the compulsion to "salvage" insect-affected forests by intensively logging them for fear of such areas going to commercial waste.

Climate change appears to be playing a significant role in some insect outbreaks, the most important example being mountain pine beetle in British Columbia. With fewer days of deep freeze in the winter to kill the larvae, they instead flourish over time and expand their range. The increased logging that has followed the path of this insect, which may soon jump from lodgepole to jack pine, is a major force that is changing the shape of caribou habitat.

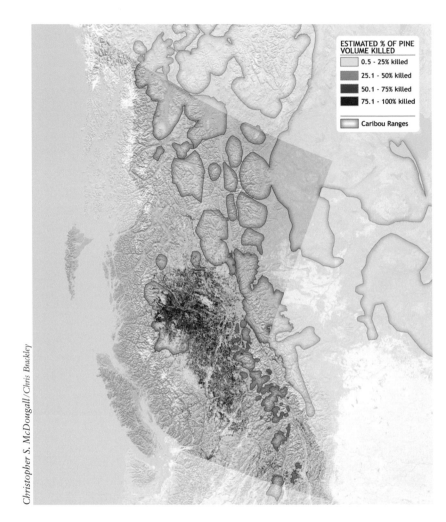

Christopher S. McDougall/Chris Brackley

ESTIMATED % OF PINE
VOLUME KILLED

0.5 - 25% killed
25.1 - 50% killed
50.1 - 75% killed
75.1 - 100% killed

Caribou Ranges

Map 2.2. *The extent of mountain pine beetle damage relative to mountain caribou distribution in British Columbia (1999–2006).*

Wolves and grizzly bears are also natural threats to individual caribou, following them as far as their calving grounds in tundra environments. For boreal forest and mountain caribou, predator pressure can be relentless; it is one important factor that appears to explain why and how individual caribou space themselves. Indeed, there is much evidence that an underlying force driving the evolution of caribou behaviour and ecology is the risk of being chased, ambushed, killed, or eaten. Simply put, caribou need space to keep one or two steps ahead of predators. Although caribou make up only a small component of the diet of boreal bears and wolves, even low levels of predation can threaten the viability of a small caribou population.

The harsh environments that are home to caribou in the High Arctic are periodically characterized by particularly severe winters, or freezing in the fall, or any weather pattern that can interrupt the generally fragile course of life. One misstep — a hoof through the ice, the inability to get food for days at a time — can lead to many more deaths than might occur under more normal weather conditions.

These are only a few of the natural disturbances that caribou have had to contend with, long before the arrival of human-induced land use changes. The difference now is that such natural phenomena, through which caribou have persisted for millennia, can serve as tipping points when acting in combination with unprecedented people pressures.

VULNERABILITY OF CALVES

Paradoxically, although they have adapted to more demanding environmental conditions than their deer cousins, caribou in some respects are inherently more vulnerable than other hoofed mammals. Compared to moose, deer, and elk, for example, caribou have a lower reproductive potential: females typically do not produce young until over two years of age, and then have only one calf per year. Making it through the first year of life can be an enormous challenge for a calf. In the first six weeks, its precarious, wobbly state renders it vulnerable to a whole suite of threats, including predation, drowning, starvation, abandonment, or random accidents. At the same time, adults that may be rearing calves or otherwise contributing to the next generation can die as a result of predation, human hunting, disease, starvation, or accidents such as avalanches, falls, or even motor vehicle collisions.

Simple mathematics dictates that the production of calves must be enough to keep pace with the mortality rate suffered by adults. Typically in large-bodied herbivores, a small difference in adult female survival dictates whether a population increases or declines. Variation in calf survival is somewhat less important, unless it becomes a trend — then a decline can be accelerated. In fact, keeping up with mortality is the only mechanism for a population to re-

David J. Tilley

Having survived the most vulnerable period of life, this moulting yearling from Newfoundland will have about two more years until it reaches adulthood.

"Indeed, less than five minutes after being born, the calf levered itself upright on what appeared to be a very generous helping of legs. It was comical how long they were — four stiltlike limbs wedged under a tiny body, each jerking its own way as new nerves short-circuited under the paper-thin skin. Struggling for control, the calf pitched forward and toppled, staying on the ground only as long as it took to gather itself up and try again." — Karsten Heuer, from *Being Caribou*. Seattle: The Mountaineers Books, 2005.

main on a more or less stable path. While other animals are capable of making up for that deficit by producing larger or more frequent litters that survive easily, the physiology of caribou and the harsh environment they live in do not put them in the same league. This increases the stakes for caribou when it comes to recovery from disturbance — be it natural or caused by people. While decline of a herd can be measured in terms of calf production and survival, caribou populations can decline for any reason, with or without development pressures. This is the essence of a common controversy: whether the declines now being witnessed would be happening without pressures from human activities, and whether it is even possible to link changes in caribou populations to human-caused pressures.

Female caribou travel less during the calving and post-calving periods in the spring and summer months, when they show their strongest fidelity to calving and post-calving ranges. This reduced movement renders individuals more vulnerable to, and less able to recover from, disruption during this most sensitive part of their life cycle. Migratory tundra caribou that congregate on the calving grounds are more vulnerable because all the cows of the herd are present and their calves are born within a few days of each other. At

Serge Couturier

This calf from the Rivière George herd is less than 24 hours old. Even a newborn caribou calf can stand, walk, and join its mother and herd within a matter of hours.

this time, cows are especially alert and responsive to danger. But they cannot afford too many interruptions to their foraging, which they need to supply milk to their calves.

There is good reason for the rush to calving grounds for migratory tundra, boreal forest, and mountain caribou alike. Regularly, the conditions elsewhere are not nearly as good: the cows arrive and give birth usually in time to eat high-quality forage, as the leaves and flowers bud out while the snow melts. So there can be a high price to pay if the cows don't make it on time. For example, in 2000 and 2001, unusual and extensive snow cover prevented Porcupine caribou herd cows from reaching their usual calving grounds in Alaska. Instead, females gave birth to their calves wherever they were at the time while en route, and the resulting survival of these calves was markedly reduced. The post-calving period of about three to five weeks after birth — when the calves are consuming green vegetation as well as the cow's milk — is also a particularly critical time. This period foretells their future growth, because it has a direct link to their own ultimate size as well as that of their future offspring. Even beyond the post-calving period, it is the calves in a caribou population that are at the greatest risk of death.

In any given area, the calving period is highly predictable, occurring in late May or early June, depending on the latitude. With most births in a caribou population generally occurring within the space of two weeks, calves typically make up as much as 30 percent of a population for this brief period. However, by the time those calves reach independence, about half will have died. As a rule of thumb, for a population to remain stable from one year to the next, at least 15 percent must be calves that have survived in that year.

Mother and calf along the Thelon River, likely part of the Beverly herd.

THE NEED FOR SPACE

Bigger is better (and necessary) when it comes to accommodating all the needs of a caribou population. This is obvious regarding the lifestyle of migratory tundra caribou. But even sedentary mountain and boreal forest caribou, which disperse when calving, generally maintain maximum space between females. Therefore, herds of a sufficient size to maintain viability will inhabit very large areas. This space is often the key to recovery from natural disturbances on their range, and if there is enough room to steer clear of new, unexpected stimuli (such as development activities), they will be better off.

Caribou generally occupy areas where alternative prey, such as moose and deer, are not numerous enough to support robust predator populations. As a result, depending on the time of year, boreal forest caribou are generally found in regions with old coniferous forest, peat, or wetland complexes, and in high-elevation areas. These habitats are typically nutrient-poor, lacking sufficient vegetation to support moose and deer. However, such areas are most important not because they directly provide food or shelter to caribou, but rather because they indirectly maintain low predator populations at the regional or population level. Therefore, habitats across the range of a caribou population must not be suitable for supporting alternative ungulate populations in order to best maintain caribou viability.

Caribou are not as efficient at escaping into safe terrain as more nimble sheep and goats. So in western North American predator-prey systems, which can be composed of up to six other ungulates and four to five large predators, caribou are hands down the most vulnerable. As a result, they are usually the first ungulate species to decline, and the last to recover. This puts caribou at a disadvantage relative to other species when they inhabit a shared range, particularly during calving. The caribou's survival strategy is to create as much space as possible between themselves and their predators, as well as between themselves and other prey that might attract those predators.

Caribou create space between themselves and other animals by virtue of the big, rugged places they inhabit.

Caribou will also use areas where the environmental conditions (such as snow) give them an advantage over predators. But in areas where a wolf population is sustained by other prey species, these predators can actually eliminate a caribou population because they are such easy pickings, being easier to kill than moose, for example. And since other food species are available, the wolf population may not be affected as caribou decline.

It is the caribou's need for space that gives rise to concerns about what happens when industrial development encroaches on its habitat. For example, timber harvesting is one of the most extensive human-caused disturbances in boreal forests. Although fire is also an important and extensive disturbance, it tends to be sufficiently patchy and isolated in terms of when and where it occurs that fire-affected areas do not support increased predator densities. Most important, fire does not bring roads with it. In comparison, timber harvesting is never isolated, but rather is part of a regional economic development process. As such, industrial forest operations and their accompanying roads typically eventually cause habitat change and increased predator densities over a large area. Habitat transformations caused by other land use footprints, such as well sites, pipelines, and seismic lines, are also sufficient to cause caribou populations to decline.

Unlike the extensive impact of timber harvesting, mining is often presented as an intensive industrial activity, i.e. the actual mine occupies a relatively small area and therefore has only localized impacts. However, with their associated pits, berms, dust, and noise, mines located on migration routes can deflect caribou from their normal lines of travel. Mines need to be serviced, often by a more extensive seasonal or permanent road network, which obviously reaches out beyond the mine itself. Also, any mining-related contamination problems can spread far and wide, especially if they enter a larger water drainage system. Furthermore, the exploration phase of mining is definitely an extensive actively, i.e. it is spread out over a large area, and numerous exploration projects are often underway at once along migration routes or in calving and post-calving areas. Sometimes exploration can be conducted from the air, or from small camps dispersed broadly across the land, in which case impacts on caribou may be lower. However, this assumes that measures to protect caribou are implemented, such as minimum levels for overflights and shutting down operations during the migration, calving, and post-calving seasons. Again, all these factors become potential problems because of the caribou's fundamental biological need for space.

Hydroelectric development can also be an issue through access roads, transmission line right-of-ways, and the dams themselves. "Run of the river" technology notwithstanding, most hydro development still floods large areas, which can affect caribou range. For example, removal of the northern portion of their traditional calving area due to such flooding probably caused the decline of the Lac Joseph herd in Labrador.

SAFETY FROM PREDATORS

Most boreal forest and mountain caribou populations that are being monitored within ranges subjected to forest harvesting are in decline. The evidence suggests that such activity alters a critical caribou-predator relationship, resulting in reduced recruitment of calves into the herd and lowered survival rates. The principal driver of this appears to be habitat change. The relatively

A large tundra wolf surveys caribou country near the Back River, Nunavut.

high reproductive potential of moose and deer allows them to take ready advantage of flushes of young vegetation that arise after forest disturbance, allowing predators to reach higher population densities than they might otherwise in regions where caribou occur.

Migratory tundra caribou choose calving ranges in part to maintain safe distances from most predators. If forced to calve elsewhere, due to a failure to reach the calving ground or a calving area that has been rendered unsafe due to development, excessive predation can be a consequence.

It is difficult to disentangle various pressures on caribou, but since predators leave dramatic evidence of dead animals behind, it is always tempting to "push the predator button" and mount predator control programs when it comes to management decisions. However, decision makers often fail to separate the *proximate* from the *ultimate* factors of caribou decline; in this case, while predators may produce the proximate final death blow, often it is ultimately habitat change precipitated by industrial development that triggers the changes in predator populations that increase the pressure on caribou. Fraction-of-a-second reactions form a caribou's margin between escape and death, so it is only reasonable to expect subtle consequences of habitat change to be linked with vulnerability to predation. As such, management decisions should respect and address those other causes for caribou decline as well as, perhaps even as a condition of, reducing predator numbers. As the respected biologist Frank Banfield observed in the 1950s regarding migratory tundra caribou, "We must not delude ourselves by laying the entire blame for the caribou decline upon the wolf. It should be remembered that large caribou herds existed in the past in spite of a relatively uncontrolled wolf population. Now, when caribou are becoming scarcer, we covet every caribou taken by a wolf."

A science-based perspective refuses to make predators into either devils or angels, but instead tries to figure out when they are a limiting factor on a caribou population and when they are not, as well as the underlying reasons behind their pressure. It must be stated, however, that when herds have passed beyond a certain point, society must accept the consequences of a decision to conserve those herds at all costs. Under such circumstances, "controlling" predators by removing or killing them may be the only option. Not even strict habitat protection may be enough to conserve caribou once the whole system has shifted enough to put caribou in real peril.

FOOD

Food requirements are paramount for all caribou. Migratory tundra caribou travel to the calving and post-calving areas to take advantage of "green up" for the health of the calves and cows that need an influx of good nutrition at this time of the year. Summer wanderings are also food-related, as well as being influenced by mosquitoes and warble flies. And of course winter habitat must provide sufficient forage, usually in the form of lichens, for caribou to make it through to spring. Therefore, anything that affects availability of food, from fires to industrial development to insects to ice to altered distribution of vegetation due to climate change, can increase the inherent vulnerability of caribou. Some Alaskan researchers think they are already seeing replacement of preferred lichens by vascular plants that are less desirable for caribou — a result of widespread warming.

Mountain caribou are particularly exposed to dramatic differences in snow depth, which in turn determines whether they can access arboreal versus terrestrial lichens. Fires, predators, industrial development, and backcountry recreation (such as heli-skiing) can all displace these caribou from prime feeding areas.

The influence of human-induced habitat changes on caribou nutrition remains poorly understood. It is important to note that poor nutrition can result in much more subtle negative impacts on caribou than out-and-out starvation. Undernourished animals may be weakened to the point where they succumb more easily to disease or predation. Inadequate nutrition can also decrease calf production and recruitment in a population. A caribou's life requires a strong body for constant travelling, swimming, and surviving temperature extremes. Therefore, it stands to reason that this species is very sensitive to both the quantity and quality of its food resources.

Andrew Leith Macrae

This abundant ground lichen is eaten by caribou, therefore it is commonly called "reindeer lichen" or "caribou moss."

David J. Tilley

A caribou cow forages on an arboreal lichen commonly called "old man's beard."

An early autumn bull browses on alders.

THE DANGER OF SMALL POPULATIONS

When caribou are reduced to small populations, they are all the more susceptible to bad luck and even extinction. Recent research has indicated that populations composed of fewer than fifty individuals are ultimately destined for extinction, whereas ones with at least three hundred animals provide safer ground. Most small populations are isolated from neighbouring populations and surrounded by hostile, degraded habitat, further contributing to their vulnerability. This is the case for mountain caribou in the southern part of their distribution in British Columbia, and for many boreal forest populations in the southern portion of their current distribution in Alberta, Saskatchewan, Manitoba, Ontario, and Quebec.

Another group in this situation is at the northern extremity of North American caribou distribution, namely Peary caribou in the High Arctic. Here, some of the dozen or so sub-populations of Peary caribou on different islands may have been brought to the brink by inclement weather affecting their food supply. This makes them more vulnerable to additional pressures such as human harvest, climate change, and industrial activity (mining and hydrocarbon exploration and development).

Endangered mountain and boreal forest caribou populations are best known for high-profile campaigns to protect their forest habitats from industrial development. But in their current precarious state, they are also vulnerable to plain bad luck. One incident, such as a poaching event or an episode of bad weather, could wipe out significant portions of a population already barely

Peary caribou search for food under the snow in the High Arctic Islands.

hanging on. Obviously, such incidents, which would be buffered by a more robust population, could mean the difference between survival and extinction for a small, vulnerable herd.

Translocations have been used to add to existing caribou populations or to restore them to previously occupied habitat. This has occurred in the South Selkirk Mountains of northern Idaho, the Charlotte Alplands of southern British Columbia, and the Lake Superior shore of Ontario. The rationale behind such caribou reintroductions is that they may buy precious time or help to maintain a local caribou population in its current range. For example, 103 animals were translocated into the South Selkirks between 1987 and 1998. While this population is still highly endangered, with only about thirty-five animals, transplants appear to have enabled it to persist for the time being. Other reintroductions have ended in failure. In Maine, for example, the introduced caribou succumbed to the meningeal worm, or brainworm (*Parelaphostrongylus tenuis*), a parasite normally associated with white-tailed deer; or they were killed by bears; or they just plain disappeared. A concern with any translocation is to move in animals with similar, if not identical, habitat associations and genetic makeup as those that are already there. Another tool that is just beginning to be used to aid the recovery of small, isolated caribou populations on the brink in Alberta, British Columbia, and the Yukon, is captive breeding or maternity enclosures to protect pregnant caribou and calves during the period when they are most vulnerable in the wild.

Often when a species (such as the grizzly bear or wolf) has been persecuted on a continental scale, what's left behind are isolated, vulnerable small populations that sadly "wink out" over time. Some of these local extinctions, for example wolves in Yellowstone, have been reversed through reintroductions. A similar effort is being made for both the plains and wood bison.

However, everyone associated with these species restorations will immediately advise others not to let the situation get to this very expensive, last-ditch point. The parallel plight of small, isolated caribou populations on the periphery of their current North American distribution should be instructive in this respect. Let's learn from these and other natural resource collapses, by acting early to bring about more chance of success at less cost.

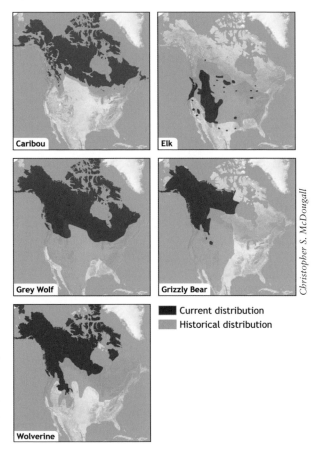

Map 2.3. *Like caribou, other large mammals in North America (such as elk, grey wolf, grizzly bear, and wolverine) have experienced range loss over the past century, with the greatest pressures occurring in the latter half of the 1800s.*

INCLEMENT WEATHER AND ACCIDENTS

One factor that renders caribou vulnerable is the unpredictability of northern environments. Even though caribou possess impressive adaptive capabilities, we have seen that bad weather or snow conditions can limit mobility and inhibit access to high-quality food. Both weather and generally treacherous conditions render caribou vulnerable to accidents, which can result in deaths, sometimes with significant impacts on populations.

Weather that results in ice forming as a hard glaze on the ground, or as a crust on or layers in the snow, has been implicated in a number of the major ungulate die-offs, including Peary caribou. Temperatures warm in spring or fall when there is already snow on the ground, which then melts or absorbs rain, before refreezing. These situations contrast with the more usual condition, in which temperatures from the first snowfall throughout the rest of winter remain below freezing and the snow remains powdery and easier to dig through.

River crossings on migration routes usually result in some drownings every year, especially by mothers and their calves in years when the snowmelt is late. In September 1984, ten thousand caribou drowned crossing the Limestone Falls on the Caniapiscau River in northern Quebec. Heavy rain and the recent release of water from the reservoir upstream conspired to create unusually high flood conditions, causing what Tom Bergerud has referred to as "the mother of all accidents." Avalanches have also been known to take down caribou residing in montane areas. While most such documented deaths have been limited to a handful of animals at a time, cases of mortalities numbering in the hundreds have occurred in Alaska and Norway. One concern is that in order to avoid areas used by humans, mountain caribou may be squeezed into sub-

The first day of spring in caribou country, east of Yellowknife, NWT.

Wild reindeer — victims of an avalanche. A minimum of 250 animals were killed in late February 2006 (exact number is not known). Svarthoe (Black Mountain) in the Dovrefjell mountains, Norway.

optimal areas that are prone to avalanches. There was one strange incident on a tundra plateau in Alaska in 1972 when fifty-three caribou were found dead in a heap; the final conclusion as to the cause of this incident was that they were struck by lightning. Deaths caused by drowning, avalanches, and even lightning strikes likely occur more frequently than we realize, since humans are still unable to witness the vast majority of caribou wanderings.

INSECT HARASSMENT AND PARASITES

We have already discussed how forest insects, such as the spruce budworm and mountain pine beetle, can affect caribou habitat. But insects can bother the caribou as well, literally to death. Anyone who has travelled in caribou country does not need to be convinced that hordes of blackflies and mosquitoes can drive any living thing mad. For migratory tundra caribou, add to these the likes of nose-bot and warble flies, which pursue caribou relentlessly to lay their eggs on their legs or nostrils. Once the nose-bot grubs hatch out, they live in the caribou's mouth, causing coughing and breathing problems. The warble fly grubs migrate to underneath the skin on a caribou's back, where they emerge through holes that make a seriously infected animal a sorry sight. Such insect harassment plays a key role in the places caribou seek out: windy expanses can provide relief. Coastal plains often provide this refuge during the calving and post-calving seasons. Insects also account, in part, for why the great migratory herds often travel together in tight groups. This minimizes exposure for animals toward the middle. In addition

to influencing their movements, minimizing exposure to insect harassment means frequent interruptions to foraging, so that caribou can end up too undernourished in the fall to become pregnant.

Farther south, white-tailed deer have been carriers of the brainworm parasite, which can be transferred with disastrous consequences to both moose and caribou where these ungulates overlap. This has led to concern about habitat changes that cause deer to move into ranges where caribou are found, or vice versa.

Glen and Rebecca Grambo

Warble fly grubs give new meaning to getting under your skin.

OVER-HARVEST

Over-harvesting is a potential problem principally for migratory tundra caribou, which are still heavily hunted and relied upon by northern communities. However, the underlying issue relates to caribou population cycles. Hunters become accustomed to high levels of harvest while caribou are increasing or have reached peak numbers, which makes it difficult to hold back or reduce the harvest when numbers decline. Further, there is often a lag between the time when numbers begin to go down, and the time when that decline is actually known and resulting reduced harvest levels take effect. So for a period of time, one factor (heavy harvesting) can be reinforcing the other (population decline).

Hunters tend to be understandably skeptical of population assessments by scientists and managers that fly in the face of what the hunters themselves are seeing on the ground; scientists and managers are understandably skeptical of anecdotal observations by hunters that contradict what their aerial and telemetry survey techniques are telling them. For the sake of the caribou, however, the object of the exercise should be to get the best of both world-views. Thankfully, as

Paul Zakora

What's left after a successful hunt.

concern grows over widespread caribou declines in the North, there are also growing signs of people coming together in this respect.

There are multiple factors that make caribou inherently vulnerable to over-harvest. First, they can occur in such large numbers in one place that it is easy to overestimate their abundance, and many can be taken at once when they congregate on a regular basis in places that are accessible to people, for example at a river or highway crossing. Second, the number of calves born every year can be very different from the number successfully recruited into the population. Third, some telemetry technologies necessary for tracking such a wide-ranging species have been used to more easily locate animals for hunting purposes. This has recently been addressed by no longer posting caribou locations in "real time." Finally, caribou are relatively easy to shoot, and thus vulnerable to excessive or wasteful harvesting. Even though boreal forest caribou are rarely the principal target of hunters, a group of caribou congregating on a lake can fall easy prey to hunters on snowmobiles, resulting in a significant portion of a population being wiped out in a single event.

On the other hand, hunters are often a valuable source of essential information for wildlife conservation, such as providing information about caribou movements and condition. Aboriginal hunters in the Far North traditionally avoid caribou calving areas, unlike prospectors or oil companies. Elders in particular are concerned about unethical hunting practices, especially by community members and others who do not show caribou the respect they deserve. And caribou are still so important in some areas — as a source of affordable, nutritious meat and for other social and cultural reasons — that hunters themselves have a direct long-term interest in not over-harvesting these animals.

CHAPTER SIX

Pressures of the Past

CARIBOU HAVE BEEN on the North American continent for as long as 2 million years, and in the course of their tenure have survived multiple ice ages, even while other mammals became extinct. The secret to their success was likely their multiple adaptations to extreme temperatures and their ability to move and follow the shifts in vegetation. Caribou fossils have been located in North America as far south as West Virginia, where caribou existed during the last Ice Age eight thousand years ago. At that time, spruce, pine, and fir boreal forest habitats extended farther south, while ice sheets covered the North. Upon the retreat of the glaciers, forests advanced northward with the accompanying climate warming, as did caribou (at a much slower pace), to where they reside today. It is the various adaptations that caribou made to these different emerging habitats, in the mountains, forest, and tundra, that account for the different caribou behaviours and ecotypes that challenge our urge to classify this species today.

Caribou have always served as a primary source of meat, clothes, and other materials for people sharing their range. Since ancient times, humans took advantage of the predictable behaviour of these animals. So it is not surprising that caribou patterns of distribution shaped those of humans as well, as camps and settlements formed in spots where the caribou would come year after year. When they did not arrive, people would often starve.

Oral tradition and archaeological evidence indicate that the opportunity to hunt migratory tundra caribou was most profitable at two times during the migration: during the late spring on the way north to the calving grounds, and in the fall during the southward return to the wintering grounds. There is also evidence of caribou being hunted at other times of year, but they were usually intercepted while on the move. Although the technology of hunting has changed, these seasonal harvesting traditions continue today.

In late spring, river crossings were predictable but often occurred across frozen terrain. A frequently used method to capture caribou then was to build hedges or fences. These were several kilometres in length, often made from stones or animal skins, with openings at various intervals across which snares would be stretched. In this way, hundreds of caribou would be deflected, lured, and captured while attempting to cross the erected

David J. Tilley

Swimming caribou were easier, but not necessarily easy, prey for ancient hunters.

John A. Nagy, GNWT

Boreal forest caribou, happened upon on open lakes, represented a relative bounty of riches for the fortunate hunter.

barrier. Sometimes Inuit families used the same fences over multiple generations, as they required large groups to build and operate.

On the return migration during the fall, rivers would be free flowing, and the most efficient way to hunt was to intercept swimming animals and spear them from kayaks.

Neither the spring nor the fall technique required European technology. The caribou fence was the most efficient at capturing large numbers of caribou, persisting even after guns were introduced, and there is still evidence of these out on the land. These hunting events, which happened a few days a year and could result in the death of many hundreds of caribou at one time, caused much shock in non-Aboriginal observers wrestling with their perception of "wanton slaughter" rather than the reality of pulsed harvests when the animals were available. Taking from this bounty on the few occasions it offered itself was understandable and necessary for subsistence purposes under such circumstances. However, the persistence of this traditional attitude, and the large numbers of animals still harvested, presents both perceived and real conservation problems today, especially when there are many other pressures acting on caribou at the same time.

By contrast, during winter months, caribou were more dispersed in boreal forest areas and more apt to congregate in small groups, particularly on lakes. At this time, they would also present a relative bounty of riches, although less numerous, less predictable, and only available to those who opportunistically came across them.

CARIBOU AND THE FUR TRADE

Europeans in pursuit of the Northwest Passage instead landed on the shores of Hudson Bay and established the commercial fur trade under the control of the Hudson's Bay Company in the mid 1600s. Historical records indicate that early European observers were impressed by the huge numbers of caribou they saw, particularly compared to wildlife on the overexploited continent they called home. Alaska was subject to a very different history during this time; its original colonists were Russians, who discovered the area in 1741. Their primary interest was also in establishing a commercial fur trade that focused on sea otters, foxes, and fur seals, which was directed by one company, the Russian American Company.

The rapid inland expansion of the Hudson's Bay Company fur trade after 1783 increased the company's dependence on in-country provisions. Traders encouraged local residents to hunt caribou, and it wasn't long before this new pressure was evident, as company men commented on the decreasing success of hunts. In the early fur trading period, the commercial caribou trade was largely limited to local hunting in the area of the posts. By the late eighteenth

Kim Y. Bennett

Caribou near Winisk on Hudson Bay, where some of the early caribou hunting associated with the fur trade first occurred.

century, however, large-scale commercial hunting began to develop. At first this was limited to caribou tongues, which contained rich fat reserves, could be cured, and were easy to transport. Later, the difficulty associated with transporting other caribou products, such as heavy loads of meat, compelled the posts to send out entire parties of company men to native camps for the specific purpose of trading in caribou. As a result, trading posts began to handle large quantities of flesh, tongues, fat, and skins, which were used for such diverse purposes as lamp fuel, sinew-thread, hide robes, winter clothing, shoes, and snowshoes — all vital provisions for life in the harsh hinterland.

Aboriginal hunters harvested more caribou for this emerging market than they would have traditionally; they also shifted to year-round hunting with the help of muskets. Though caribou numbers likely surpassed the requirements of local native populations for a reasonably stable food source, the rise of the commercial caribou trade undermined this, making food shortages an increasing reality. And because they were beholden to the company, many hunters began hunting more selectively for commercial purposes, or acting as middlemen. These activities removed them from regular subsistence hunting and gathering.

The fur trade had two different effects on caribou numbers. At first it reduced caribou to very low numbers in some places, so low that few caribou were ever again available for trade. This state of scarcity, along with the decline of the industry itself, led to a release of pressure on caribou, which then allowed populations to rebound by the latter part of the nineteenth century.

The fur trade was not the only force draining caribou resources. In the late nineteenth century on the western Arctic coast of Alaska, Inupiat and Inuvialuit hunters were participants in a skin and provision trade with American whalers. The creation of a market for wild meat to supply whaling ships affected the Porcupine, Central Arctic, and Western Arctic herds of the Yukon and Alaska.

"Although the Lowland Cree believed that the caribou they killed would return to replenish the stock, the hunting of caribou beyond the limit of sustainable harvest was also linked to the Hudson's Bay Company's policy of exerting pressure on the Lowland Cree to supply increasing quantities of skins and meat." — Victor Lytwyn, historical geographer from *Muskekowuck Athinuwick: Original People of the Great Swampy Land*. Winnipeg: University of Manitoba Press, 2002.

THE SETTLEMENT FRONTIER

The story of the expansion of human settlement in the United States and southern Canada during the late nineteenth and early twentieth centuries has been told many times. Called by some historians the "Era of Overexploitation," this was when the number of unexplored areas in the southern part of the continent dwindled to none. Towns and farms sprouted, supported by a rapidly expanding road network. Wildlife populations, forests, unbroken grasslands, and indigenous peoples were all generally thought to stand in the way of progress. The impressive bison herds of the Great Plains — some 30 million strong — and the passenger pigeons that once darkened the sky and took days to pass, became extinct in the wild. Large predators, such as grizzlies and wolves, experienced their greatest range loss during this time, becoming extinct on the prairies as human populations, along with their farms, ranches, roads, and new communities, began to creep west and north. Guns reached a new level of sophistication with the introduction of repeating rifles in the late 1800s. The building of transcontinental railroads also provided access into regions hitherto uninhabited by non-Aboriginal settlers.

The Far North did not escape this push. In Canada, politicians in the south were convinced that northern regions were capable of supporting large human populations through agriculture, and they were aware of the rich potential for other natural resources, especially gold. The commercial economy continued to expand in the late nineteenth and early twentieth centuries, with an influx of trappers, traders, explorers, whalers, and miners from the south contributing to further reductions of caribou numbers in the Mackenzie Valley and other northern areas. Ironically, the federal government was preoccupied with hunting by Aboriginal peoples, and they went so far as to impose legislative controls on caribou hunting in the Northwest Territories. Many politicians were also enamoured by the idea of replacing the northern hunting economy, which they considered to be wasteful, with a large-scale caribou domestication program, in effect modernizing and commercializing the production of wildlife resources.

Although hungry eyes were on the North for resource potential, little actual development occurred north of the railroad line in Canada. The fur trade had grown beyond its peak, and many of the North's animals — including beaver and otter — went through a prolonged period of recovery from past overexploitation. Despite recurring northern visions, such as Canadian Prime Minister Diefenbaker's "Roads to Resources," most of the Far North was simply too inaccessible and unproductive to hold much interest for settlement, or even for resource extraction activities. After all, who would want to move their family to "the Barrens?" This situation has changed in the past thirty to forty years, during which time resource exploitation interests have become very real indeed.

Migratory tundra caribou have historically occurred in large enough numbers to attract the most hunting pressure.

Jeremy Harrison

Although the Russians had dabbled in other development interests in Alaska, such as coal and minerals, there was very little settlement, and furs were the only resource that was profitable. Once those began dwindling, and other resource ventures such as coal and minerals failed, Russia lost interest in Alaska and sold it to the United States in 1867. The infamous gold rush that began in California made its way up to Alaska by the late 1800s, bringing with it many people and the need for infrastructure. Salmon fisheries were an additional interest, with the first canneries built in the 1870s. Towns, telegraph lines, and roads were constructed, and the Alaska Railroad was completed in 1923. Until oil was discovered in Prudhoe Pay four decades later, however, the northern part of the state, where most caribou ranged, remained undeveloped.

THE GEOGRAPHY OF CARIBOU RANGE RECESSION AND POPULATION DECLINES

Although caribou in the northern parts of their North American distribution are now showing disturbing early warning signs of decline, we have witnessed the most severe impacts at the southern edge of their distribution: it is in the south where all the major range loss has occurred. Caribou have been extirpated from approximately 60 percent of their historic extent of occurrence in Alberta and 40 percent in British Columbia. In Ontario, half of historic woodland or boreal forest caribou extent has been lost, having crept northward at a rate of thirty-four kilometres per decade from 1880 to 1990.

In the lower forty-eight states, caribou were once known to roam in Washington, Idaho, Montana, Minnesota, Wisconsin, Michigan, Vermont, New Hampshire, and Maine. Today, only one remnant population still resides in northern Idaho and Washington. Caribou disappeared from New England and the Maritimes in the early part of the twentieth century, and from the Great Lakes region by 1940. This northward range recession occurred in tandem with human settlement, especially the development of roads, during a time when gun technology made it increasingly easy to shoot and kill large numbers of caribou.

As we move progressively northwards, caribou are generally more remote from human influence. Indeed, caribou have experienced no discernible range loss in any of the northern jurisdictions of Alaska, Yukon, Northwest Territories, and Nunavut. In other words, they still occur in the same general areas they have for millennia. This may change for Peary caribou as the polar ice cap melts. However, for now in the North, it appears not so much overall *range* that has been adversely affected as *population numbers*, especially in the western Canadian Arctic. For example, the Porcupine herd declined from 178,000 in 1989 to 123,000 in 2001 (a 31 percent decline); the Cape Bathurst herd from 17,500 in 1992 to 2,400 in 2005 (an 86 percent decline); Bluenose West from 98,900 in 1987 to 20,800 in 2005 (a 79 percent decline); Bluenose East from 104,000 in 2000 to 66,600 in 2005 (a 36 percent decline); and Bathurst from 472,000 in 1986 to 128,000 in 2006 (a 73 percent decline). The Beverly or Qamanirjuaq herds are only now being surveyed after a long hiatus, but they too are both suspected to be in decline.

Newfoundland caribou in winter twilight on the barrens.

What is causing these caribou declines, and whether they are within natural rates of population fluctuation, are key questions. And we have already seen that many caribou populations subjected to severe declines resulting from overexploitation in the past, for example during the fur trade, have long since recovered. But a disturbing feeling throughout the North now is the looming sense of unprecedented change of a different sort altogether. There is widespread concern about allowing a southern model of development and exploitation, which has put caribou genuinely at risk elsewhere, to move unchanged and unimpeded into the North.

HAVE CARIBOU EVER COMPLETELY DISAPPEARED?

Apart from the extirpation of local populations, especially in the southern part of boreal forest and mountain caribou distribution, there is only one documented case of the extinction of what was at one time thought to be a bona fide caribou subspecies — the Dawson caribou *(Rangifer tarandus dawsoni)*, from the Queen Charlotte Islands/Haida Gwaii. This is a remote archipelago of several hundred islands on the edge of the continental shelf, about eighty kilometres west of British Columbia and sixty kilometres south of the Alaskan panhandle.

We are indebted to John Broadhead, long-time resident of Haida Gwaii, for his sleuthing and account of what may have happened to this unique animal. Compared to its relatives on the mainland, the Dawson caribou appears to have been shorter in stature (about one metre at the shoulder), pale in colour, with much smaller antlers.

Zoologists and early settlers debated whether elusive herds of caribou ever existed on the Queen Charlottes, but the Haida knew better. The fossil record for caribou dates back forty thousand years, and the Haida have been there for about twelve thousand. We now know that caribou were once a prominent part of Haida diet and technology: worked fragments of bone and antler indicate they were used for needles, wedges, awls, and spear, arrow, and harpoon points. All that remains of the caribou themselves are a few skulls, pelts, antlers, and some photographs of a pair of hides with the heads still attached, from animals collected in 1908. The best parts were patched together by the B.C. Provincial Museum to form what John describes as "a heroic taxidermic effort to create a single type specimen."

Many theories have been advanced with respect to what happened to the Dawson caribou, but it appears that as a result of rising sea levels as the glaciers melted, these animals were faced with a reduced domain, hostile climate, and the disappearance of the plants they had come to depend on for nutrition. The caribou "eventually grew smaller, with stunted features and ultimately less resilient constitutions," John says. They likely persisted until the late 1930s, and then were gone.

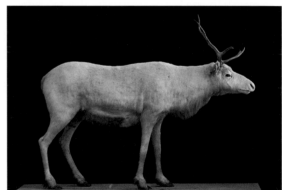

Image courtesy of Royal B.C. Museum.

A taxidermied version of the Dawson caribou, assembled from pieces at the B.C. Provincial Museum.

Recent DNA studies indicate that Dawson caribou were not lineage distinct from mainland animals, so the subspecies classification is now debatable. Nevertheless, the story of the Dawson caribou is one of extirpation of a once robust and abundant disjunct population of animals, brought on by climate change. As such, their story should be instructive.

CHAPTER SEVEN

Pressures of the Present

IN THE PAST, the principal direct human impacts on caribou were limited mostly to overexploitation. Today, the picture is dominated by real and potential land use changes through industrial activity, interacting with continued exploitation of the caribou themselves.

In the southern boreal forests, the pressures emanate from human settlement and agriculture, as well as from forest clearing with accompanying roads. About half the commercially accessible boreal forest right across the continent has already been committed to logging, with an accompanying spiderweb of roads. Many of these roads remain open long after logging trucks have stopped using them, thus providing access to otherwise remote areas by hunters and other predators of caribou, such as wolves.

In western North America, in addition to logging, recreation is now posing an additional threat to fragile mountain areas. The same terrain that is favoured for many forms of winter recreation — such as snowmobiling, heli-skiing, snowcat skiing, and backcountry skiing — also serves as the best habitat for wintering caribou. And recreationists take advantage of expanding industrial road networks to open up new, previously inaccessible playgrounds. The newest snow machines don't even depend on roads; they are capable of traversing rugged terrain in search of mountain vistas and powder snow.

In the far northern areas of Alaska and Canada, we are currently well into a period of intense planning, exploration, and the beginning of significant exploitation. Although the presence of crude oil was suspected for more than a century on Alaska's North Slope, it wasn't certain until 1968, when the vast oil field under Prudhoe Bay on the Arctic coast was confirmed. Plans for a pipeline were underway within a year. In 1977, the Trans-Alaska Pipeline System was

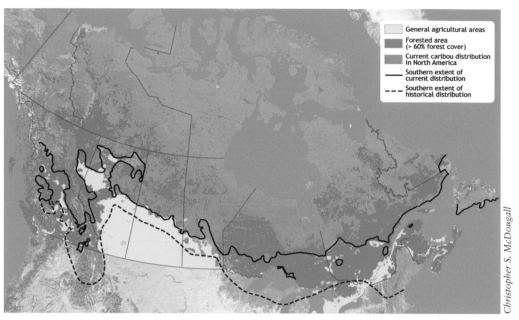

Christopher S. McDougall

Map 2.4. *Agricultural use and accompanying settlement has been implicated in historical range loss of boreal forest caribou in Canada.*

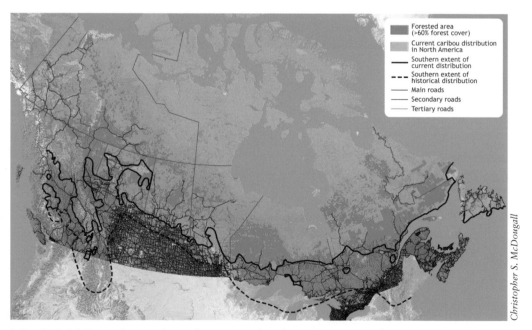

Christopher S. McDougall

Map 2.5. *Major road networks and regions with at least sixty percent forest cover within current and historical caribou distribution in Canada. From British Columbia to Quebec and Newfoundland, forestry and its associated roads have been the primary "opener" of forests in recent history.*

completed, and oil began to flow from Prudhoe Bay over the mountains to Port Valdez, eight hundred miles to the south on the Pacific Ocean. Airstrips and roads, all requiring gravel, connect distribution centres to camp facilities and drilling sites. The North Slope Haulroad became the James Dalton Highway when it was opened for public access in 1995. Since then, truck traffic has increased substantially. In 2007, significant new oil and gas leases were made available on additional "petroleum reserves" in northern Alaska, where the impact of this industry has already posed widespread concern for the Porcupine, Teshekpuk Lake, Central Arctic, and Western Arctic migratory tundra caribou herds.

In addition to the existing oil pipeline across Alaska, there is now pressure to build a new gas line south from the North Slope. One all-Alaska route would terminate at Valdez; the alternative

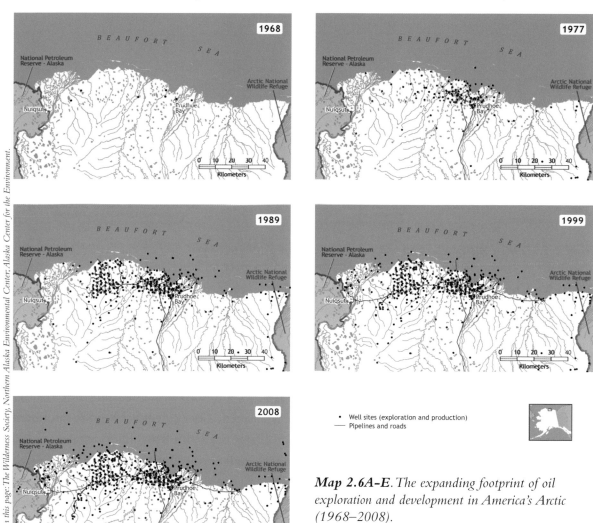

All maps on this page: The Wilderness Society, Northern Alaska Environmental Center, Alaska Center for the Environment.

· Well sites (exploration and production)
— Pipelines and roads

Map 2.6A–E. *The expanding footprint of oil exploration and development in America's Arctic (1968–2008).*

doubled in size since the mid-1990s, are already sixteen years ahead of schedule. The pace, size, and purpose of oil sands development have become perhaps the highest profile environmental debate, not just in Alberta but throughout Canada and North America as well. Concerns also include impacts on more distant areas, for example gas development in caribou habitats of the Mackenzie Valley provides the gas that provides the heat that provides the steam that provides the heat to warm, process, and transport oil sands product. Record oil prices could soon bring a similar boom to northern Saskatchewan.

Jiri Rezac/WWF/Polaris

Jiri Rezac/WWF/Polaris

Seismic lines cut regular patterns through the boreal forest in the oil sands north of Fort McMurray, Alberta.

Well pads and service roads in the oil sands.

The skyrocketing oil production in Alberta exacerbates two other significant land uses already well established in the region: forestry and agriculture. More than 60 percent of Alberta's boreal forest is tenured by forest companies and has been harvested since the 1950s; 20 percent of the forest cover in the Peace River lowlands has been converted to agriculture in twenty years. Of concern to caribou populations — already in decline in the region — are the cumulative effects of all the linear features and land clearing that come with overlapping industrial activities. These include roads, seismic lines for geophysical exploration, transmission lines, pipelines, clear-cuts, and oil and gas extraction sites. Research has documented that the intensity and extent of habitat change in the region already far exceed the levels of natural disturbances that have been historically experienced by caribou.

In the eastern Barrens and boreal forests, minerals have been the principal objects of interest, especially diamonds, uranium, and gold, in lockstep with rapidly rising commodity prices. Developing a mine can be a prolonged process. It begins with exploration, often initiated through a prospecting permit, which conveys the exclusive right to explore in a given area. Sometimes a mineral claim is staked as result of exploration under such a permit; sometimes a claim is staked on other public lands for the purpose of subsequent exploration. In either case, it's a first-come, first-served "free entry" system that permits virtually anyone who asks to explore or stake a claim almost anywhere, unless the area has been legally withdrawn from industrial development. If the claim holds promise, drilling and bulk sampling may follow, with careful analysis of the results. And in a few cases, a mine is actually planned, subjected to an environmental assessment, and built. Although less than one percent of the area originally explored ever amounts to a commercially attractive mine, it is important to anticipate, at an early stage, the possible impacts of many years of exploration, as well as the full development of a mine. Experience dictates that once a valuable mineral has been uncovered, development is a foregone conclusion if economically feasible. Further, if an area is subject to mineral exploration or development, it is not available for other purposes, such as protected areas for conservation.

All stages of the mineral exploration and development process outlined here are currently underway in numerous locations across caribou habitats, making this the largest mineral rush in Canadian history. Four operating diamond mines have already been established in the Northwest Territories and Nunavut (Ekati, Diavik, Jericho, and Snap Lake); another is approved and on the way in northeastern Ontario (Victor). A sixth, Gahcho Kue near the proposed East Arm National Park in the

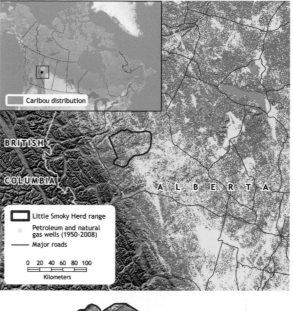

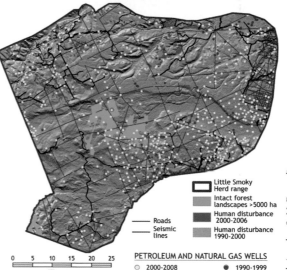

Christopher S. McDougall

Map 2.8. *The Little Smoky population is the southernmost caribou population in Alberta. At about eighty individuals, this isolated and declining herd is situated within a sea of oil and gas development. The second map depicts recent (1990–2006) industrial impacts within this range.*

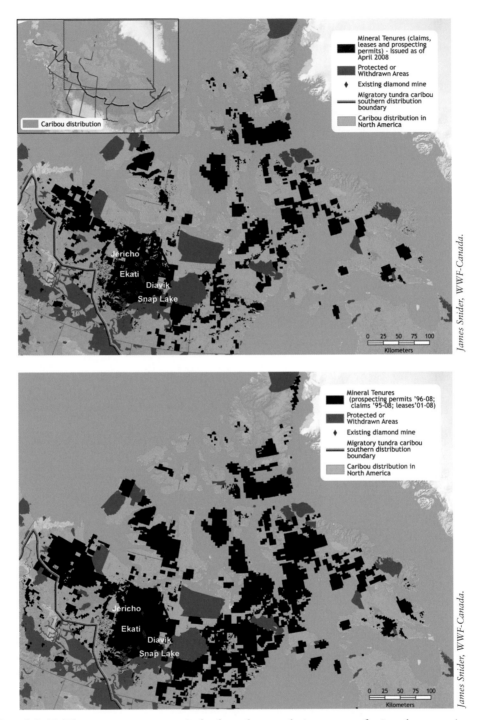

James Snider, WWF-Canada.

Maps 2.9 and 2.10. *These two maps successively show the cumulative extent of mineral tenures (prospecting permits, claims, and leases) active in one year (2008), and those allocated over approximately ten years (1998–2008), in the Northwest Territories and Nunavut. Protected or withdrawn areas have been important in keeping at least some areas free of such industrial commitments within caribou ranges.*

Coal mine adjacent to mountain caribou habitat in the Rocky Mountains, British Columbia. Caribou winter in parkland and windswept alpine areas above the mine.

Aerial view of Ekati Diamond Mine, Northwest Territories.

Northwest Territories, is moving through the environmental assessment process. Extensive diamond exploration and sampling continue and are expanding rapidly throughout caribou ranges in these and other Canadian jurisdictions.

There is already a long-established uranium mining industry in caribou winter range in northern Saskatchewan. Currently, uranium exploration is very active on a similar geological formation (the Thelon Basin) that extends from the southeastern Northwest Territories to western Nunavut, through the calving and post-calving areas of the Beverly and Qamanirjuaq herds, and the spring and fall migration routes for other migratory tundra caribou as well. The first uranium mine in Nunavut will likely be established within a decade in the post-calving area of the Beverly and Ahiak herds. Further uranium exploration is underway seemingly everywhere in the North, including Nunatsiavut — the Inuit portion of northern Labrador — which became so concerned about this in 2008 that it voted for a three-year moratorium. Nunavut Tunngavik Incorporated (NTI), which represents all Inuit beneficiaries of the Nunavut Land Claim Agreement, has recently changed the previous Inuit policy of opposing uranium development. In fact, NTI is now a participating financial partner in the uranium business, citing the need for economic development in Nunavut.

A new $270-million port and road (211 kilometres long) at Bathurst Inlet is one of three port and road projects proposed for the central Arctic coast in Nunavut. These projects have also reached, or will soon reach, the environmental impact review stage. The Bathurst road would pass through the calving and post-calving area of the declining Bathurst caribou herd to service an iron mine as well as the existing diamond mines in Nunavut and the Northwest Territories. Such a road would also make more mines possible in the future. This route would connect with the winter road that now services existing mines from Yellowknife, enabling an eventual permanent road from that city on Great Slave Lake in the Northwest Territories, all the way northeast diagonally across the central Arctic to the coast in Nunavut.

Finally, northern hydro-development is of renewed interest in provinces like Manitoba, Quebec, and Labrador, especially for the benefit of energy-hungry jurisdictions like Ontario and the United States.

Although the exploration and planning phases of most of these projects can be conducted relatively remotely, not many of them will be possible without roads — the backbone of any development. In addition to the Yellowknife to Bathurst Inlet possibility in the central Canadian Arctic, new main roads are proposed along the Mackenzie Valley in the west, and between Manitoba and Nunavut farther to the east (from a northern Manitoba community to Churchill to Rankin Inlet and perhaps to Baker Lake). Service roads bring fuel, supplies, and new people into remote areas. This enhances connectivity between Aboriginal communities hitherto inaccessible by road, and shifts winter ice roads to permanent status, in keeping with the anticipated increase in traffic and the year-round needs of local residents. Roads are commonly planned and constructed to service infrastructure and to transport materials; wildlife considerations seldom factor seriously into such decisions. The extent to which roads will serve to extend and intensify the footprint of a new project is seldom factored into environmental assessments, let alone the role they will play in inviting future development interests into frontier regions.

Northerners have greeted being on the cusp of such widespread development with everything from unbridled enthusiasm, to staunch opposition, to caution (expressed in the form of terms and conditions). However, especially in the Far North where there is still a significant dependence on food from the land, virtually everyone has rallied around one universal concern: What will happen to the caribou?

Rankin Inlet's welcome sign is a blend of the old and new, as caribou antlers frame the image of a local hockey hero.

MEASURING IMPACT

In light of the new pressures outlined above, how do we know whether caribou, or other animals for that matter, are suffering negative impacts as a result of human development? What changes indicate whether caribou are being adversely affected, and when should we become concerned?

Effects on wildlife from human activities such as resource exploration and development can occur in several different ways, ranging from modest effects on individual animals to species extinction.

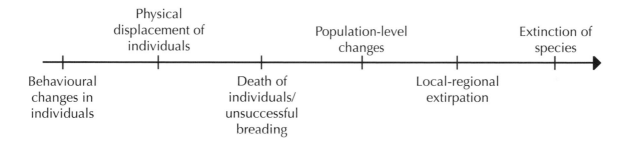

At one end of the continuum, the changes may be strictly behavioural in nature, evidenced by individual caribou altering usual patterns of feeding or resting in response to a particular disturbance or a new stimulus, such as noise. These kinds of changes may come about because caribou need to be more vigilant or ready to take sudden flight. Individuals can also be physically displaced by the activity in question, moving away, for example, to avoid encounters with a road or other infrastructure. We should be still more concerned when the activity results in the deaths of individuals, for example though new hunting pressures in the region or through the failure to breed an adequate number of new individuals into the population. We are now moving into population-level concerns that occur when too many individuals in a population die in successive years, or when not enough young are born or safely make it to adulthood: in other words, births cannot keep up with deaths. Finally, when population-level declines occur at a scale where it is no longer possible to sustain the populations, the result can be actual extirpation from some regions, and ultimately the possible extinction of an entire subspecies or species. Unfortunately, different caribou in different parts of North America can be placed at every point on this continuum.

Behavioural changes and movements of individual caribou in relation to development activities include ceasing foraging and walking away when approached by vehicles at distances of less than 0.8 kilometres in at least one study. Panic and strong escape reactions of migratory tundra

Liv S. Vors

Boreal forest yearlings and cows in Woodland Caribou Provincial Park in northern Ontario.

caribou to low-flying helicopters and small fixed-wing aircraft have also been documented, with individuals sometimes running hard for lengthy periods that continue even after the aircraft has left the immediate area. In one investigation of the effects of petroleum exploration on boreal forest caribou in Alberta, those individuals that were exposed to loud noise moved significantly faster than those that were not. Behavioural disruption has even been documented for the relatively benign activities of ecotourism, when caribou are simply being watched, photographed, or filmed. Individual animals spend less time resting and foraging, and more time standing and being vigilant, with possible impacts on their energy reserves. Responses to such disturbances are not universally negative. Caribou are frequently spotted in the vicinity of industrial infrastructure (most famously pipelines), and herds have continued to inhabit areas below the flight paths of low-flying military aircraft. However, no one understands the long-term responses to sustained disturbances over time, or what levels impact on breeding success, the fundamental cornerstone of population persistence.

In northwestern Ontario, caribou were displaced eight to sixty kilometres from a traditional wintering area in years when a logging road was snowplowed and used for log hauling. Elsewhere, caribou decreased use of and movement through oil complexes over time. Boreal forest caribou have been found not to return to traditional wintering areas following the establishment of road networks and clear-cuts. During the construction phase of a hydroelectric project in Newfoundland, caribou were less likely to be found within three kilometres of the site than prior to that development. Physical disturbance from industrial infrastructure, such as roads, drilling sites, and seismic lines, has resulted in caribou avoiding habitats beyond the actual development footprints by many kilometres. Although the available evidence suggests that caribou avoid seismic lines (which are not particularly wide) by only a few hundred metres, the tendency of these linear features to occur at high densities means that there is little to no room for caribou in between. In the western segment of the Central Arctic herd in Alaska, the area of concentrated calving has gradually shifted inland to the south, away from the infrastructure associated with oil fields along the coast. In contrast, farther east, calving behaviour has been unchanged in a relatively untouched landscape.

Caribou needs will have to be addressed as new roads are built in the North.

Documented impacts beyond behavioural changes or physical displacement include decreased frequency of nursing in migratory caribou in response to helicopters, which had consequences for the survival of those calves into adults. In southern Labrador, female caribou from the Red Wine Mountains who were exposed to military jet flights experienced lower calf survival than those who calved outside the flight paths. For the Central Arctic herd of Alaska, not only was there a shift in calving areas, but also the birth rate was significantly lower for those females exposed to development. A concern for mountain caribou is that in areas of heavy use by snowmobiles or heli-ski operations, particularly within subalpine parklands, caribou may be displaced into steeper, more avalanche-prone terrain where mortality risks are higher.

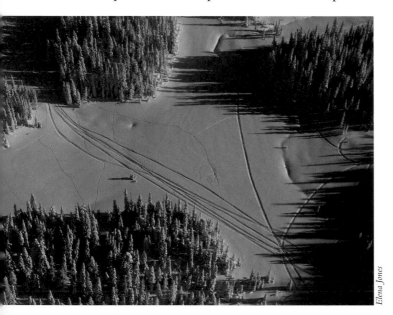

Evidence of both snowmobiles and mountain caribou in the same habitat in Northern British Columbia.

The reaction of individual caribou can often be a harbinger of greater effects down the line. Indeed, population-level impacts of any kind are often the most difficult to evaluate. Only in the past twenty years, when researchers have executed carefully designed studies and followed individual animals over time, have some of the answers begun to unfold. Such studies help by documenting the chance of survival for caribou, how many young are born, and how the population itself has changed in response.

Linking development and population declines, while the cause for most concern, is also difficult to evaluate and to separate from other factors. To begin with, population size itself is difficult to measure, particularly for those residing in forested habitats (sedentary boreal forest and mountain ecotypes). These caribou are typically widely dispersed, so population boundaries are difficult or impossible to assess. Determining population declines requires following the caribou for two decades or longer. In one unique study in Norway that followed the progressive impact of industrial development on wildlife over a ten-year period, the authors documented declines in density as high as 92 percent. On the other hand, the Central Arctic herd of Alaska actually grew in size from five thousand to thirty-one thousand animals during the thirty-year period that oil development expanded on the North Slope. However, what is usually not mentioned is that the harvest of the herd is restricted to a very low level. This illustrates the difficulty in attributing population changes to development pressures, when other management actions and/or natural population fluctuations may be occurring at the same time. Range recession is still harder to determine because it generally occurs over even longer periods, and therefore can only be discerned through careful monitoring over equally broad time frames. In any case, it is these population-level changes that give rise to the greatest concern to conservationists, especially when they reach the point of placing caribou on official species at risk lists.

SPECIES AT RISK

When a species or population is recognized to be under threat of extinction, it is often subjected to a period of scrutiny, primarily by governments, to determine whether it merits special attention beyond routine management. This has become a necessary red flag for numerous species on the North American continent. In Canada, Threatened, Endangered, and Special Concern species are classified by the Committee on the Status of Endangered Wildlife in Canada (COSEWIC), under the umbrella of the federal Species At Risk Act.

Peary caribou have been designated as Endangered in Canada due to population declines.

Once COSEWIC has advised the federal government about the conservation status of a species or population, there is a sometimes protracted round of consultations that can (for example, in the case of Peary caribou) take years before the government actually designates the species under the Act. Many, though not all, provinces and territories have similar designations at their respective jurisdictional levels. In the United States, the Endangered Species Act governs the assignment of federally threatened and endangered species, and individual states have their own lists.

It should be stated that the purpose of prudent wildlife management is to make sure a given species never reaches the point of having to be classified under these legislative tools. And while caribou are not considered to be under threat of extinction in large parts of their range, including Alaska, Newfoundland, and across the Far North, some populations of caribou have indeed been classified as endangered or threatened under American and Canadian endangered species legislation. These comprise classically endangered small, isolated populations, such as those in the Gaspésie Park of Quebec, southern British Columbia, or the Selkirk Mountains of Idaho and Washington. But they also include the Peary caribou of the High Arctic, endangered, we think, by weather conditions that have made food unavailable. And all boreal forest caribou are

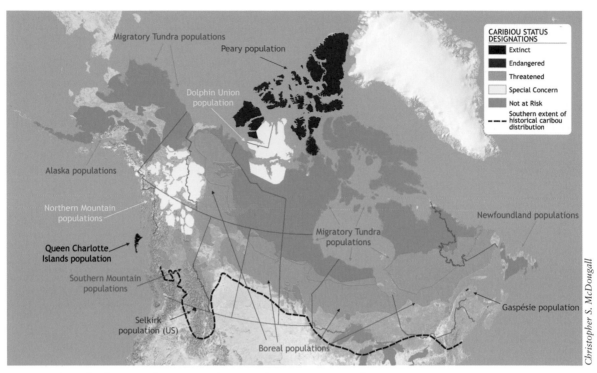

Map 2.11. Federal status of various caribou populations across North America.

designated as Threatened because of the significant range loss they have experienced through the continual encroachment of human activities.

Perhaps more important is the fact that species at risk legislation in both the United States and Canada requires the preparation of recovery plans for listed species. And more and more of these are now appearing for listed caribou populations, ecotypes, and subspecies. Recovery planning means working with a cross-section of people and agencies with a stake in recovery. Although this can make for a cumbersome, even controversial and protracted, planning process, it does mean that the eventual recovery plan should have the support that is essential for its implementation. Recovery plans are significant because they say quite clearly what needs to be done to conserve the species or population under consideration, and thus serve as a kind of test for our social resolve. Are we, or are we not, prepared to do what needs to be done for caribou? This question is effectively answered by how readily recovery plans are implemented.

The very fact that caribou are increasingly showing up on official species at risk lists, coupled with widespread declines in more abundant populations, should be sufficient warning that something needs to be done sooner rather than later. One of the things that often stymies or complicates recovery efforts is our level of knowledge with respect to the population under consideration.

David J. Tilley

Newfoundland caribou are officially considered "not at risk," although there are mounting concerns about some populations that are experiencing dramatic declines. In response, the Government of Newfoundland and Labrador has increased investment in caribou research to investigate the source of these changes.

David J. Tilley

the Bluenose herd in the Northwest Territories was in fact three different herds with three different calving grounds. The enhanced ability to follow individuals and to document the causes of death also provided helpful new information on the impacts of development. Techniques to capture caribou became more efficient and less invasive, particularly with new helicopters in the early 1990s.

In the last ten years, satellite telemetry and genetic analysis have greatly helped scientists to address the most challenging questions about caribou. Satellite collars, deployed since 1996, are ideally suited for wide-ranging species whose radio collar signals can easily get lost over the long distances they wander. With the new collars, however, the signal gets transmitted up to satellites, then researchers sitting at their desks (often half a continent away) download it.

Serge Couturier

Caribou biologist Serge Couturier is checking the wear of the teeth of this female caribou from the Rivière George herd to assess her age seconds before release. She will carry this Global Positioning System (GPS) collar for two years, providing a tremendous amount of data to biologists.

Genetic research — using DNA techniques born in the late 1990s — is yielding further information on movements, as well as measuring the genetic variability within and between individual populations. This is helping answer questions about how to classify caribou and the relationships between different populations. Individual caribou can now even be identified through analysis of their droppings, which holds promise as a non-invasive survey technique, particularly for boreal forest populations.

Systematic surveys have been undertaken on a more formal basis for many migratory tundra caribou since the 1970s, and have generally concentrated on individual populations. The frequency of surveys depends on many factors, ranging from available funds, perceived urgency, and even weather. Numbers for some herds, such as the Ahiak population in the Canadian central Arctic, are almost completely unknown; others, such as the adjacent Bathurst herd, are better understood because they have been followed every year for a decade or more. Most migratory tundra herds have at least some satellite collars attached to individual members of the herd.

Just understanding where caribou occur — the first step of any knowledge about wildlife — is no easy feat. In tundra habitats, aerial surveys are easier during the calving season, when animals congregate. As a result, we have a pretty good fix on the location of important calving grounds on the tundra right across North America.

In boreal forest regions, where caribou disperse during calving, the range is less defined and much more challenging to describe, let alone determine with precisely drawn boundaries. Often, spring calving sites are dispersed around the same general area as their lichen-rich winter habitat. Some researchers visit probable calving sites (based on information provided by local people) to investigate whether calving has taken place. Also useful are accidental sightings assembled over the years. During snow-free months, the telltale caribou tracks are of course largely absent, and the individual brown bodies are impossible to spot through the trees — especially when caribou are on their own and trying to hide. For many boreal herds, however, calving sites are simply not known, so the location of the calving grounds remains a guess based on the distribution of known cows during the calving period.

In the last twenty years or so, more and more scientific work on caribou has focused on their sensitivities to various environmental changes, both natural and human-caused. While there is broad general agreement about the nature of caribou responses to such impacts, the application of that science remains a source of debate. When uncertainty prevails, many argue for a "precautionary approach," which entails erring on the side of conservation. A related principle is that the "burden of proof" should be on those proposing change, especially large-scale industrial developments, to prove that such projects will *not* harm caribou, rather than others having to prove that they *will*.

David J. Tilley

Caribou in autumn in a bog on the Topsail barrens, Newfoundland.

CHAPTER EIGHT

Pressures of the Future

IT IS DIFFICULT to project precisely what the future will bring for caribou, given the current uncertainly around how temporary some of the population declines may be on a population-by-population basis. And although mineral, oil, and gas exploration is currently occurring right across caribou range, how much of that will translate into operating mines, wells, and pipelines is unclear. For example, some of the specific energy mega-projects being considered for the western Arctic, especially the new Alaska pipeline and the Mackenzie Gas Project (likely with an accompanying road along the length of the Mackenzie Valley), were still in the planning stages or undergoing regulatory hearings at the time this book was written. However, these projects have progressed to the point where there is a general feeling that they, and more like them, are inevitable. And if only some of these proposals move ahead, they will still transform the North. Most interesting will be the terms and conditions associated with project approvals, especially the provisions that are made for caribou.

While precise predictions may not be possible or wise at this point, the overall direction of events is relatively clear: *the pace and scale of industrial development in caribou habitat will only grow, and they will put the future of this species in North America increasingly at risk.* Ample experience has shown that once one mine or oil field is developed, the chances of nearby development occurring increases substantially. Roads constructed to service the first project make it that much easier to contemplate the next one. These are the origins of the notion of cumulative effects — the impact on the environment that results from the incremental and additive impact of other actions in the past, present, or future.

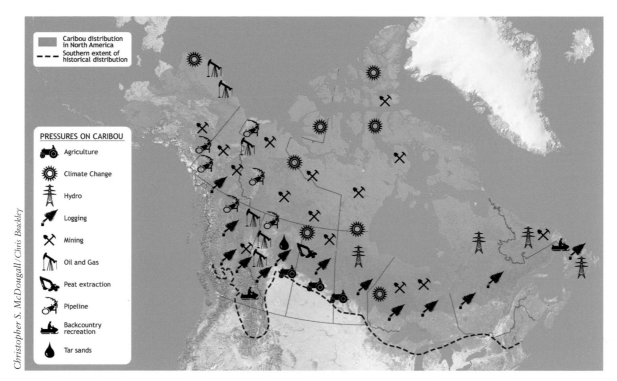

Caribou distribution
in North America
- - - Southern extent of
historical distribution

PRESSURES ON CARIBOU

Agriculture

Climate Change

Hydro

Logging

Mining

Oil and Gas

Peat extraction

Pipeline

Backcountry
recreation

Tar sands

Christopher S. McDougall / Chris Brackley

Map 2.12. *Geography of chief present-day and future pressures on caribou across their current distribution in North America. Roads and hunting are not depicted.*

TEN LITMUS TESTS FOR THE FUTURE

We believe there are a few specific planned activities that will serve as litmus tests for the future of the North, and for the future of caribou. In other words, whether these projects move forward, and the extent to which they accommodate caribou, will serve as indicators of the ultimate success or failure of caribou conservation in North America.

Perhaps heading the list is a decision to *permanently protect the calving grounds of the Porcupine caribou herd* on the 1.2-million-acre coastal plain portion of the Arctic National Wildlife Refuge in Alaska. Although it represents only one calving area for one herd and only five percent of the entire Refuge, this issue has become the highest profile example for many as to whether caribou will be respected at the end of the day. As things stand, this area *could* be opened up by an act of Congress, which is why pro-drilling forces keep bringing it forward and why it has become as precedent-setting an issue for them as it has for the other side. There's no doubt that if the Refuge were opened up, then other sacred places would no longer be sacred.

Second, mineral exploration is proceeding unchecked; in fact, it is actively encouraged in several locations on or near traditional caribou calving and post-calving areas, especially in

Nunavut. These could be crucial to the future of barren-ground caribou, not just in Nunavut but also far beyond. For example, the calving and post-calving areas of six of the eight herds found in the Northwest Territories lie outside that territory, one in the Yukon/Alaska (Porcupine herd) and five in Nunavut (Bluenose East, Bathurst, Ahiak, Beverly, and Qamanirjuaq). Although it is important to maintain healthy caribou habitat right across their range, these herds are not going to recover if the most sensitive habitat — the calving grounds that are crucial to their regeneration — is compromised. Therefore, we believe *the extent to which Nunavut changes direction and becomes more concerned about protecting critical caribou habitat, especially calving and post-calving areas,* is another pivotal indicator for the future of caribou in North America.

Third, taking an even broader perspective, *of the 21 or so recognized North American migratory tundra caribou calving areas, only one is permanently protected.* That is the calving area for the Bluenose West herd, which is located almost entirely inside Tuktuk Nogait National Park in the Northwest Territories. Three other calving areas occur partly within protected areas: Half of the Beverly herd's calving area is within the Thelon Wildlife Sanctuary in Nunavut, but the remainder outside the sanctuary is being heavily staked for diamonds and uranium (even though it has been recommended as a Special Management Area in the Thelon Wildlife Sanctuary Management Plan). Although the Ahiak herd's calving area is almost entirely within the Queen Maud Gulf Migratory Bird Sanctuary, this is an area that could permit industrial activity when the birds aren't there; in Nunavut, prospecting permits have been recently approved that include land within the Sanctuary (even though this area has been recommended to become a year-round protected National Wildlife Area by the nearby Hunters and Trappers Association of Gjoa Haven, specifying concerns about the caribou). The famous Porcupine herd calving area, although it is in a U.S. National Wildlife Refuge, has still been proposed for opening up to oil drilling (even though this has been vigorously opposed by the most affected users — the Gwich'in people of Alaska and Canada). It is difficult to understand the lack of attention, and in some cases the blatant abuse, that caribou calving and post-calving grounds have received in North America. If the respective political jurisdictions are serious about conserving caribou for the future, then a change in these policies will be another crucial litmus test for the future of this species. Caribou management boards, scientists, and local people have all repeatedly recommended the highest level of protection for these areas.

Fourth, a crucial issue for caribou right across North America, but particularly in Canada north of sixty and in several northern boreal regions, will be *whether locally conducted land use planning will be allowed to set the context for both conservation and industrial development.* So far, industrial permits have been issued in advance of reserving conservation areas by the same federal department responsible for both (north of sixty, that is Indian and Northern Affairs Canada). In the provinces, a number of First Nations have objected and sued over mineral

Alex Hall

Only one of the twenty-one or so major calving grounds has been permanently protected for migratory tundra caribou in North America.

Glen and Rebecca Grambo

Tundra landscapes such as these are now experiencing the most extensive mineral rush in Canadian history.

Andrew Leith Macrae

A reclusive bull is spotted through trees scattered across an esker near Whitefish Lake, NWT.

year-to-year and generation-to-generation changes in snow and ice conditions, along with the resulting movements of resident wildlife species. However, the pace and trajectory of future trends at a global scale give rise to concerns about irreversible impacts. With the debate having finally shifted from whether human activity is causing Earth to warm, to how such effects can be mitigated or adapted to, the notion of global tipping points — critical points at which key components of the Earth's system are abruptly pushed into different states — is coming to the fore. Such fundamental shifts could happen when a small change brings about large and irreversible consequences. European scientists have recently identified a short list of such "policy-relevant tipping elements" around the globe, which include the melting of Greenland and West Antarctica ice sheets, Arctic summer sea ice, a shutoff in Atlantic thermohaline circulation, and (particularly relevant for caribou) boreal forest dieback and loss of permafrost and tundra.

High-latitude warming is already well on its way. Over the past thirty to forty years, the Arctic has experienced a warming trend, which has been most intensely felt in western Alaska and the central Canadian Arctic. Even in the more southerly boreal forests, a trend toward hotter, drier summers, increasing fire events, and more violent but less frequent rainstorms is already evident. Interestingly, northern Quebec and Labrador so far show little sign of being affected.

There has already been fairly extensive documentation of the observations of local people in the Arctic who have witnessed changes due to warming temperatures in the 1990s, compared to previous decades. Such changes have included increasing year-round temperatures, earlier spring melts, and later freezes in the fall. In general, summer is longer, and the weather has become more erratic, with frequent changes in the freeze-thaw cycle. There are also both documented and consistent anecdotal accounts of insects, birds, and mammals normally found farther south increasing their range northwards.

Some impacts on caribou are already apparent. For example, when icy layers form on top of snow, it is difficult or impossible for caribou to access food. As caribou time calving season so closely with peaks in the annual flush of vegetation, there is a real danger of a mismatch: caribou migration and calving is cued by changes in day length, whereas plants respond more to changes in temperature. In Greenland, where spring temperatures have risen an average of 4°C over the past decade, caribou have been arriving at their calving grounds as much as two weeks too late. Both the digestibility and nutritional content of plants peak fairly soon after they appear and decline rapidly thereafter, and four times fewer calves are surviving each year.

Other impacts on caribou can only be surmised at this point, based on computer modelling or occasional anecdotal evidence. The effects of climate change are likely to be felt principally through the redistribution of vegetation itself. The general prediction is for longer and warmer seasons, increases in precipitation in some areas, a northern shrinkage of permafrost, changes in soil moisture, and concomitant shifts in vegetation communities. As preferred caribou foods are

George W. Calef

Mountain caribou bull in velvet, Mackenzie Mountains, NWT by George Calef,
author of Caribou and the barren-lands.

found farther and farther north, it is possible that some populations will get squeezed between the northernmost extent of their food supply and the Arctic coast. Some lichen-rich areas may be replaced or diluted by vascular plants, which are not only less preferred by caribou but also attract other ungulates with all the accompanying problems they bring for caribou, especially parasites and predators.

Warmer and wetter summers are projected to lead to an increase in insect pests for both caribou and their habitats, and these changes have already arrived in some areas. In forested environments, the rising influence of insects such as mountain pine beetle will lead to fundamental changes in the availability of forested habitat for caribou, as is unfolding in British Columbia. In tundra environments, habitats are selected by caribou explicitly to provide relief from insect harassment. More time spent coping with insects during summer months, when energy is needed to raise calves, is expected to lead to lower recruitment and reproductive success in some caribou populations.

Among the other predicted effects of climate change are increasing frequency and severity of forest fires in boreal forest areas, which will likely change the quality of winter habitat for caribou right across the mid-North. Fires are also expected to become more frequent in some tundra areas where current vegetation will be replaced by woody shrubs. Larger areas may become devoid of both terrestrial and arboreal lichens for winter food. Reduced area in large patches of older, conifer-dominated forest reduces the ability of caribou to separate themselves from predators. And more availability of foods may invite higher numbers of moose, deer, and elk into caribou country.

Reuters/Rock Arssenault

It is quite possible that some of these negative impacts might be offset by some relatively positive changes for caribou. For example, warmer winter weather could reduce caribou energy expenditure, although this is also likely to increase the frequency of rain and consequent snow/icing events. Available forage may increase in some areas, due to a longer and warmer growing season. In multi-species predator-prey systems, caribou might be at an advantage relative to moose, deer, and even wolves, if changes in precipitation resulting in deeper snow are a consequence of climate warming.

While broad trends related to climate change are somewhat predictable, the magnitude and direction of these changes are impossible to predict at the scales at which most planning occurs. And despite the fact that most observers agree that climate change is truly occurring, it is still considered too big or too long-term to include in most resource development and conservation plans. This reflects widespread uncertainty about its specific impacts on wildlife and ecosystems. Therefore, how climate change actually plays out on the landscape is a key issue for the future of caribou. Indeed, we could well add an eleventh, umbrella litmus test for the future, namely the extent to which governments will finally commit to real measures to reduce greenhouse gases.

CONCLUSION

DESPITE THEIR INHERENT vulnerabilities, caribou have overcome and adapted to a formidable suite of challenges — everything nature and people have thrown at them over centuries. Yet there are storm clouds on the horizon for even this most resilient of wildlife species: they are beginning to show up on species at risk lists; they have disappeared from significant portions of their southern range; and normally abundant populations are experiencing widespread, synchronized declines. Of most concern are the challenges ahead for caribou: habitat loss, new industrial pressures, over-harvesting, and climate change While humans have long looked to the North as a source of rich natural resources, the prospects for true transformation of the landscape have never been more real than they are now.

It is one thing to outline the past, present, and future challenges for the North and caribou; it is quite another to address what we can *do* about these from here on. If we are to move beyond blithe optimism on one hand, or fatalistic hand-wringing on the other, then it's time to take key steps to ensure that caribou stay with us for the long term.

Glen and Rebecca Grambo

SECTION THREE

KEY STEPS FOR CONSERVING CARIBOU

INTRODUCTION

THE FATE OF caribou is tightly bound to the future of the North. But equally, caribou may help determine the fate of the North. This is because caribou are still sufficiently widespread and still sufficiently important both culturally and economically throughout much of the North that they could well help sort out what happens there. Moreover, the sensitivity of this species to the changes that threaten to sweep across the region serves as a barometer of human restraint. In other words, if caribou populations dwindle or disappear, it is a signal that many less visible components of these northern ecosystems face similar fates. By the same token, if we can maintain areas where caribou are able to retain population numbers within the natural range of variability, they will be the foundations for conservation success. If humanity is not prepared to make decisions that respect this crucial northern species, then are we prepared to respect nature at all in this part of the world?

In many areas of the North, caribou conservation is rising to the top as a pivotal issue, as important as the other socio-economic concerns that preoccupy the average citizen. Under such circumstances, it is possible to contemplate a future where leaders who are not prepared to do the right thing by caribou will risk not getting elected. Conversely, those who do come aboard will be in power. Businesses that will not take meaningful steps to protect caribou and their habitats will not get project approvals, while those who do take action will prosper. And large areas will become permanently protected, so that caribou will still be around long after the oil, gas, diamonds, uranium, and gold are gone. Although the people in the North who feel this way may seem like a tiny fraction of the larger North American population, and therefore hardly a lever for change, it is important to remember that northerners are the ones who will

Glen and Rebecca Grambo

Signs of caribou animate the land.

" As we extend our roads, communities, mines and pipelines more and more in the caribou ranges, are we collectively nibbling away the space where caribou have long adapted to the shifts in weather, climate, and predators? Do we have enough respect for caribou that we will not allow them to slip between our fingers?" — Anne Gunn, from "What Price the Caribou?" *Northern Perspectives*. Ottawa: Canadian Arctic Resources Committee, Volume 31, Number 1, Spring 2007.

and should take the lead in deciding what happens to their homeland. Furthermore, with North America's remaining unprotected wilderness areas positioned in the North and on the front line of a changing climate, the North is becoming increasingly important and relevant even for those who do not reside there

However, there are still a significant number of people, even in the North, who will never be champions for caribou. For them, economic development is an imperative for disadvantaged communities to climb out of poverty. Opportunities on the horizon pose a possible solution to unemployment rates as high as 90 percent, and hope for youth who face an otherwise troubling future. Farther south, boreal forest caribou are sparsely distributed and historically have never been particularly important for local hunters, who, quite frankly, prefer moose. For them, caribou conservation can serve as an unhelpful symbol of urban-manufactured visions of wilderness that stand in the way of community prosperity. In fact, the very notion of "wilderness," which usually suggests a pristine landscape absent people, is culturally strange and irrelevant for many people in the North.

The truth is that most northerners are trying to navigate their way through this conflicting, soul-wrenching maze of options so crucial to their future. And they are intelligently struggling to make such decisions for themselves, rather than having them foisted upon them by outside forces. In a globalized economy, to what extent there still *are* outside forces is an interesting question. For now, however, let us suppose that caribou *were* accepted as arbiters for the future of the North. How would we measure whether the right decisions were being made? In other words, what are the key steps that need to be taken to conserve caribou?

Answering this question plunges us into the forbidding sea of public policy …

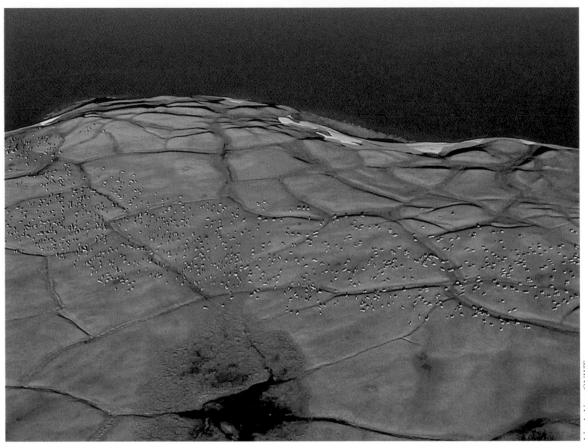

Migratory tundra caribou are dwarfed by their far northern land, ice, and water.

CHAPTER NINE

A Cautionary Tale About Policy

WE BELIEVE A discussion of public policy should focus not just on the usual suspects, namely governments, but on the many other parties who need to be at the table for caribou conservation as well. These include Aboriginal peoples (who are often governments themselves), scientists, NGOs, and industry representatives, among many others. "Policy" here shall be understood as a fairly high-level statement of intent or set of principles from which concrete decisions and future actions are meant to flow. As such, it is important to note that having a policy on something merely sets the stage for what really counts: actions on the ground that make some measurable difference, in this case, for caribou.

What follows is a policy planning cycle that is commonly observed by governments at the national level; others imitate it at different levels in both the private and public sectors. It serves as both a humourous and sobering platform to illustrate the often protracted process for initiating needed conservation action, but it is not intended in any way to belittle the hours of honest effort invested by people at all levels trying to make a difference for caribou. In fact, it is intended to support their efforts by making sure their investment in policy making *does* make a difference.

1) An issue arises (for example the decline of a species or ecosystem) and attracts public concern, resulting in calls for "the government" in particular to "do something."
2) Government may try some stop-gap measures, usually well intentioned and based on the best short-term advice they can get, but limited by urgency and budget constraints.

3) These actions don't solve the long-term problem, and someone (often those outside government who have studied the issue, particularly those in academic circles) states publicly that the real problem is "We have no *policy*" on the issue, for example a national policy on the conservation of biodiversity, or even on caribou themselves.

4) At this point, there is often a conference of some kind, with invited keynote speakers, panels, and papers on subjects such as "Towards a Policy on …," followed by published conference proceedings and recommendations to governments on how to proceed. Historically, these have been gatherings of outside "experts," although increasingly they are beginning to involve the people who live in the area where the issue has developed and who are most affected by it as well.

5) Also at this point, it will likely be determined (again often by those outside government) if the national policy being contemplated needs to be embedded in turn in a broader international commitment of some kind, which can lead to a very time- and energy-consuming political exercise to arrive at an international agreement or treaty (for example the Convention on Biological Diversity) or bilateral or multi-lateral agreements with subsequent wrangling over who's on official delegations, schedules of ratification, coming-into-effect dates or conditions, meetings of the parties, sanctions for non-compliance, etc.

6) Once a national policy has been arrived at, with or without an international backdrop, there is often a need for state, provincial, or territorial policies, designed or modified to contribute to the national one and to reflect the respective responsibilities of these non-federal jurisdictions. In the Far North, this must extend to Aboriginal representatives and legally mandated resource management boards in Alaska, the Yukon, and the Northwest Territories, and to a plethora of other elected and Designated Inuit Organizations in Nunavut. This is a very important step in the policy making process everywhere in the North, including the provinces, because if the appropriate/affected parties have not had meaningful input into the resulting policy, it will go nowhere.

7) Once these various national and sub-national policies have been arrived at, there often follow strategies (or a strategic plan) to implement the policy; action plans to implement the strategies; implementation plans to implement the action plans; and then, finally, some specific actions. (Not to be forgotten

are the monitoring plans, to help judge whether the actions are in fact taken and are making the desired difference.) Of course, each of these planning steps in turn must be "transparent and fully participatory," or they are unlikely to be broadly supported or effective.

Although every step of this tortuous path can be intellectually justified, the obvious problem here is that if we wait to take action until such a policy planning process has played itself out, the objects of the exercise, in this case the caribou, are no better off. In fact, they will likely be worse off through neglect, while everyone has been cloistered away planning to save them. Often field staff are diverted from what they alone do well to take part in the exercise, but it badly needs their practical perspectives. There are frustrating examples where the various multi-party planning steps take so long (sometimes years) that by the time everybody is ready to actually *do* something, the money has run out, or there's been an election, or the situation on the ground has changed, resulting in the original policy becoming outdated. Then the entire process starts over: policy is revisited, action plans are reworked, etc., with no meaningful action being taken at all.

This state of affairs has been dubbed "dynamic inaction." In other words, it creates the illusion that something is being done about the original problem, and worse, the participants in the process honestly believe that to be so. Lest this analysis appear too tongue-in-cheek or cynical, when the above process was outlined to at least one former Canadian minister of the Environment, his good-natured response was, "My God, you've found us out!"

The point here is not to dismiss all this good effort, but to keep it under control and to go into it with our eyes open, making sure we do not allow perpetual planning to rule the day. We must never confuse process with progress, or progress with actual results. Caribou will not be conserved simply by plans to do so. But we do need a map to know where we're going and when we've arrived.

"My theory is we get bogged down in process for so long, the resource suffers while we are trying to figure out what the process is …We can't let this go on forever, and I'm thinking particularly of the caribou situation, the Porcupine caribou herd in particular on the Yukon side. I know my government is looking very closely at the situation on this side, the Bluenose herds and the decline there. I know my government is not going to wait until the Porcupine herd declines by 70–80 percent; we cannot do that. We have a responsibility to the resource and to the users to step in and make a decision. I would like to see governments step up to the plate and fill that responsibility." — Doug Larsen, biologist, Government of the Yukon, from "What Price the Caribou?", *Northern Perspectives*. Ottawa: Canadian Arctic Resources Committee, Volume 31, Number 1, Spring 2007

It is important to note that much of the practical responsibility for conserving caribou in Canada resides at the provincial and territorial level. Correspondingly, with the large majority of caribou in the United States living in Alaska, policies and actions at the state level are often most relevant for the conservation of this species. At the jurisdiction level, there are a growing number of "caribou problems," many of which are reaching crisis proportions, especially regarding boreal forest or mountain caribou herds at risk and migratory tundra herds in dramatic decline. These issues have served not only to catalyze short-term actions (as noted previously), but also to short-circuit the more convoluted policy-making process because of the urgency to do something. Unfortunately, it almost always takes a crisis to speed things up.

The shortcomings of policy without actions are pretty obvious. But actions without policy can also be problematic, because they tend to not hang together. One action doesn't relate clearly to another, and they may even undermine each other. Collectively, they don't add up to something that makes a difference because they aren't guided by some overarching set of principles.

Accordingly, for the purposes of caribou, rather than explore institutional processes, we offer a single discussion of key policies and the actions that should flow from them.

Glen and Rebecca Grambo

The test of good caribou conservation policies is whether they help keep caribou out on the land.

CHAPTER TEN

International and Continental Backdrop

CONSERVING CARIBOU IS part of the larger challenge of saving life on Earth. WWF's 2007 *Canadian Living Planet Report* indicates that American and Canadian citizens represent the second and fourth highest per capita ecological footprints of seventy-four countries surveyed, measured on the basis of built-up land and per capita consumption of food, fibre, timber, and energy. Worldwide, humanity's current consumption trajectory will require the resources of two planet Earths by 2050. If everyone in the world had the same ecological footprint as the average American, it would consume the resources of 6.8 planet Earths by 2050; 4.3 Earths for the average Canadian lifestyle. As the WWF report bluntly states, "Since we only have one Earth, it's clear that something has to give."

The impact that our ecological footprint is having on the world's and North America's biodiversity is truly breathtaking, and the pace of change bears no resemblance to natural rates of species loss or ecosystem change. The cumulative effects of human activity have largely brought about this situation. When one takes into account the cumulative impact of eight natural capital expenditures in Canada and parts of Alaska (transportation and urban development; oil and gas development; mining; large dams; forestry; commercial fishing; aquaculture; and agriculture), the overall picture is one of continental pressures on biodiversity moving northward. In the words of WWF's report, these pressures are "penetrating the boreal forest and creeping into some of our northernmost regions" — in other words, into caribou country. This does not include the additional pressures of manufactured pollutants or invasive species, whose effects are even more challenging to model and quantify.

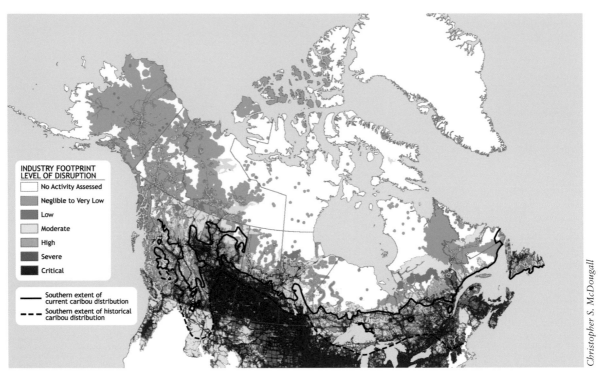

Map 3.1. *Cumulative industrial impacts within current and historical caribou distribution in North America.*

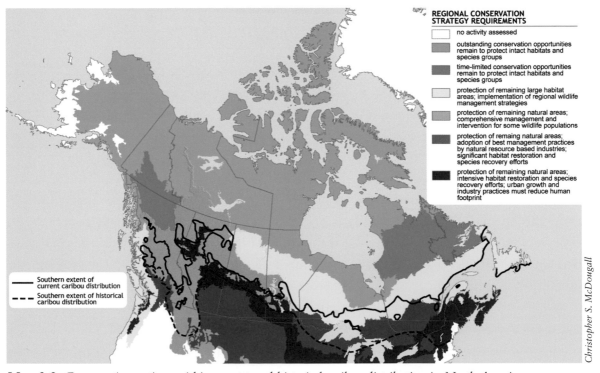

Map 3.2. *Conservation options within current and historical caribou distribution in North America.*

The geography of caribou conservation varies across the North and is dictated by both the nature of the pressures and the degree to which caribou populations have already been adversely affected. Honouring this diversity sets the stage for discussing what our conservation policy options are, in order to constructively do something about the current situation. There are some "frontier" areas where we still have exceptional opportunities to conserve biodiversity, and others that have their backs to the wall and will need significant restoration. Overlaying this map of conservation strategy options with the distribution of all the different kinds of caribou in North America reveals a number of parallel strategies that should be the starting point for conservation policy.

Specifically, for those populations of caribou that are known to be at the highest risk of extinction (for example Peary caribou in Nunavut and the Northwest Territories, mountain caribou in southern British Columbia and Quebec, and most boreal forest populations in Alberta), policy must be directed at emergency measures *to stop declines immediately and to buttress or restore populations before they are lost forever.*

For those populations of caribou that are known to be seriously declining (such as boreal forest caribou throughout the southern portion of their North American extent of occurrence and some migratory tundra herds such as the Cape Bathurst herd in the Northwest Territories), the policy must be *to ensure that these populations never become endangered and that steps are taken to return them to natural rates of population fluctuation.*

For herds that appear to be in decline, but which may be within natural population fluctuations (including the Porcupine herd shared by Canada and Alaska, most of the migratory tundra herds in the Northwest Territories and Nunavut, the Leaf River herd in Labrador, and Newfoundland caribou), caution and careful monitoring should be the policy order of the day.

"Increasingly, industrial development activities associated with energy and mineral exploration and extraction in the Alaskan Arctic are encroaching on wildlife habitats and threatening wildlife populations through habitat loss, expanded legal and illegal wildlife harvest, and environmental contamination from industrial pollutants entering wildlife food chains ... Although an environmental assessment is required under the National Environmental Policy Act ... there has been relatively little effort made to undertake follow-up assessments of the actual impacts of the projects once they are approved.... Assessment of the consequences of cumulative impacts from multiple interrelated projects taking place over extended periods has only recently been attempted though analysis and synthesis of past studies." — David R. Klein (lead author), from "Management and Conservation of Wildlife in a Changing Arctic Environment," Chapter 11 of the *Arctic Climate Impact Assessment*. Cambridge University Press, 2005.

"Trial and error is not a valid approach when dealing with an endangered species [such as Peary caribou], the 'precautionary principle' should be applied." — Frank L. Miller, research scientist emeritus, Canadian Wildlife Service, from "What Price the Caribou?" *Northern Perspectives.* Ottawa: Canadian Arctic Resources Committee, Volume 31, Number 1, Spring 2007.

Here the conservation goal must be *to ensure that modern pressures on these herds don't combine with population declines to place their long-term future in jeopardy.*

And for herds that appear to be more or less stable, or to be fluctuating within historical rates of change (such as boreal forest caribou in intact forests of central Canada, northern mountain caribou, the Western Arctic and Central Arctic herds in Alaska, and the George River herd of Quebec–Labrador), the

Serge Couturier

Migratory tundra caribou (from the Rivière George herd crossing the Rivière Koksoak in late October) still present a remarkable image of northern abundance.

policy should be *to maintain and regularly monitor the current state of affairs to make sure these herds never become either threatened or endangered.*

Each of these scenarios carries with it its own set of challenges and trade-offs. On one end of the spectrum, the populations at greatest risk of extinction will usually require intensive management along with the decision to conserve them. This battle will not always be won, and it may involve temporary measures that many will find difficult to contemplate, such as predator control, when protecting habitat is not enough. Restoring caribou may necessitate the arduous and expensive task of translocating individuals from elsewhere into habitats where risks have not necessarily been eliminated. This is not guaranteed to succeed and also runs the risk of usurping limited resources at the expense of actions that can be taken to prevent such crises elsewhere. Safeguarding the future of caribou populations for which pressures are not imminent will call for proactive, precautionary planning that may involve sacrifice of unknown economic opportunities.

In any case, no matter *what* the current status of a given caribou population, from endangered to abundant, there is an important motivation for conservation. Therefore, if the conservation of caribou is an explicit goal, any policy in both the United States and Canada that affects caribou would have to recognize and support a tapestry of conservation options, depending on the different situations caribou face in different regions. These approaches need to be pursued under a strong umbrella policy commitment *to conserve the caribou species as a whole, in its full genetic diversity, throughout North America.* Although such a policy commitment is not a precondition for meaningful action (in the sense that its absence should not be used as an excuse for doing nothing), it would nevertheless provide overarching guidance and motivation for caribou conservation at various levels.

There is certainly no lack of international backup for such a continental commitment to caribou conservation. Both Canada and the United States are signatories to the international Convention on Biological Diversity (1992), which calls on both countries to have national biodiversity conservation strategies and federal endangered species legislation, among many other things. Although the United States' Endangered Species Act was enacted long before, in 1973, the international convention certainly served as the catalyst for a long-awaited federal Species at Risk Act in Canada, which came into force in 2004 after several aborted attempts to create the legislation. Apart from this, Canada and the U.S. are individually or together party to more than twenty-five international treaties, conventions, or agreements, all rife with resonant conservation obligations that could be cited as justification for getting on with the job of conserving caribou. Therefore, we likely don't need any more of these; rather, we need a greater effort to live up to those that already exist.

More specific to caribou, there is now an international organization dedicated to assisting all Arctic countries with the scientific and technical aspects of conserving migratory tundra

Serge Couturier

Migrating caribou from the Rivière George herd on the move in late July.

caribou — the CircumArctic *Rangifer* Monitoring and Assessment Network (CARMA), formed "in response to the need to co-operate and co-ordinate monitoring efforts across the North." Although CARMA has focused primarily on migratory tundra caribou to date, this organization could provide a model to extend its scope to other caribou ecotypes. There is also a precedent for a formal international treaty on caribou known as *The Agreement Between Canada and the US on the Conservation of the Porcupine Caribou Herd*. Although the International Porcupine Caribou Management Board is currently inactive due to lapsed formal participation by the United States, the structure was set up to conserve this high-profile herd, which migrates across the international boundary between Alaska and Yukon. The agreement does succeed in providing an important means for bi-national technical co-operation aimed at meeting information and management needs of this herd.

CHAPTER ELEVEN

Specific Steps and Responsibilities

USUALLY A DISCUSSION of policy steps begins and ends with governments, and in what follows we have indeed focused most heavily on the need for improved leadership and commitments from the government sector. But the future of caribou and the North will rest in the hands of multiple players, with no one entity being solely responsible. In northern Canada, Aboriginal peoples (Inuit, First Nations, and Métis) not only frequently insist on being treated as governments, they actually *are* the government, through a numerical majority in the elected legislatures of Yukon, Northwest Territories, or Nunavut and/or through management boards and other bodies established as a requirement of legally binding land claim settlements. In Alaska, although the situation is constitutionally different, Native Americans serve on management boards, regional corporations, and other bodies that effectively give them a definitive say regarding the future of caribou. In other words, co-management of this species is the dominant trend in both countries as far as migratory tundra herds are concerned.

It is important to note, however, that in the provinces and within the ranges of most boreal and mountain caribou populations, First Nations tend to be politically behind, still working to assert and legally protect Aboriginal and treaty rights, as well as advancing land claims. Further, the move toward formal co-management of natural resources is considerably less advanced in the provinces, especially in terms of being legally mandated, than it is in the northern territories. This means that such arrangements are still being "invented" among First Nations, provincial governments, industry, and other parties. Nevertheless, First Nations everywhere often voice the desire to engage in "government-to-government" discussions and negotiations regarding the future of their lands, waters, and wildlife.

It follows that governments and Aboriginal organizations should have similar or shared policy-making roles for caribou. This, of course, brings with it similar levels of political accountability, along with all the other expectations that can be reasonably levelled at governments. No one can have the authority of government without the responsibility as well. Of course, the standing challenge for most Aboriginal governments is adequate financial resources, in order to effectively exercise both their authority and responsibility.

Healthy migratory tundra bull in autumn, in the area of the headwaters of the Thelon River, NWT.

We have devoted the balance of this section to a description of specific actions required to achieve caribou conservation. Although there are many nuances to this list — because activities need to be tailored to particular circumstances, caribou herds, and geographies — we believe that several emerging principles apply. Having stated what we think each of these principles and policies should be, we then offer some observations regarding what the situation actually was in various regions of North America at the time this book was written. This gap between the steps that need to be taken to conserve caribou and what is actually happening is something we feel needs to be narrowed as soon as possible.

INFORMED, ENGAGED, AND FORTHRIGHT LEADERSHIP

Leadership in conservation comes from all levels, from grassroots efforts to national political leaders. We need to link at all levels and to work together. Grassroots leadership is fundamentally important, for example when a committed individual steps forward for a conservation cause. Conservation success stories are full of such individuals. It follows that having the personal attention of the leader of any organization can make a huge difference for moving forward on just about any issue. Caribou are no exception. Informed, engaged, and forthright leadership, therefore, is a responsibility — perhaps the most important responsibility — that cuts across all sectors.

As far as governments are concerned, it is rare, and some would say unrealistic, for senior political leaders to be well-versed in the nuances of caribou conservation or the steps necessary for achieving this goal. Yet it is precisely this knowledge that is necessary for making key decisions that affect caribou. Where such knowledge does exist, it is often a casualty of changing governments, with the unfortunate result that new regimes have to begin from square one on caribou conservation, rather than building on previous momentum. Therefore, the first step toward engagement in caribou conservation for the leader of any government — the president, prime minister, premier, governor, or grand chief — would be to have a standing policy of participating in an unfiltered meeting, one-on-one, on a regular basis with those individuals responsible for wildlife in that jurisdiction. There the leader needs to ask, "How are caribou doing, what more do we need to do, and how can I personally help out?"

Such conversations need to be forward-looking and action-oriented, not a numbing bureaucratic account of everything being done or, a list of ways to put the best face on government inaction. The idea is to help the leader become aware of the current situation and what needs to be done about it. It would give him/her a basis upon which to inject subsequent questions into the system, and provide him/her with sufficient information to informally ask appropriate constituents, "How do *you* think we're doing on caribou?" Also welcome would be the occasional visit by leaders to caribou-focused gatherings — which are increasing in frequency — to further learn, and to demonstrate personal interest and concern.

Grappling head-on with the challenges of conserving caribou will inevitably bring increasing appreciation of the trade-offs this entails. If society chooses to keep caribou on the landscape, leaders will have to be forthright about both the benefits and costs that society will experience as a result. By the same token, if leaders choose to pursue economic development at the expense of caribou survival, gone are the days when they should try to convince the public that we can indeed have it all — we cannot.

As far as corporate leadership is concerned, at least three general models appear to be emerging, which could be summarized as follows:

David J. Tilley

Spring photo of a caribou still wearing its winter coat.

1. "We comply." — Many companies advertise that their corporate policy is to comply with all regulatory requirements. While this may involve considerable time and expense, it is largely unappreciated by the public because it is regarded the bare minimum that is expected of industry. After all, such a policy effectively only amounts to obeying the law and, as such, doesn't

really constitute leadership in any meaningful sense of the word. However, companies that are consistently found to be *out* of compliance, hence breaking the law, should be identified as not meeting even the minimum requirements for corporate responsibility.

2. "We will do it, if all the others will as well." — Companies in this category offer to do something that is a cut above the rest of their industry, provided everyone else is required to do so as well. In this way, they are not put at a competitive disadvantage for demonstrating "leadership." Also, the fact that they led the way results in a broader change right across their corporate sector. This is a policy commitment that deserves support, but of course if the rest of the industry doesn't come aboard, either voluntarily or through regulation, nothing will have changed. So this, at best, is conditional leadership.

3. "We will do it, whether or not others follow." — This is the company that says it will take certain steps, in this case to help conserve caribou, whether or not anyone else does, because they believe it's the right thing to do, or for competitive advantage in the marketplace. This kind of leadership is unconditional. It involves breaking from the pack and actually leading. These are the companies that are the first to embrace best practices (trying to minimize impacts on the environment and caribou) or other corporate policies that go well beyond either regulatory requirements or what they think everyone else is prepared to undertake.

The authors' personal assessment of the current political leadership in North America, jurisdiction by jurisdiction, would likely only be subjective and provocative. Moreover, our assessment would be transitory, because such leadership changes more often than caribou populations rise and fall. However, we would observe that grand chiefs in the Far North are likely already engaged in the kind of leadership-oriented meetings we have suggested, on a frequent and ongoing basis. Presidents and prime ministers likely are not, while premiers and governors are probably somewhere in between. Ministers and senior bureaucrats responsible for natural resources and wildlife are generally reasonably well-briefed regarding caribou issues, especially because of their importance to northern voters, businesses, and NGOs.

Of course government policy often flows from the political ideology of the leader and the people around him/her (*not* necessarily from their political party, as there have been conservation advocates of all political stripes at one time or another). Therefore, regardless of party affiliation, high expectations of any elected leader should be the order of the day. If we have low expectations of politicians, we passively hand them the option to deliver on just that.

As far as corporate leadership is concerned, there are many reasons why some companies have decided to lead from the front, but by doing so they have indirectly created a second tier of companies that aren't "there" yet. And if the market rewards the most environmentally responsible companies, it won't be long before the others follow suit. However, there is often a jittery initial period when real sector leaders are not sure whether their commitments will pay off in terms of the bottom line and when the second tier companies stay on the sidelines watching to see what will happen. That is

"We're making plans to do harvest surveys, and try to do a better job monitoring. We're going to have to work with people on regulations and monitoring the whole harvest, which is a very big step. Outside our boundaries, we want to work with Yukon and get our surveys done, and then the other big issue is to start the process for the calving grounds, talk to Nunavut, initiate those discussions, and then of course, there's getting the federal government to be a more visible and supportive member of the process." — Honourable Michael Miltenberger, Minister of Environment and Natural Resources, Government of the Northwest Territories, from "What Price the Caribou?" *Northern Perspectives*. Ottawa: Canadian Arctic Resources Committee, Volume 31, Number 1, Spring 2007.

David J. Tilley

This Newfoundland caribou bull shows mature antlers and a swollen neck, typical of the rut, or breeding season.

precisely when concerned consumers need to jump in and help fashion social change by giving preference to companies that are "walking the talk."

While some companies have made certain forest conservation commitments, such as not buying paper produced from mismanaged boreal forest caribou habitat, there is still no mining or oil and gas company that has voluntarily signed up for the "conservation first" principle, for example by voluntarily staying out of areas proposed for protection, including migratory tundra caribou calving areas. There are certainly many other important commitments that industry can, and we hope will, make to help with the long-term conservation of this flagship species right across its forest, mountain, and tundra distribution. Perhaps when being "caribou friendly" becomes a widespread criterion for the decisions of investors, we shall see more rapid change and leadership in this regard.

GOVERNMENT POLICIES

For governments, including elected Aboriginal organizations with equivalent powers, we suggest a series of standing policy commitments regarding caribou in Canada and the United States. These do not constitute *everything* governments need to undertake in cooperation with others, but we feel that with these policy building blocks in place, most of the rest of what is needed would flow from them, and we would collectively be much better positioned to conserve caribou for the long term:

Sequence Conservation First

The prevailing pattern of land use in North America is driven by an accumulation of piecemeal decisions over many years. For example, a community might have begun as a collection of individual dwellings with just one (or even no) road, and no accompanying plan for how and to what extent the community would grow in coming years. After some time, the decision could have been made to build connector roads, with bridges for water crossings, and more structures in the town itself, followed by a mill, mine, fuel depot, or some other industrial complex, or perhaps an airport or regional government office. In the North, most conversion of natural habitat has proceeded in a similar bit-by-bit fashion, usually driven by natural resource extraction or centres of government. Development patterns have largely been a result of responses to perceived economic opportunities, and the land was thought to be so bountiful that restraint wasn't really necessary.

As we have already discussed, most caribou range loss has occurred in the southern part of their distribution. But there are significant areas where there is still an opportunity for proactive planning under a completely different paradigm. The "conservation first" principle states simply that when making land use decisions, conservation decisions should be made first, while they are still possible. For example, local residents should be given the opportunity to identify and reserve areas they want to protect in advance of industrial development. And such areas are often important habitats for caribou.

One conventional way to address the "conservation first" principle is through locally driven land use plans that set conditions often called "conformity requirements," or these plans may zone the landscape for both conservation and other uses. However, in reality the reverse has often occurred: extensive commitments have been made, in particular to the forest, mining, and oil and gas industries, in advance of land use planning. This has resulted in industrial commitments being made inside areas proposed for protection and, vice versa, protection being proposed literally over top of areas where commitments have already been made to industry. In other words, poor sequencing of land use planning and decisions by governments has led to a first-class traffic jam that serves no one's best interests.

Right now, many Aboriginal groups right across Canada are invoking Supreme Court rulings regarding the "need to consult," in order to effectively stop many industrial developments until they have had a chance to devise a longer term plan for their lands and natural resources, which

"The 'development pending' reality exists for almost all of the boreal forest caribou habitat at the wilderness edge [say the last 150 kilometres before the northern limit of the logging in the provinces], and for much of the area in the far northern reaches of the provinces and territories as well. Here, few *new* decisions need to be made to cause these forests to be cut, roaded, or mined. Simple day-to-day business, using the permits and infrastructure already in place, will see this change happen.

"This situation exists as an artifact of the way Canadian governments have viewed wilderness. In the 19th and 20th centuries, we saw the forests of Canada as a limitless free resource from which we could build towns, employ new immigrants, and create wealth. Laws were constructed that gave highest priority to development and commerce, and largely ignored the needs of nature. This was not done with malice, but rather out of a mistaken belief that nature was without limit in its ability to provide more resources or to repair itself after we took what we wanted. As a result, our mining, forestry, and hydro legislation does not require the needs of wild nature to be considered before development proceeds, and almost none of our laws require that some wild areas be identified and left aside before, or even as part of, the approval of new industrial activity." — Tim Gray, from *Woodland Caribou: The Politics of Conservation.* (unpublished), Toronto: WWF-Canada, 2007.

include caribou. Notice that this is not a matter of being against all industrial development; it's a matter of getting the sequencing right, so that people can plan where they want to see such economic activity. In other words, "conservation first" is a *condition* of development approach, not an *anti*-development approach.

In many cases, since the industrial development train has already left the station in advance of the conservation train, we are facing a "conservation *also*" situation in most of the North: conservation decisions now need to made parallel with, rather than in advance of, other land use commitments.

It is obvious that policies targeted at conserving important caribou habitats are going to have to embody the "conservation first" and, where necessary, the "conservation also" principles.

Yearling caribou in spring, Newfoundland.

David J. Tilley

Otherwise, caribou will simply be left with whatever habitats fall between the cracks (if any), rather than what they truly need. Throughout the Far North, there are some examples of land areas where proactive land use planning at large scales is beginning to emerge, along with the usual examples where "conservation also" is the name of the game.

In the Northwest Territories portion of the Mackenzie River watershed, significant recent progress has been made by providing at least interim protection to large areas proposed by Dene communities in advance of a decision regarding the Mackenzie Gas Project ("conservation first"), and parallel with uranium exploration east of Great Slave Lake ("conservation also"). For example, the Gwich'in, Sahtu, and Dehcho First Nations have all produced land use plans that have resulted, among other things, in more than 12 million hectares of various natural areas being temporarily withdrawn from industrial development. And in 2007, the Akaitcho Dene around Great Slave Lake spearheaded the largest land withdrawal for protection in Canadian history — nearly 10 million hectares, much of it important for caribou. Many more areas are awaiting interim withdrawal from industrial development in the Mackenzie River Basin, and caribou conservation has been a major motivator for these additional proposals.

Alaska has become a classic battleground for both "conservation first" (the ongoing struggle to protect the coastal plain caribou calving grounds of the Arctic National Wildlife Refuge) and "conservation also" (the expansion of oil and gas development into new areas of the North Slope). Virtually all of this is occurring within the ranges of Alaska's principal migratory tundra caribou herds. The recent decision by the United States federal government to offer up huge additional areas in the Chukchi Sea for oil and gas leases, before a ruling was made under the Endangered Species Act on the status of polar bears there, was a clear example of getting the industrial cart before the conservation horse. The caribou herds, whose coastal ranges intersect this development zone, have similarly been placed at increased risk by Alaska's approach: making industrial commitments first, then dealing with the conservation fallout second.

For more than twenty years, the Gwich'in First Nations and the governments of Canada and the Yukon have remained steadfastly united in opposing drilling in the Arctic National Wildlife Refuge. In fact, four governments on the Canadian side (Canada, Yukon, Gwich'in, and Inuvialuit) have collaborated to establish national parks (Vuntut and Ivvavik) as well as other protected areas on the Canadian side to protect important habitat for the Porcupine caribou herd. It must be noted, however, that habitat protection by itself is not the only insurance against population declines, if it does not proceed in tandem with harvesting policies — a recognized issue on the Yukon side of this herd.

Even while standing firm on the position of protecting important habitat for the Porcupine herd in Alaska, Canadian governments (Canada, Nunavut, and elected Inuit organizations) have shown no particular restraint in promoting industrial activity in the calving and post-calving grounds of a number of other migratory tundra caribou herds, especially in Nunavut. Nunavut has taken this position despite community requests (from within Nunavut and the Northwest Territories) and recommendations from co-management bodies such as the Beverly and Qamanirjuaq Caribou Management Board, to permanently protect important caribou habitat, especially calving and post-calving areas. Perhaps the forthcoming government-initiated caribou strategy will consider such protection. If so, it should be strongly supported. If not, Nunavut will have resisted any form of a territorial Conservation Areas Strategy, while resource development proceeds apace. There is an urgent need for Inuit to better incorporate caribou conservation into plans for land use and economic development.

Caribou deserve conservation planning in advance of development if the big spaces they require are to be maintained.

David J. Tilley

In northern Quebec, commitments have been made to extensive hydroelectric developments in advance of conservation planning, although that province has committed to dramatically increase the overall amount of protected area in the province to 8 percent of its total area. How much of this will benefit the North and caribou remains to be seen. Labrador is making plans to go down the same path, with the proposed damming of the Lower Churchill currently undergoing environmental assessment. This project would flood parts of the ranges of at least two caribou herds. The Innu have worked hard to design an overall plan for their territory that would give priority to conservation areas but also welcome environmentally responsible forestry and mining operations.

Across the extent of occurrence of boreal forest caribou, virtually every political jurisdiction is currently wrestling with policy challenges associated with deploying "conservation first" in the northern boreal landscape. Although land use planning processes of various forms are being proposed or developed, only a few so far show promise of heading in that direction. The Poplar River First Nation in Manitoba has proposed and received preliminary approval for a land use plan for both conservation and development that features a six-hundred-thousand-hectare protected area in boreal forest caribou habitat. The last word has certainly not been spoken in the northern boreal forest, but decisions so far have revolved around "conservation also" principles — similar to the southern boreal, where extensive commitments have been made to the forest industry and to companies mining the oil sands. Caribou have been at the very centre of this debate. The Canadian Boreal Forest Conservation Framework has articulated a formal statement that strongly advocates a "conservation first" approach to planning right across the boreal forest and taiga, with at least 50 percent protected, complemented by industry best practices on the remainder. Supported by First Nations, NGOs, and industry leaders, this has provided a platform from which land use decisions in key regions of Canada have elevated "conservation first." Significantly, a coalition of unlikely bedfellows, including NGOs and industry, have recommended to the Alberta government that there be a moratorium on new leases in certain parts of the oil sands until decisions about conservation lands have been made in the same area. The policy promise to sequence land use planning up front in the northern boreal found its way into recent provincial elections in Alberta, Manitoba, and Ontario, and no doubt will in other "caribou provinces" as well.

Ensure Habitat Protection

A package of recommended actions to achieve caribou conservation must inevitably include habitat protection as an essential element. When an area is protected for caribou, the implication to most would be that it would be off-limits to activities that result in habitat change. Increasingly, however, terms such as "effective protection" have emerged to describe the hoped-for outcome for caribou, while industrial development is supposed to proceed in a manner that has little or no negative impact on the population in question. This can be looked at from two different but complementary standpoints: first, how much habitat is enough to buttress caribou against the ill effects of change within their ranges; alternatively, how much development within a range is too much for a population to persist? Certainly precise numbers will elude us, because every range is different enough to preclude generalizations. However, we are gathering enough experience across the distribution of caribou that some patterns are beginning to emerge. For example, analyses in the published literature now suggest the proportion of range that needs to be beyond a certain distance from development, or the proportion of range that is affected by both natural and human-caused disturbance. Understanding both is necessary to ensure persistence of the caribou

Sarah Ashleigh Couchie, Anishinabek/Ontario Fisheries Resource Centre.

A rare photograph of a boreal forest caribou shielding her newborn calf from the rain on an island in Smoothrock Lake, northern Ontario.

populations. Developing knowledge of such thresholds will ultimately help us to manage levels of disturbance in caribou ranges, within defined levels of risk.

An almost universal recommendation made time and again by local residents, scientists, and caribou managers is to protect the calving grounds of migratory tundra caribou herds. The calving and post-calving period is regarded as the most critical phase of the caribou life cycle, when cows and newborn calves exhibit the most pronounced sensitivity to any kind of human disturbance. Since members of this caribou ecotype concentrate during calving, often using different areas within a larger traditional calving ground year after year, these calving grounds offer identifiable candidates for protected areas. Few caribou experts would venture that this is the *only* measure necessary to conserve caribou, because other parts of caribou range serve vital functions as well, and frequent disturbance to caribou during other parts of their life cycle can have serious consequences for individual animals or at the population level. Further, populations can still be over-harvested whether or not their habitats are protected. Nevertheless, protection of calving and post-calving areas should anchor any policy for conserving caribou.

For boreal forest and sedentary mountain caribou, areas that serve as calving grounds are more elusive in nature. Female caribou give birth in solitude, and although they remain largely faithful to specific calving areas, it is not generally possible to delineate an area that serves as a calving ground for the population at large. Unlike some other species at risk, boreal forest caribou do not have specific needs that can be safeguarded through protection of particular habitat features. Due to low population density, boreal forest caribou populations often cover very large areas (thousands of square kilometres), and population-level responses to disturbance are known to be driven by habitat changes within distances that are measured in kilometres rather than metres. Although an overwhelming body of evidence suggests that boreal forest caribou are affected at very low thresholds of disturbance, absolute protection of habitat at large scales is seldom employed as a management option.

Most governments prefer to mitigate the effects of development on caribou and other species at risk, rather than prohibit industrial activities altogether. Such a compromise-oriented policy obviously minimizes conflicts with resource extraction interests. It is for this reason that many governments are not inclined to mandate strict protection of habitat for the purposes of caribou conservation in recovery strategies and other land use policies. But it is difficult to envision how caribou conservation can be achieved without a stronger government commitment to safeguard caribou habitat from industrial incursion and habitat change.

As of April 2008, more than 650 active mineral dispositions (prospecting permits, mineral claims, and mineral leases) had been granted by the federal government, mostly for diamonds and uranium, in the traditional calving grounds of the Beverly and Qamanir-juaq caribou herds in Nunavut. The proposed road to access a new port on Bathurst Inlet would pass through the Bathurst herd's traditional calving area. As indicated in Section Two of this book, despite a continuing chorus of scientific and community-based recommendations, just one of 21 or so migratory tundra caribou calving grounds has been regulated as permanently off-limits to industrial activity in Canada. At best, such areas enjoy only seasonal protection during the calving and post-calving periods, which begs the question: What would happen if a year-round mine or drilling operation were ever established in a caribou calving or post-calving ground? This may soon happen in Nunavut.

David J. Tilley

Providing adequate protection for the sensitive areas where caribou raise their calves should anchor any conservation policy.

In British Columbia, there have been encouraging recent announcements of large areas reserved for mountain caribou conservation, though whether enough area has been strictly protected — versus area designated for "special management"— is the subject of ongoing controversy. Even less clear is whether this measure will stave off the steep declines being experienced by the endangered southern populations.

Dave Gustine

Protecting habitat is key to any caribou population. Mountain caribou habitat in Beas-Prophet watershed, north central British Columbia.

"But as government, we have to look at the whole public interest, aboriginal, consumptive or non-consumptive; it even goes beyond that, to the intrinsic value of the resource. We have an obligation to the caribou and the other wildlife populations just to make sure that they're there, even if nobody uses them. I take that very seriously as well." — Doug Larsen, biologist, Government of the Yukon, from "What Price the Caribou?" *Northern Perspectives.* Ottawa: Canadian Arctic Resources Committee, Volume 31, Number 1, Spring 2007.

Avoid Over-Harvest

As is the case with protecting caribou habitat, a general policy commitment to ensure safe levels of harvest is more easily stated in principle than implemented on the ground. Nevertheless, of the more than two million caribou in North America, many thousands are taken every year, particularly migratory tundra caribou, and mostly by Aboriginal people. So making sure this number is sustainable must be at the centre of any caribou conservation policy.

First, we should probably address the issue of hunting caribou at all, as some animal rights or welfare organizations may take exception to conserving caribou "just to kill them." The fact is that in the North there is a deep interest in conserving caribou precisely because they *are* harvested. For example, a socio-economic study contracted by the Beverly and Qamanirjuaq Caribou Management Board has indicated that the harvest of these two herds alone is worth over $20 million per year to the many communities that still depend on them. Therefore, a conservative comparable number for all twenty or so migratory tundra herds in North America would be $100 million per year. Here we protect habitats *for* hunting, not *from* hunting, because such traditional uses are really the only ones that stand a practical chance of competing with industrial uses of the land, such as mining and oil and gas development. Furthermore, Aboriginal people have constitutionally entrenched rights to continue to hunt, fish, and gather natural resources. That said, there is a legitimate argument to be made for conserving caribou for their own sake, for their ecological role in northern ecosystems, and for other non-consumptive uses such as viewing and photographing, especially when such uses benefit northerners as well.

A policy directed toward avoiding over-harvesting of caribou is complicated by many factors that must be addressed:

First, harvest levels will be impossible to set without the backdrop of reliable, current, and regular monitoring information regarding not just the numbers of animals in a harvested population, but also the natural mortality and recruitment rates, population trends, and overall health or condition of the herd. An additional requirement is to have agreement across user groups regarding these numbers and assess-ments, which will require their full involvement. The starting point is to agree on what people want to see for a herd, for example a slow or rapid rate of recovery, or other possible scenarios. Harvest

Jeremy Harrison

Many caribou are enjoyed simply as company along the way down a northern river in NWT.

"Response to 'outside' opinions stems partly from previous experience with some organized animal rights activists and some who see hunting as a threat to animal welfare or conservation. Indigenous hunters, who view their dependency on local resources as sustainable in contrast to the heavy dependency by southern urban dwellers on non-renewable resources, perceive such urban-based organizations as a threat to their way of life." — David R. Klein (lead author), from "Management and Conservation of Wildlife in a Changing Arctic Environment," Chapter 11 of the *Arctic Climate Impact Assessment*. Cambridge University Press, 2005.

levels cannot be set until people decide what they would like to see for the herd's future.

It should be clearly determined who is respon-sible for setting and enforcing safe levels of harvest. In northern Canada, this responsibility is shared across governments and renewable resource man-agement boards dominated by Aboriginal peoples, subject to the needs of conservation and public safety, which reside ultimately with the territorial governments. In Alaska and the boreal provinces, responsibility resides more clearly with state and provincial wildlife agencies. A co-management ap-proach is evolving in Alaska through bodies such as the Board of Game, regional advisory boards, and the International Porcupine Caribou Man-agement Board. This distribution of responsibility in both Canada and the United States has led to competing assertions of authority, even legal ac-tions, when one body feels its mandate is being encroached upon. But by far the best and most realistic way of proceeding is collaboratively, which leads to the best chances for agreement on the proposed levels and distribution of harvest, no matter who determines them.

Decision makers must also be aware of the role that increased access to the herds plays in the human harvest of caribou, especially via roads and aircraft, and whether that access can be realistically controlled. Increasingly, information regarding the movements of radio- or satellite-collared animals is not made public in real time, since that information has been used to access herds for hunting purposes. The few but major highways in Alaska, Yukon, and the Northwest Territories are continuing sources of controversy regarding the role they play in facilitating both legal and illegal caribou hunting. This concern should be kept in mind when more roads are proposed in the future. Concerns have also been voiced regarding the hunting impact

Migrating caribou move so freely and in such large numbers that cross-border co-operation is often key to their conservation.

"All of the user First Nations and Inuvialuit have settled their land claims and have some authority to make hunting regulations within their territories. These indigenous governments can take an active role in developing consistent hunter education strategies and voluntarily impose harvest restrictions on their beneficiaries if they deem it necessary. In addition, mandatory restrictions on aboriginal harvest are allowed for conservation and public safety reasons under all land claims.

"Some examples of harvest management measures might involve: imposing harvest quotas to all harvesters or to particular groups of harvesters, limiting harvest in particular locations, limiting harvest to particular seasons, limiting or eliminating harvest of cow caribou, and limiting or eliminating harvest of rutting bulls ... Sensible, uniform regulations throughout the range, developed with hunters, will improve hunter compliance with recommendations and regulations. Making small changes in hunting practices now may prevent the need for crisis management later." — Porcupine Caribou Management Board, from "What Price the Caribou?" *Northern Perspectives.* Ottawa: Canadian Arctic Resources Committee, Volume 31, Number 1, Spring 2007.

of roads penetrating through formally remote northern areas in the boreal forest of the Canadian provinces.

What is the quality of the information regarding caribou harvest? It is difficult to get a handle on how well caribou harvest is reported and therefore actually known, including the numbers, age, sex, and condition of animals being taken.

Next, there is an ethic of respect for caribou out there on the land, but is it being lost as elders pass on? This would be reflected in such things as efficient hunting (low rates of wounding and loss), proper field preparation, and complete utilization of the animals with minimal wastage. Upholding such an ethic requires that irresponsible hunters be dealt with, especially by their peers. These are often the lead concerns of elders and the subject of word-of-mouth education efforts within northern communities. In fact, of sixty-three proposed actions voted upon, "developing codes of conduct for harvest" was ranked the second highest priority by participants at the 2007 Northwest Territories Caribou Summit, garnering just one vote less than "protecting the calving grounds in the NWT and Nunavut."

Are some user groups given preference over others? This is an especially sensitive concern if harvest quotas are introduced. Potential competitors include Aboriginal hunters, non-Aboriginal residents, and guide-outfitters who bring in non-resident hunters. Another question on many hunters' minds is, "If we have to reduce our harvest (and endure the hardships associated with that), will there be some accompanying effort to reduce the number of caribou taken by predators through some kind of predator control programs?"

"Given our diversity as people and organizations, and the complexity of the problems facing caribou, what can or should we be doing? An overarching answer is respect, starting with respect for each other's views. Caribou ecology is complex — causes of declines interact, and simply blaming one factor or another is unproductive ... Respect includes being knowledgeable about caribou and about the views of people who depend on caribou and people who are concerned about them." — Anne Gunn, from "What Price the Caribou?" *Northern Perspectives*. Ottawa: Canadian Arctic Resources Committee, Volume 31, Number 1, Spring 2007.

"By hunting better, perhaps no one will have to be asked to hunt less." — Porcupine Caribou Management Board, from "What Price the Caribou?" *Northern Perspectives*. Ottawa: Canadian Arctic Resources Committee, Volume 31, Number 1, Spring 2007.

Lastly, it is important to know which caribou are being harvested, particularly in cases where migratory tundra and boreal herds co-mingle during the winter. This is a real issue in cases where some populations are considered to be at risk of extinction and the others are not. On the Ungava Peninsula, where the numerically robust George River migratory tundra herd shares its winter range with considerably less secure popu-

"The path to harvest reduction has been established by law. When you have subsistence rights and a conservation issue, every other alternative from a harvesting point of view has to be addressed first, resident harvest and non-resident harvest, before you can touch First Nations harvest. However, if you ask me — Bruno Croft, not the [government] biologist — I would say something like, we have to elevate ourselves above the rhetoric, the blaming games, and the politics and things that stall the process, and spread hardships if we can." — Bruno Croft, biologist, Northwest Territories Environment and Natural Resources, from "What Price the Caribou?" *Northern Perspectives.* Ottawa: Canadian Arctic Resources Committee, Volume 31, Number 1, Spring 2007.

lations of the Red Wine and Lac Joseph boreal forest caribou, any hunting of caribou in areas and at times of range overlap could have negative population-level consequences for herds that are already in decline.

All of the issues outlined above are alive, in one way or another, in virtually every North American jurisdiction with caribou, especially migratory tundra herds. In some cases, for example in the Northwest Territories, this has resulted in lawsuits by outfitters regarding the adequacy of the information upon which harvest control has been based, as well as challenges to the legal mandates of competing bodies to manage caribou. In Labrador, national press attention has been occasionally focused on Aboriginal harvesting from the Red Wine caribou population, judged to be seriously at risk already. Most objective observers would say there are still examples of over-harvesting caribou out there on the land, but the challenge is to do something constructive about it.

Legal actions notwithstanding, probably the only productive way through these issues is to keep on talking in order to arrive at co-operative solutions. Generally speaking, there does appear to be a broad-based commitment to do just that, especially where there is shared concern about caribou declines. In the best-case scenarios, caribou are so important to northerners that the species has served to bring everyone to the table. Furthermore, caribou have caused each party to take responsibility for being part of the solution.

Where there is disagreement about the causes of caribou decline, arriving at consensus solutions becomes significantly more challenging. For example, where hunting, resource exploration and development, and climate change are occurring simultaneously across the range of a declining population, it is seldom clear which agent is causing greater harm, although all factors together may exert more pressure than can be reasonably withstood.

"If we take steps now, we'll hear the thunder again." — Danny Beaulieu, Resource Officer, Northwest Territories Environment and Natural Resources, quoted from his address to the Northwest Territories Barren-ground Caribou Summit. Inuvik, 2007.

Undertake Regular Monitoring and Research

It is impossible to take informed steps to conserve caribou if we do not have an adequate understanding of the overall status and health of caribou populations that is updated on a regular basis. Surveying caribou, which usually range across vast areas in the course of a year in remote, inaccessible locations, presents a formidable challenge. In all cases, it is necessary to deploy airplanes at considerable expense, and there are generally small windows of opportunity to execute surveys. Accomplishing this takes a clear commitment by governments to fund and undertake caribou surveys on a regular basis.

Adele Curtis

In the fall, the velvet on the antlers of a bull caribou begins to loosen and fall, an act that precedes the shedding of the antlers themselves.

175

Assessing the impact of exploration and development activities on a caribou population cannot be reasonably accomplished in the absence of adequate knowledge of the population before the project begins. Such information must obviously be gathered to establish a basis against which to compare future changes. Following this, a monitoring program must be designed that is appropriate to detect population-level changes and, where possible, to differentiate those changes due to the project from those due to natural variability. For long-lived, wide-ranging species like caribou, this is a challenging and expensive enterprise. New development projects are being proposed in areas where knowledge of caribou abundance and distribution is inadequate or non-existent, thereby stretching both the capability and credibility of environmental assessment processes that are evaluating possible impacts.

While methods have been reasonably standardized for population surveys of migratory tundra caribou, no standard, widely used survey technique for boreal forest and mountain caribou has been developed. The absence of such a standard increases the challenge of comparing survey results for different populations. An independent body, such as CARMA, could help determine basic monitoring and research protocols that would serve as an agreed-upon minimum for any jurisdiction with caribou. In fact, a trusted third-party peer review group is likely an important component of caribou monitoring efforts everywhere; this would include the degree to which Aboriginal or local knowledge is being effectively integrated. Combining such knowledge with aerial survey information is easier said than done, given the fundamental differences in the nature of the information. But there is increasingly widespread acknowledgement that this needs to be the goal, and more and more examples of it actually happening.

Quite apart from monitoring, ongoing research that addresses areas of uncertainty continuing to affect management and conservation should be supported and encouraged by government. Such research should back up monitoring efforts to make sure that the questions being asked and the places being surveyed continue to make sense (see discussion of the role of science in caribou conservation later in this section).

"The information we have is all of the caribou are in decline, most of them quite significantly … The issue is, of course: Is this just a cyclical occurrence that some folks have indicated has happened over the years, or is it a situation where the decline may be deepened by the climate change issues, the resource development pressure, the harvesting, and all the other contributing factors overlaid onto what in the past may have been a more natural kind of trend?" — Honourable Michael Miltenberger, Minister of Environment and Natural Resources from "What Price the Caribou?" *Northern Perspectives.* Ottawa: Canadian Arctic Resources Committee, Volume 31, Number 1, Spring 2007.

Unfortunately, caribou biologists, like any group of people, have occasionally made mistakes, in their case by drawing conclusions from their work that turned out to be wrong. These errors are often cited, especially by northerners, as throwing doubt on what the "experts" have to say. Biologists are told they weren't looking in the right places, or at the right times, or otherwise didn't listen to the advice of local residents. Less famous are the pronouncements made by scientists that have turned out to be right. Only regular and transparent collection of all types of available information will bring the clearest results.

An additional issue is that many Aboriginal people, especially elders, have ethical reservations about techniques such as capturing and tranquilizing caribou, or putting tags or radio and satellite collars on the animals. They find all this to be disrespectful. Yet the ability to follow the fate of individual animals is the only way to address many key questions, such as survival and reproductive success of a population, important habitats (including calving areas), extent of movements, and even population numbers. Some non-invasive techniques, such as the analysis of genetic information from caribou droppings, hold promise, but there is still a long way to go before more invasive techniques can be abandoned entirely. Concerns such as these demonstrate that as important as *what* information is gathered, is *how* it is gathered.

There is no doubt that local people must be involved in the caribou monitoring process by obtaining their agreement; by genuinely seeking their advice on logistics and survey assumptions; by employing them in the field in the data-gathering so they can tell other community members how it was done and why; and by translating results, reporting back, and testing conclusions against what the people who live there have experienced in the past and are actually seeing now.

The role of Aboriginal leaders, of course, is to encourage co-operation and participation of hunters, elders, and community leaders in such a process.

All of this needs to be built into a policy of monitoring caribou because it leads to better quality science; it at least minimizes the chances of mistakes; and it generates the kind of credible information that is most likely to be actually used for conservation purposes. Above all, it reflects mutual respect.

It follows that common access to caribou databases is key to the success of caribou monitoring. In Canada, territorial and provincial governments are generally considered

David J. Tilley

An over-wintering caribou craters for food in the boreal forest.

custodians of wildlife, and by extension custodians of information about such wildlife. Other parties cannot usually gain access to wildlife information without special permission under the data-sharing agreements governing its use. The same is generally true for Alaska, although the process of accessing information is generally less onerous in the United States. Aboriginal peoples have provided very valuable information though harvest surveys and interviews about traditional use, some of which they now regard as proprietary. If we're not careful, this tendency to hoard information on all sides can result in a climate of mistrust among the different parties interested in caribou conservation. This is not only counterproductive when it comes to taking action, it is a serious waste of money if it leads to everyone gathering their own, redundant information about caribou. The task is likely too large for any one player, even governments, so it is important that everyone involved helps out to the extent that they are able. The goal should be to share information that all agree is the best basis for management decisions.

In general, monitoring and research funds have been victims of major budget cuts in federal, provincial, territorial, and state wildlife programs over the past ten years right across the North. The priority of many natural resource ministries or departments is to facilitate, rather than to proactively plan for, development activities with proper sequencing of conservation concerns.

In Canada, the federal government largely withdrew from caribou monitoring activities north of sixty in the early 1990s, leaving serious data gaps for migratory tundra caribou such as the Beverly and Qamanirjuaq herds, which has undermined their management. This is only now starting to turn around for these particular herds, with significant new contributions from Indian and Northern Affairs Canada, along with some financial support from industry and NGOs. The lack of recent monitoring information is cited by industry as inconclusive evidence of their impacts; they argue that they should be allowed to proceed unless there's evidence they are actually causing harm. On the other hand, lack of information is cited as a reason for caution by management boards and NGOs.

The Northwest Territories has published an ambitious but necessary management strategy for the eight migratory tundra herds whose entire or partial ranges occur in that territory. This plan urgently needs financial support, especially for monitoring activities. Nunavut has done some important vegetation studies, but (apart from Peary caribou) it has no real handle on the population status of most of the thirteen migratory tundra herds found there. It is hoped that the government of Canada will recommit to participating more actively in caribou monitoring in the northern territories, as such work is unlikely to be adequately funded without greater federal engagement.

For boreal forest caribou, some jurisdictions, including Alberta, British Columbia, and Newfoundland and Labrador (in some cases aided by substantial investment from industry), have undertaken comprehensive radio-collaring efforts that have resulted in a solid picture of the location and status of multiple boreal forest or mountain caribou populations. In others, like Ontario and Saskatchewan, little or no investment in such activities has yielded a comparatively poor idea of habitat condition and population health in key areas of caribou range. Thankfully, this trend is showing recent signs of change: caribou monitoring has ratcheted up a few notches, especially as the requirements of both federal and provincial species at risk legislation begin to take effect.

Industry, particularly forestry and mining, has helped both logistically and financially with caribou surveys in some areas. Individual companies have their own site-based databases that have not been fully accessed by other players in caribou conservation. This too is changing for the better, which should be encouraged, because the quality of this information appears to be excellent, and it should be available for the broader caribou conservation effort.

Paul Zakora

Summer migration of the Bathurst herd, about one hundred kilometres north of a mine site in the NWT.

The next section of this book, profiling the different kinds of caribou across North America, provides further information on the current status of caribou based on monitoring work to date. What emerges is a patchwork, based on uneven knowledge, because long-term caribou monitoring and research have been maintained in only a few areas. There are many more areas where such work has been interrupted or never initiated in the first place.

179

Reconcile Industrial Development with Habitat Protection

We have used the term "conservation first" to refer to identifying specific areas for caribou where no industrial development should take place. But reconciling industrial development with habitat protection provides a conservation approach called "best practices," whereby development happens and needs to be mitigated.

Best practices are absolutely essential to biodiversity conservation and should be embraced with the same enthusiasm as the more popular protectionist strategies, for several reasons: economic development can provide important benefits to people, especially in the North; we are not ever going to be able to provide strict protection to the full range of habitats required by caribou (and we may not need to); and most companies are committed to best practices in any case, since this is either legally required or confers a market advantage and makes good business sense.

Key habitat for the Chisana mountain caribou herd that spends time in Alaska, Yukon, and northern B.C.

Best practices are usually assured by governments (including Aboriginal organizations such as Regional Inuit Organizations, which issue permits on Inuit Owned Lands), through regulatory requirements, and through various licences or permits that need to be obtained and obeyed as a condition of an industrial project being allowed to proceed. Different jurisdictions have different standards in this respect, and certainly different levels of enforcement. However, at the policy level relating to caribou, we suggest the starting point for best practices should be a logical extension of the options already outlined: *No exploration or development should further endanger an endangered population, worsen the decline of a threatened one, increase the decline of a declining one, or destabilize a healthy one fluctuating within natural limits.*

To do anything less than obey regulatory conditions would be to break the law, leaving a company (or government) subject to legal action and penalties, (or electoral defeat). Whether compliance with regulations is actually having the desired effect on caribou also needs to be monitored by the company, by government, and increasingly by an independent monitoring body with representation from affected communities. And whether regulations are in fact adequate needs to be periodically reviewed by government and independent researchers.

The key to continued thriving caribou populations in all habitats will be maintaining options. With their formidable space requirements and sensitivity at certain times of year, caribou require the latitude to move in response to disturbance or habitat loss resulting from exploration or development or other impending changes, similar to the way they have navigated natural disturbances in their ranges. Proactive planning at the population range level can ensure that industrial development (including road networks) accommodates natural level of disturbances, rather than adds to them in a way that exceeds the threshold of overall habitat disturbance for caribou. These spatial options are what allow caribou, with their inherent resilience, to adapt or adjust. By the same token, with sufficient time to recover from

Paul Zakora

Calving grounds for the Bathurst herd in the area of the Wright and Hood rivers, west of Bathurst Inlet.

"When we consider habitat problems relating to human activities on caribou range, we must remember that annual range is only as good as its weakest link. That is, little or nothing is gained by protecting only calving ground areas, if we do not also protect adequate amounts of summer, autumn, winter, and spring ranges. It is the entire range of the animal that determines its well-being." — Frank L. Miller, research scientist emeritus, Canadian Wildlife Service, from "What Price the Caribou?" *Northern Perspectives*. Ottawa: Canadian Arctic Resources Committee, Volume 31, Number 1, Spring 2007.

population lows and to follow natural vicissitudes, their capacity to rebound has been demonstrated time and again. However, the reality is that such options are increasingly limited. Where there was some exploration or development activity, more is planned. With the increasing sophistication of both industrial and hunting technologies, the pressures on caribou are becoming relentless. When populations remain seemingly stable in the face of change, the usual response is to push them still further, without sufficient knowledge about when caribou collapse could occur.

In addition to maintaining options, the entry of industrial development into caribou country necessitates planning at spatial and temporal scales appropriate for caribou. The area used by this wide-ranging species for all parts of its life cycle over the course of the year can extend into tens of thousands of square kilometres. This is larger than a municipality, a forest management unit, and just about any customary planning unit. We have already seen that risk to a boreal forest caribou population will increase if habitat transformation (natural and human-caused) occurs on about 30 to 40 percent of its range, resulting in higher alternate prey and predator densities. Therefore, to conserve that population, any land use planning process must consider the entire spatial extent of the population range, which will be particularly challenging where population range boundaries are unknown, or where planning units are constrained by other factors.

Time scales are also important, because the default position is to pursue a business-as-usual approach that makes decisions on a piecemeal basis. This has important consequences for caribou because, as a long-lived species, it takes time for effects to play out to the point where their population shows signs of being harmed. As a consequence, some effects on that population may not be felt until after the development has been allowed to proceed too far. Or it may be difficult to ascertain whether population changes are natural or the result of industrial disturbance.

While reconciling industrial development with caribou habitat protection may be a reassuring concept, it is difficult to implement and to assess in practice, even when all involved are genuinely committed. In fact, whether this is even possible, let alone achieved, has been the source of debate. But that should not stop us from putting the principle out there as a standing policy and doing our very best to make it a reality.

On the positive side, inviting industrial development into the North can bring economic benefits to communities that are ready for them, if not overdue. The truth is that most northern communities, like people everywhere, are split on the merits of economic development versus conservation. They want to believe they can have them both, and in some cases they probably can.

Industry thrives in an environment where the rules are clear, and on occasion they have been helpful in coming forward, often with NGOs and Aboriginal groups, to urge governments to make land use decisions expeditiously and to establish regulations that provide greater certainty for business investment. Most businesses now recognize that they need a "social licence" to operate, so they need to know how to go about getting that.

The business community can bring technical expertise and information to the table, for example on geology or forests. They also bring management know-how, logistic support, an ongoing presence out on the land, and potential financial resources for caribou research and monitoring activities. Increasingly, industry is accumulating experience with various techniques to mitigate the impact of its activities on caribou: flying higher over or totally avoiding calving areas when they are occupied by caribou; building berms and fences to try to divert caribou around industrial installations; experimenting with different forest harvesting patterns; or instructing employees on how to minimize their disturbance of animals.

On the negative side, industrial activity at virtually all stages inevitably has *some* disturbing influence when it contacts caribou. And sometimes the right thing to do for caribou is not cost-effective, especially when that means no industrial activity at all, for example shutting down operations during the migra-

"A lot of people who work at the mine still have a connection to the land. Even though they have a good income doesn't mean they go to the grocery store and just buy cans of beans. The caribou and the whitefish are still out there, they're harvesters as well." — Fred Sangris, Chief, Yellowknives Dene, from "What Price the Caribou?" *Northern Perspectives*. Ottawa: Canadian Arctic Resources Committee, Volume 31, Number 1, Spring 2007.

David J. Tilley

Spring caribou moulting their winter coats are not always a pretty sight, but they will be better off for it once the temperature changes.

"In Alaska, the federal government, primarily through the U.S. Fish and Wildlife Service, assumes a much greater role in regulation of the harvest of wildlife than in other states ... federal laws mandate that rural residents of Alaska, comprised mostly of indigenous peoples, should receive priority over urban and non-resident hunters in harvesting for subsistence use of the annual surplus of fish and wildlife from federal lands ... Since federal lands in national forests, wildlife refuges, national parks, military and other federal reserves, and federal public domain lands constitute 60 percent of the total land area of Alaska [1.48 million square kilometres], the federal role in management and conservation of wildlife in Alaska is unique among states. This federal-state partnership in management of Alaska's fish and wildlife resources has been both controversial and complex and has contributed to political polarization between urban and rural users of fish and wildlife resources." — David R. Klein (lead author), from "Management and Conservation of Wildlife in a Changing Arctic Environment," Chapter 11 of the *Arctic Climate Impact Assessment*. Cambridge University Press, 2005.

tion or calving season. Protected areas deny miners, petroleum geologists, and industrial foresters access to the very resources around which their businesses revolve. Although industry is well-served by a business environment of relative certainty, it has a history of lobbying in advance for regulations and land use decisions that are best for them, rather than for local residents, the natural environment, and caribou.

Furthermore, the economic benefits held out by industry often make people want to believe that caribou will not be seriously impacted, when in fact they will. Or caribou may be judged as simply less important than the new economic opportunities being offered by industry to needy communities, especially to youth. Such decisions may seem short-sighted to outsiders, but they can be desperately important to those most affected.

In our experience, most major resource companies — forestry, mining, and oil and gas — are in compliance with regulatory requirements. This is a meaningful part of their corporate culture, and violations are usually accidents or exceptions to the rule. Of course that doesn't mean that accidents don't happen, and in a northern environment, the consequences of these (such as oil spills) can be significant. The extent to which we are being asked to accept accidents as inevitable is the extent to which certain activities should not be permitted at all in such a vulnerable place.

While most of the major corporations have sufficient resources to try to do things right, the same cannot always be said of small exploration companies or construction contractors. These businesses may cut corners, often claiming they don't have the financial resources of the major players to always do the required thing. They also commonly claim that many of the regulations they have to meet are either unreasonable or unnecessary.

Suzanne Barger

Caribou in the vicinity of oil and gas infrastructure in Alaska.

"After five years of fierce public debate and a steadfast refusal to protect habitat, the B.C. government recently decided to adopt all elements of the Recovery Strategy, including protection of critical habitat. In October 2007, the government announced its Mountain Caribou Recovery Implementation Plan. This widely supported plan will protect a total 2.2 million ha (380,000 of it new) of mountain caribou range from logging and road building; capturing 95 percent of the caribou's high-suitability winter habitat. They will also manage human recreational activities within the areas outside strict protected areas, manage predator populations of wolf and cougar where they are preventing the recovery of caribou populations, manage the primary prey of caribou predators, support adaptive management and research, implement effective monitoring plans for habitat, recreation, and predator-prey management, and institute an effectiveness monitoring strategy. The key difference between B.C.'s plan and all the others across Canada is simple: they have chosen to listen to the best advice that science and civil society can provide and protect habitat as a key component of their approach." — Tim Gray, from *Woodland Caribou: The Politics of Conservation* (unpublished). Toronto: WWF-Canada, 2007.

In Alaska, there has been ongoing tension regarding who sets policy regarding best practices, whether it be the federal Bureau of Land Management and state Department of Natural Resources, whose primary mandates are to further development, or the federal Fish and Wildlife Service and state Department of Fish and Game, for whom caribou are a key client. However, the same tensions in principle reside within virtually every North American jurisdiction that harbours caribou. Certainly industry assurances that they could drill within the Arctic National Wildlife Refuge without negatively affecting caribou have been a long-standing point of debate, as are claims that some North Slope industrial installations do not negatively affect caribou but in fact attract them. Because of the stakes associated with such claims, they have been the subject of much research and counter-research, leaving the public somewhat mystified as to where the truth really lies.

Of real concern is when regulatory requirements are just not adequate for caribou conservation. For example, in Nunavut permit conditions for exploration work include Caribou Protection Measures, which are supposed to protect caribou while they are in calving and post-calving areas and using designated water crossings, enforced through federal government legislation. However, evidence to date suggests that these measures are not adequately enforced, and would not be adequate even if they were enforced. Nunavut's new Wildlife Act and its regulations do not include accurate boundaries for caribou calving areas, in which a similar version of these protection measures is supposed to provide seasonal protection to caribou.

In many ways, Alberta is on the front line of woodland caribou conservation. This province has invested enormous industrial capital in considering the best practices elements of caribou conservation strategies, but not those elements that require deferrals or no industrial activity from forestry and oil and gas interests.

In Ontario, there has been considerable research into how logging practices might be modified to help conserve woodland caribou, with guidelines that are cutting edge but still based on the untested hypothesis that good quality habitat will grow back in time, allowing caribou populations to recolonize previously logged and roaded areas. As in Alberta, the most difficult and least pursued option for government and industry is to leave large areas unlogged for long enough periods that caribou will return. Temporary loss of habitat due to large forest fires has made embracing this option even more difficult, as have difficult economic times for the forest industry.

The concept of "Critical Habitat" inherent in the endangered species legislation in both the United States and Canada holds promise as a tool for identifying habitat elements necessary for the recovery of caribou populations at risk, as well as identifying what might be done to protect those habitats. As noted previously, significant new work is being undertaken in this regard, for example by the Canadian federal government.

"'The Alberta Government has adopted this plan as Alberta's Woodland Caribou Recovery Plan with the exception of the recommendation in Section 7.2 relating to a moratorium on further mineral and timber allocations on specific caribou ranges.' Thus, in one short sentence, the Alberta Government has made it clear that even when a herd is facing an immediate threat of extirpation [Little Smoky Herd], new logging, oil and gas, or other industrial licenses will continue to be placed in its habitat. They have, however, proceeded with other controversial aspects of the plan, such as predator culls and penning of pregnant females until they give birth. Few expect these measures, in the absence of habitat protection, will long delay the disappearance of this species in these critical areas." — Tim Gray, from *Woodland Caribou: the Politics of Conservation* (unpublished). Toronto: WWF-Canada, 2007.

The Canadian government is identifying Critical Habitat for boreal forest caribou under the federal Species at Risk Act.

"In Ontario, constrained by maintaining and increasing timber harvest levels, the Ministry of Natural Resources has failed to address the survival of caribou in recent land use planning. As a result, only one of the hundreds of parks created since 1995 was designated to provide habitat for this species [Wabakimi Wilderness Park]. At the level of forestry operations, the government has chosen to site large new clear-cuts and primary roads in remaining occupied caribou habitat, rather than concentrating harvest in already fragmented areas and conserving the remaining intact areas. The result is ongoing loss of viable habitat, backstopped only by a hope that caribou will return to these large cutovers if and when they regenerate to mature conifer forest." — Tim Gray, from *Woodland Caribou: The Politics of Conservation* (unpublished). Toronto: WWF-Canada, 2007.

Address Climate Change

There is no doubt that climate change stands to have a significant long-term impact on caribou, as part of the climate-vulnerable North. As such, appropriate governmental policy must address it. However, many volumes have already been dedicated to climate change, so we will not pretend to give it an in-depth policy treatment here.

Succinctly, we believe that both Canada and the United States should commit to the goal of a 30-percent reduction in greenhouse gas emissions by 2020, and 80-percent by 2050, based on 1990-level emissions. This would be an appropriate North American contribution to reaching a global average target of 50-percent reductions by 2050. And we agree with many others that the global goal should be to confine average surface temperature increase to no more than 2°C. Such a policy commitment would be in keeping with the findings of the Intergovernmental Panel on Climate Change, and it would stand a chance of avoiding some of the worst consequences of this global threat.

How will spectacular northern landscapes, and caribou, be affected by climate change?

In our view, such a policy goal would best be met on two fronts: First, the demand side of the North American energy equation should be revisited through significantly greater commitments to absolute reduction in energy use and to conservation, efficiency, and appropriate end-use. Second, the supply side of the equation needs to be addressed through greater emphasis on transitional and renewable energy sources.

Right now, neither Canada nor the United States is committed to anything close to the above policy goal, and of course climate change will continue to be an overarching issue addressed directly at the international level. Tribute should be paid to the Inuit who have spoken so eloquently about the need to take action now, especially through the leadership of Nobel Prize nominee Sheila Watt-Cloutier, past head of the Inuit Circumpolar Conference.

Caribou are also being sideswiped by the indirect effects of climate change and underlying North American energy policy, through attendant oil and gas development, pipelines, and mining for both coal and uranium in the North. Consequently, it could be argued that unless we successfully address the larger issue of climate change and its related contributions to humanity's ecological footprint, all the other governmental policy suggestions we have made regarding caribou won't amount to much in the long term.

RESEARCH PRIORITIES AND THE ROLE OF SCIENCE

Curiosity will always drive research; scientists virtually never have enough information and can always come up with more that needs to be gathered. The priority for caribou should be focused on enhancing our understanding of impacts of exploration and development activities on populations and learning to apply such knowledge to mitigate negative effects. Research is needed to better understand thresholds of human harvest, as well as our industrial footprint with its corresponding deterioration in habitat quality. How much of this can be tolerated by caribou, and what are their minimum protection needs? Scientists also need to better understand the ecological forces driving growth and decline of caribou populations so that we can better identify natural conditions and differentiate them from those that are our responsibility.

Glen and Rebecca Grambo

Migrating caribou tirelessly file their way across the tundra.

Caribou defy definitive statements, even when they are urgently needed. This has led to some erroneous pronouncements regarding their status in the past. Consequently, no one wants to panic and declare a caribou population to be headed for extinction, proposing management hardships on everyone involved on order to save them, only to learn that the caribou were simply in a cyclical state of decline that eventually reversed itself. On the other hand, certainly no one wants to be proven by hindsight as having been complacent while presiding over the loss of a caribou population. These potential mistakes flow from the problem of projecting the current state of affairs too far into the future — virtually always the wrong thing to do with caribou.

So it's a tough call, and it is arguably more responsible to caribou to err on the side of caution. However, it's easier to argue the precautionary principle from a distance than to live with the day-to-day consequences felt by the people who are being asked to take fewer caribou or none at all. Invoking the precautionary principle can also mean asking a community to forego potential economic opportunities that come with a new project, or asking society at large to bear higher oil prices due to decreasing availability. Often it is argued that these consequences will be short-term only, and everything will be better in the long run for both people and caribou. But the consequences are felt nevertheless. Some genuine appreciation of these realities, and sympathetic proposals to address them, would go a long way to patching up some brittle relationships between scientists (and NGOs) and affected northern communities.

Scientists also face a further challenge that is often beyond their control, namely the interpretation that is attached to their work, especially when acting on it carries political or economic consequences. For example, numbers can be lifted out of context to make a situation sound better or worse than it really is, depending on who is latching on to the scientist's work. Ideally, misinterpretations could be minimized by scientists' clarifying, when briefing decision makers, what their work does or does not indicate. But even this is not always adequate. Perhaps the only recourse is to speak up when

"I think there are some big differences, and big problems with trying to use the past to predict the future in this case. When caribou declined before, they could stay away from harvest pressure, from disturbance, they could avoid us. They can't anymore. There's access by winter roads, there's access by aircraft, there's all sorts of activities across their ranges. So we can't assume that the future will be just as in the past; we have to deal with it in that cautious manner. The caribou have demonstrated the ability to rebound from lows in the past, but we have to make sure we give them the ability to do that in the future."
— Ray Case, biologist, Northwest Territories Environment and Natural Resources, from "What Price the Caribou?" *Northern Perspectives*. Ottawa: Canadian Arctic Resources Committee, Volume 31, Number 1, Spring 2007.

work is misused— there are certainly many examples of this happening, but it's a tall order when a scientist's job may be on the line.

With computers beckoning from the warmth of the big city, it is tempting for some scientists to become "caribou experts" without laying eyes on the real thing, feeling the land under their boots, or meeting the people who have such a huge stake in the results of their studies. "Getting out there" is in order, however, because it will measurably improve the quality of a scientist's work. Experience in the field leads to better, more relevant questions, and it helps all of us avoid those obvious mistakes we never would have made if we had actually "been there."

Involving the people who live in a study area is an additional key step. In some parts of the North, scientists and managers are simply no longer allowed to come and go in the field without developing a rapport with the people who live there, as they must obtain the appropriate permissions and permits to conduct their work. Obtaining these is often dependent on first gaining approval from communities and regional organizations.

We have already emphasized the importance of working collaboratively with local people and integrating their knowledge into scientific work. When the two perspectives don't agree, it will be increasingly necessary to ask why. Reporting back on research findings and discussing them with community members, especially before public release, is also a common-sense gesture. It keeps the community informed and gives researchers a good heads-up on how the findings of their studies are likely to be received.

In a way, it is unfortunate that Traditional Ecological Knowledge (TEK), also known as Aboriginal knowledge or local knowledge, has become so *de rigueur* that it is now the subject itself of academic study, policy, and even legal wrangling over proprietary intellectual rights. In Nunavut, a deeper concept is now a guiding directive for the territorial government. It is called *Inuit Qaujimajatuqangit* (IQ), and it reflects the ancient knowledge of the Inuit while encompassing all aspects of traditional Inuit culture, including values, world view, life skills, perceptions, and expectations. In many cases, there has been debate about the real worth of TEK and IQ resulting in a polarized, unhelpful "take it or leave it" divide where one side rejects the perspective of the

Jeremy Harrison

Caribou are not always on the move, but spend significant periods just resting and grazing. How important are these undisturbed moments to them?

other out of hand. To be on the receiving end of this has been uncomfortable and unproductive for everyone involved. Instead, perhaps integrating TEK and IQ should simply be a matter of human respect and decency, acknowledging the obvious: that the people who have lived there for hundreds of years know something about their land and resources that others don't. Equally, someone who has spent decades testing hypotheses and rigorously gathering and analyzing data from the field is quite likely to have something to offer. So why not ask, and why not respectfully work together to get the best of both perspectives working for caribou?

In Alaska, there is currently debate about why both the Western Arctic and Central Arctic herds appear to be increasing, despite intensifying oil and gas activity in their range, while the Porcupine herd is declining, despite continued protection of important habitat such as the calving grounds. There is also ongoing controversy over the impacts that disturbances associated with the North Slope oil and gas industry (such as noise, roads, gravel pits, waste disposal lagoons, drilling rigs, and pipelines) have on caribou behaviour. Obviously those who support such activities have a vested interest in arguing low impacts, and those opposed have a vested interest in arguing high. Although much research has been focused on these questions, definitive answers have not yet emerged.

By contrast, research regarding the impacts of roads and forest harvesting on boreal forest and mountain caribou habitats has been more unequivocal, indicating detrimental effects from landscape disturbances on caribou behaviour and occupancy to four kilometres and beyond. The

A best guess in the face of scientific uncertainty is better than no advice at all when it comes to conserving animals with needs like caribou.

The tidal flats of Hudson Bay in Northern Ontario represent an undeveloped area where pro-active conservation planning, sequencing "conservation first," is still possible.

interpretation and application of such results have, however, not enjoyed universal support on the part of those with vested interests in either development or protection.

Scientists are renowned for fastening on to what they don't know, rather than what they *do*. Often their hard-won appreciation of the complexity of things, not to mention the fear of making a professional mistake, causes them to be understandably reluctant to recommend any specific course of action other than more studies. Even when advice is offered, it is couched in numerous caveats. However, in the case of caribou, those who want to develop or harvest northern resources are not so reluctant to make decisions or take action, and the government regulators being asked for a decision cannot (and should not) delay indefinitely. This puts everyone, including scientists, on the spot. A decision *is* going to be made, either with the scientists' best advice based on what they know now, or without it. (In some cases, decisions can be made conditional upon gathering critical information, but this is not always a possible way out of the decision conundrum.)

The point is this: scientific caution should not serve to disenfranchise either science or caribou. It is often better to move forward with an opinion based on the best available information, even under duress, than to incorporate no opinion at all.

TRIAGE SITUATIONS

If something less than the fundamental conservation principles outlined previously is going to be pursued in the name of caribou, that exception should be made very explicit, and public approval should be sought. In other words, step one is for governments to tell the electorate the truth, not to issue bland assurances that everything is going to be okay. For example, it may be that a triage approach is going to be taken to an endangered caribou population, whereby it is decided to effectively allow one population to become extinct or extirpated because the time, money, and effort required to save it is in limited supply, and would be better directed at other populations with better prospects for success.

We believe that if such an approach is proposed, it is important that the immediate community — and indeed all citizens of that state, territory, or province — be made aware of that decision and its likely consequences; furthermore, they should be asked in some way to sign off on it. In the case of letting a population disappear, a debate and even a vote in the relevant legislature would not be unreasonable. Governments, which are responsible for enforcing best practices, should take responsibility for trade-offs made along the way, rather than surprising everyone years later when the consequences are eventually realized.

Another case in point occurs when there is no political will to insist on habitat protection and management practices to reduce the rate of predation on caribou, because the industry ultimately responsible for these changes is so valuable socially and economically. If so, direct predator-prey management may be the only alternative. Environmentalists' first instinct is to challenge why everyone has been put into this position in the first place, but once confronted by such a choice, everyone faces a difficult decision if the caribou are to be saved.

In other situations, predator-prey management may be required to maintain caribou even if full protection of habitat *is* implemented. For example, the colonization of central British Columbia by moose has fundamentally changed the predator-prey system. The number of wolves supported by this novel prey species may be too great for caribou to be self-sustaining, even in a wilderness landscape. The decline of caribou herds in some large protected areas in southern British Columbia suggests that this may be the case. If so, the choice may well be to either accept ongoing predator-prey management or recognize that caribou can no longer be self-sustaining in those areas and allow them to disappear.

So far, we do not feel that governments have been forthright enough in explaining the trade-offs associated with triage situations. Sometimes we are told that endangered or even extirpated caribou populations can be restored by reintroducing caribou into areas where habitat has been sufficiently restored or protected to support them, or by bringing pregnant females into captivity so they can give birth without risk of predation. However, both of these are expensive, last-ditch strategies that we should seek to avoid. And if captive-bred caribou are being reintroduced, it is important that they emanate from the same genetic stock as the animals that once inhabited the area — a concern that has arisen for translocation of mountain caribou into the Selkirk Mountains and the proposed reintroduction of endangered Peary caribou in the High Arctic Islands. This issue of genetic provenance haunts conservation biology everywhere; our goal should be not just to rebuild a species' numbers, but also to maintain the full diversity of the species as it has evolved on different landscapes. Otherwise, we risk re-establishing relatively homogeneous populations, or ones otherwise genetically, behaviourally, or ecologically unable to survive or exceptionally vulnerable to disease and other environmental changes.

"Whenever management prescriptions are proposed, the differences between management of caribou solely for the purpose of increasing their number for harvest, versus the conservation of a genetically, biologically, and behaviourally distinct caribou in Canada and North America must be kept foremost in mind." — Frank L. Miller, research scientist emeritus, Canadian Wildlife Service, from "What Price the Caribou?" *Northern Perspectives*. Ottawa: Canadian Arctic Resources Committee, Volume 31, Number 1, Spring 2007.

Lonnie Brock

A curious bull in a remote region of Northwest Territories.

CARIBOU CAMPAIGNS

From the perspective of the general public, non-governmental organizations are some of the most visible actors in caribou conservation. With much of the caribou action taking place either behind closed doors or in far-flung places of the North, information campaigns led by NGOs are often the public's only exposure to caribou. Public interest can be filtered through the imagination and narrative of others, be they NGOs, governments, scientists, or industry. Perhaps this is inevitable, but who does the public tend to believe?

Like it or not, reliable polls indicate that NGOs are consistently near the top of the list of most trusted sources of information regarding public policy issues, especially those relating to the environment. NGOs score far ahead of government and industry. Governments by and large take the views of NGOs seriously precisely because of their claim to represent a significant portion of the voting public, and because much of caribou conservation is playing out on publicly -administered land. However, if NGOs do anything other than "play it straight," they stand to jeopardize this public trust, which translates into an important responsibility on their part.

One inaccurate statement can discredit what might otherwise be a factually impeccable presentation. And if the mistake is serious and public enough, it can permanently wound the organization that makes it. Because many observers lump all NGOs together, such a move can serve to discredit the whole environmental community. Years are involved in establishing a good reputation, but in seconds it can all go down the drain. And today's media are just as prepared to expose factual errors made by NGOs as they are to jump on both industry and government.

Shared, high-quality information is also crucial to collaborative problem solving. If parties around the table disagree on the facts, the chances of generating a co-operative solution diminish considerably. For example, if a First Nation does not truly believe a caribou population is in serious decline, they will obviously be less inclined to sign on for a reduced harvest. Everyone has a vested interest in accuracy, not just a version of the facts that supports a particular point of view. Despite the quip that "statistics is the straightest line between an unwarranted assumption and a foregone conclusion," good homework, including good numbers, will always be a strong point for anyone. But this is especially true for NGOs, who are most vulnerable to the charge of emotional exaggeration.

As with academic scientists, NGOs are often urban-based, generating conservation plans from offices far from caribou ranges. Yet these plans need to be implemented in the rural, coastal, or northern parts of the country. In fact, an ongoing challenge for conservation groups is to find and hire staff who were raised in, or at least have extensive experience with, these quite different cultures.

One way to bridge this gulf, if it's affordable, has been to establish regional offices or to seek out local advisors, and to actually listen to them when it comes to policy development and implementation. In fact, there has been a fundamental shift in the way conservation groups do business over the last decade or so, from top-down campaigns promoting protection of species and places regardless of what the people who live there want, to bottom-up support by NGOs of something that is championed and led by the people who live there.

The opportunities associated with this new way of operating regarding caribou are obvious. First, there should be significant congruence between the objectives of NGOs and northerners, because both want to conserve caribou for the long term. Second, NGOs will simply not be effective in the North unless they are pursuing their objectives in partnership with northerners.

At their best, NGOs are associated with asserting a strong, independent position that is not encumbered by political, economic, or selfish interests. In other words, they are supposed to stand for the right thing to do. That's why people voluntarily give money to NGOs. Along with this moral high road, however, comes the responsibility to spend the money well and to acknowledge that many other parties have a great deal of merit to their position. In other words, rarely is everyone else entirely wrong and only one party entirely right.

Serge Couturier

Two large bulls fighting during the rutting season, Rivière George herd.

The question for NGOs then becomes how to square their image of crusader for all that is right and good, with the fact that the other side actually has some good points. The answer, we believe, is to be found in the concept of being fair.

For an NGO, being fair does not mean being weak or compromising NGO principles. Many outstanding conservation successes have been obtained through multi-party negotiations, where NGOs worked hard to earn a place at the table, then worked *with* others to generate long-lasting solutions that were agreed-upon all around. Often the most effective negotiator is not the one who most powerfully asserts his/her own position, but the one who listens and understands what others need to succeed.

What does all this have to do with caribou? Just this: A policy of being fair is crucial to bridging the cultural divides spanned by caribou. Furthermore, fairness is a crucial ingredient in arriving at conservation solutions that have the best chance of being accepted by most parties, and therefore making a difference for caribou themselves.

"We are now solidly in the 21st Century and can start to blame others for the 20th. In this century, we want to protect boreal forest caribou and many other of wild nature's creations, and we want a future where nature is abundant and enjoyed by our children. We also still want wood, metal, oil, and hydro. Some would tell us these are necessarily irreconcilable wants; that we can't have them both. They may be right, but the evidence does not show that we have tried hard enough to know.

"In practical terms, saving wild nature requires spending time deciding what lands must be left untouched, at the same time as we are thinking about what we want to develop. We need to do this first in our northern forests where we have the luxury of abundance, and then roll back some of the harsher forms of human presence in our more southerly areas where we have already developed too much.

"We need to listen to aboriginal people, scientists, citizens, and business people who give us good advice on how to do this, and we need to make it unthinkable that their advice would be ignored." — Tim Gray, from *Woodland Caribou: The Politics of Conservation* (unpublished). Toronto: WWF-Canada, 2007.

CONCLUSION

OUTLINED IN THIS chapter are some policy commitments and key steps that we think need to be taken by a range of players who can help with caribou conservation. However, simply presenting these in a book will not bring them about. It is much more important that the public constituencies of each of these players send a message that caribou are important, as are policies and actions to keep them around. That means the voting public must speak up to their local politicians and government officials; member First Nations must do the same for their grand chiefs or other elected leaders; scientists must engage real issues, communicate them to the public, and exert pressure on each other to make a difference; NGO members must communicate their concerns to the leadership of those organizations; and consumers must vote with their purchases and investments to let CEOs and their boards know what is expected of them.

In other words, good policy needs to be actively advocated and monitored, not just wished for. And caribou deserve no less.

Glen and Rebecca Grambo

SECTION FOUR

EXPERT PROFILES OF DIFFERENT
KINDS OF CARIBOU

MIGRATORY TUNDRA CARIBOU

by Anne Gunn

Anne Gunn has spent most of the last thirty years working with northern people and caribou. She has spent long hours on the ground observing caribou behaviour and ecology, as well as in small aircraft counting caribou and watching their movements and distribution. Her job with the Canadian Wildlife Service and then with the Government of Northwest Territories involved research and analyses underpinning technical advice on caribou management in a variety of contexts, including co-management boards, environmental assessment hearings, and recovery planning for endangered wildlife. Mostly, Anne worked with migratory tundra caribou and Peary caribou, but she has studied northern mountain and boreal forest caribou as well. Although Anne has now retired, her interest in caribou conservation is still keeping her busy.

Glen and Rebecca Grambo

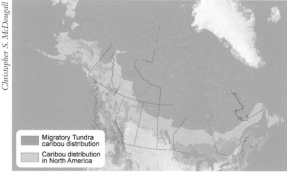

Christopher S. McDougall

Migratory Tundra caribou distribution

Caribou distribution in North America

Map 4.1.1. *Present-day distribution of the migratory tundra caribou ecotype.*

WHAT IS A MIGRATORY TUNDRA CARIBOU?

MIGRATORY TUNDRA CARIBOU are the caribou of popular imagination. The waves of migrating caribou that ebb and flow across the Barren Lands are the images of northern legends. Those caribou include the largest caribou herds in North America, with hundreds or thousands of individuals, as well as smaller and lesser known herds.

A migratory tundra caribou is the ecotype that migrates to the tundra in the spring and remains on the tundra until at least the fall. (An ecotype is a grouping of caribou herds with distinct patterns of habitat use and behaviour, according to well-known biologist Tom Bergerud.) The calving, post-calving, and summer ranges for these particular herds are on coastal and lowland tundra. While some migratory tundra caribou winter on the tundra, others head

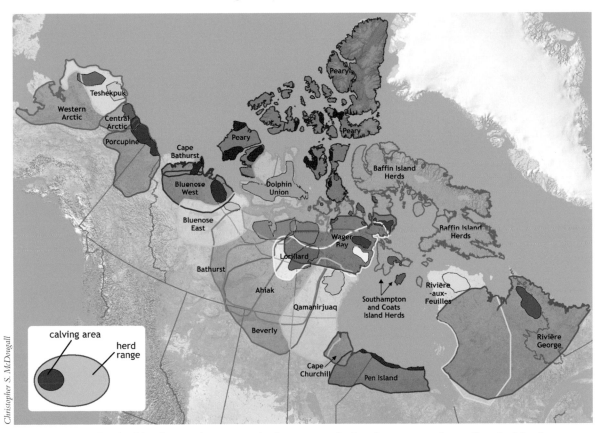

Map 4.1.2. *Individual herd annual ranges and calving grounds for migratory tundra caribou in North America. Most of the outlined annual ranges are based on the movements of satellite-collared caribou. The overlap between the winter ranges of some neighbouring herds is not uncommon and happens during some, although not all, winters. Less information has been published for the Baffin Island herds, so their individual ranges are not shown. This map shows some calving areas for Peary caribou, but more remains to be discovered about where these caribou calve, and why.*

into the boreal forest or into the mountains. Therefore, although the migratory tundra caribou ecotype is a convenient description of how all those herds behave, it can be at odds with other ways of classifying caribou, especially the ecotypes often referred to as boreal forest and mountain caribou, as explained in Section One.

LIFE HISTORY AND ADAPTATIONS

The annual cycle of the migrations of tundra caribou is an adaptation to an environment characterized by extreme seasonality and unpredictability. The caribou take advantage of the average timing of the start and end of the relatively brief plant growth season, although the onset of it varies from year to year. Caribou are also adapted to a long season when forage availability is unpredictable because of annual differences in the extent and timing of snow and ice conditions. Within that overall pattern of migration, these caribou select habitats and adapt their behaviour to reduce their exposure to the risk of predation and parasites.

The annual cycle for tundra caribou starts with spring migration. As the sun warms the snow and it starts to crust and settle in late winter, caribou trails on lakes in the boreal forest and tundra coalesce and become deeper and more defined as the caribou come together for spring migration. The cows, especially the pregnant cows, file across the tree line and onto the snow-covered tundra toward their traditional calving grounds. The cows' migration is urgent, as they steadily and purposefully press toward their destination — where they themselves were born. Meanwhile, the bulls take a more leisurely journey north, and they do not usually reach the calving grounds.

Calving grounds are termed traditional because the female yearlings learn the location by following their mothers back to the calving ground. Cows rarely switch from where they were born to a neighbouring herd's calving ground; even if they do, they may switch back. The cows' fidelity to their calving ground is striking, especially given that winter ranges of neighbouring herds may overlap in some years. Cows from two neighbouring herds may even start spring migration travelling together. But as they get farther out on the tundra, they abruptly turn and head to their respective calving grounds.

Typically, calving grounds are at the northernmost part of a migratory tundra caribou's annual range. This is to the cow's advantage, because when she arrives on the calving ground, she is at her leanest after the long winter and the demands of pregnancy. When the calf is born, the cow needs high-quality nutrition so she can produce milk for her calf. The highest quality forage is available at the time when plants unfurl their leaves and flower buds, even the buds of grasses and sedges such as cotton grass. We can track the greening-up of plants through satellite imagery.

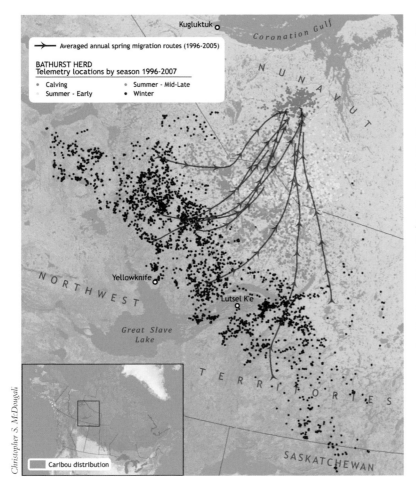

Kugluktuk

Coronation Gulf

→ Averaged annual spring migration routes (1996-2005)

BATHURST HERD
Telemetry locations by season 1996-2007

- Calving
- Summer - Early
- Summer - Mid-Late
- Winter

N U N A V U T

Yellowknife

Lutsel K'e

N O R T H W E S T

Great Slave Lake

T E R R I T O R I E S

Caribou distribution

SASKATCHEWAN

Christopher S. McDougall

Map 4.1.3. *Average seasonal routes travelled by satellite-collared cows of the Bathurst herd from their winter range toward their calving grounds (1996–2005). The point locations represent telemetry points obtained via the satellite collars and illustrate the various regions frequented by members of the Bathurst herd at different times of the year. The pre-calving migratory routes sweep north to the calving grounds, and then by late June the cows leave the grounds, travelling south throughout the summer months. Over winter the caribou spread out and south into the black spruce forests.*

For at least one herd, research has revealed that calf survival is correlated with the timing and extent of plant green-up. When spring is late and the plants are slow to green up, calf survival is poor, as the cows are struggling to produce enough milk.

Like most ecological phenomena, there is probably not just one reason for the selection of calving grounds. Besides the onset of lactation being tied to plant green-up, there may be other evolutionary advantages for caribou in gregarious calving and fidelity to a traditional calving ground. For example, calving at the northern end of the annual range delays the exposure of the cows and their calves to mosquitoes and warble flies that make their lives miserable and interrupt foraging as they try to escape this menace. This also may be the best location for removing cows and their vulnerable offspring from at least some of their predators. Wolves tend to den south of the calving grounds, and few follow caribou right out to these areas. However, some wolves do reach the calving grounds, and grizzly bears also hunt there.

The reason for a cow selecting a calving area may also include such intangibles as personal experience: she may have calved successfully there previously, or perhaps she saw her neighbours calving successfully there. Calving is also gregarious. An advantage of calving in large groups is that the sheer numbers of cows and calves may confuse predators. This safety in numbers would be helped by the fact that most calving is highly synchronized — 90 percent of the calves are born within a few days of each other in early June. There may be more intangible benefits to gregarious calving beyond our ability to measure. For example, a calving cow may benefit from being aware of what her neighbour is eating and doing. This is the realm of public information, which is the term for advantages that individuals gain about their immediate environment from other individuals in their group. Besides information about forage quality in the vegetation patches, cows benefit from the vigilance of their neighbours in watching for predators.

On the calving grounds, the newborn calves strengthen their wobbly legs within a day or two and are able to keep up with their mothers. Bouts of high-speed gambolling with other calves allow them to practise the high-speed runs and turns that will stand them in good stead with the ever-present threat of predators. Within days of calving, the cows start to aggregate and leave the calving ground. Thus begins their migration across the post-calving area, then the summer ranges. When tundra calves are about three weeks old, their rate of daily suckling drops as they forage independently.

On the post-calving and summer ranges, a caribou will alternate bouts of foraging with avoiding the harassment of first mosquitoes, then warble flies. The cows and their calves tend to head south from the calving grounds, where they meet up with the bulls and juveniles whose spring migration northward has occurred at a more leisurely pace. The rivers and lakes that were frozen during spring migration are now open water. This is usually no obstacle to caribou. The air-filled hairs of their coats allow them to ride high in the water, and their broad hooves help them to swim strongly. They tend to navigate water bodies at traditional crossing points, which they have long used and have learned are safe. But swimming across narrows in lakes and rivers is not without its dangers for the caribou. Wolves and bears may ambush them; calves and even adults may get washed away and injured by the surging currents pounding them against rocks.

During some summers, sunny skies and low winds conspire to make life miserable for migratory caribou, because these weather conditions best suit mosquitoes and warble flies. The sheer numbers of female mosquitoes drive these animals into tightly packed groups, seeking higher bare ground such as eskers where a breeze may reduce the harassment.

Warble and nose-bot flies are bee-like powerful fliers. The females of both species pursue the caribou and lay their eggs on the hairs of their legs (warble flies) or in their nostrils (nose-bot flies). The eggs hatch into grubs that either live at the back of the caribou's mouth or migrate through the body to lie under the back skin, where they grow and eventually emerge the following spring. The caribou appear to associate the emergence of the flies with the future discomfort of the grubs. These flies are more than just an inconvenience for caribou, because their immune response to the grubs is costly in using protein reserves. Caribou are highly responsive to the flies buzzing around them. They pack together in dense aggregations where caribou on the inside are less exposed to the flies. They stamp their feet and violently shiver. They stand with their heads down among the plants or blindly gallop away.

The cost of reducing their exposure to the insects is that harassed caribou spend less time feeding. The cows may respond to reduced forage intake by reducing milk production, which in turn slows down the calf's growth rate. In years when harassment is extreme, the cow protects her body reserves (and survival) by forcibly weaning the calf, whose survival then becomes in doubt.

The pattern of post-calving and summer migrations varies between herds: some caribou move forward to the coast when ocean breezes reduce insect harassment. Other herds move inland. For example, the Bathurst herd in the central Canadian barrens tends to move clockwise during the summer. The southward movements bring the caribou parallel to the tree line before they turn north and northeast back out on the tundra.

By mid-August, the first frosts have freed the caribou from insect harassment so that they can forage with only the interruption of predators. Although frosts have killed the grasses and the shrub leaves are turning to fall colours, the caribou often find a crop of mushrooms, which they avidly eat. At this time of year, from mid-August through September, the caribou are intent on rebuilding their body reserves of protein and fat. Caribou are adapted to rapid weight gain, and their body reserves determine the likelihood of cows conceiving during the rut, then surviving over winter.

Toward mid-October, the caribou begin their migration toward their winter ranges. Movements can be rapid, or they can stall for days — possibly an effect of storms. The caribou cows and bulls are together now, and the rut, or breeding period, is underway, with bulls challenging each other and following the cows. Movements skirt around the larger lakes, which are not completely frozen, so some caribou do break through thin ice. When this happens, sometimes the caribou's violent struggles extract it to safety. Other times, exhaustion takes over and the caribou perishes.

Some herds spend the winter on the tundra; some herds migrate deep into the black spruce forests. Caribou are adapted to the five or six months of snow-covered forage on their winter ranges by efficiently searching for food by digging through the snow using their broad hooves and sharp sense of smell. Typically, caribou spend the same energy digging craters in snow to reach forage as they do slowly walking. One caribou may try to save the energy of digging through the snow by displacing another caribou from its crater. Their attempts to displace each other may increase as snow deepens. While males shed their antlers following the rut, most cows are antlered at this time of the year. This allows cows to displace other caribou, and the calves benefit from their mother's place in the dominance hierarchy. Although caribou feed among the trees, they return to rest and ruminate on open lakes, where it is easier to be vigilant for wolves and even the occasional wolverine.

Caribou also have physiological adaptations to help them to survive the long winters. For example, they are able to conserve water by recycling urea. Their nasal bones are elaborately scrolled to offer a large surface area to warm the cold air as they inhale, and this also conserves moisture as they exhale. Caribou can also reduce their metabolic rate during winter. This not only lessens their forage requirements but also allows them to manage on forage that's less digestible compared to summer forage. Caribou are rare among herbivores in that their diet is often dominated by lichens (fungi and algae growing together as one plant). Lichens are relatively efficient to eat, because they often occur in dense patches and are easy to graze. Also, because this food is so dry, caribou do not require much body heat to warm themselves up once lichen reaches the rumen. Lichens are high in carbohydrates and relatively digestible, although low in protein. Caribou compensate for the low protein in lichens by selecting the evergreen parts of sedges and grasses, which increases the level of protein in their diet. The higher protein in the mixed-plant diet encourages the growth of rumen bacteria, which in turn help the digestion of the lichens.

DISTRIBUTION

Migratory tundra caribou are found on the coastal tundra of the Alaska coast and on the tundra of northern Canada east to Labrador. It seems that the larger the extent of the tundra between the coast and the tree line, the greater the maximum size of the herd. The extent of winter range, especially its southern boundaries into the Alaskan Mountains and the boreal forests, varies over decades. As caribou numbers fluctuate, the southern boundaries of their winter ranges expand and contract.

Migratory tundra caribou's annual and seasonal ranges are large — thousands of square kilometres. However, at any one time, the actual area used by the caribou is an order of magnitude smaller. This can leave an impression of vast unused spaces, but the key to survival for an individual caribou is having the space to choose where to forage and how to reduce exposure to predation and parasites. Over decades, a caribou herd's seasonal range use may shift, especially as their numbers rise and fall. Typically, for a declining herd, the boundaries of the winter ranges contract: caribou may then be found only in the heartland of their winter ranges. When herds are increasing, their winter ranges are larger and may overlap with neighbouring herds. Fidelity to calving grounds is high, and their locations are relatively predictable. There is a high degree of overlap in calving distribution in successive years; this overlap may grow cumulatively from a central axis or show a directional shift over decades. However, calving, post-calving, and summer ranges do not appear to change in size in relation to caribou abundance as much as winter ranges.

Aboriginal people have left signs of caribou hunting, such as lines of rocks or trees to guide caribou into ambush sites. The location of those sites is evidence that caribou distribution over the past centuries has been relatively stable. We also know about caribou movements over decades to as far back as a couple of hundred years, from their trails. Where the caribou trails have dug into the ground and exposed the roots of long-lived black spruce trees, the hooves leave distinctive scars, which we can age from the tree rings. And again, those scars suggest stability in caribou distribution over the longer term, unlike their boreal and mountain cousins in the southern part of caribou range. The stability of migratory tundra caribou over hundreds of years is neither surprising nor a reason for complacency. The more southerly winter ranges are already being impacted by the northward movement of roads, forestry, and human settlement; the more northerly migration routes, calving and post-calving grounds, and summer ranges are being actively explored for oil, gas, diamonds, gold, and uranium.

LOCAL POPULATIONS OR HERDS

Migratory tundra caribou have ecological parallels in the world's other gregarious migratory large-bodied herbivores, such as Saiga antelope in Mongolia, wildebeest in Africa, and Mongolian gazelle in Asia. They also have counterparts in marine mammals, such as hooded seals, fur seals, and sea lions. Those marine mammals are extensively migratory, and they too have traditional colonies where pups are born and breeding occurs. Biologists find that such species are structured as several geographic units, with a measure of independence in their population dynamics rather than one large interbreeding population. For example, satellite telemetry and tagging indicate fidelity of hooded seals to breeding colonies, suggesting that the stocks should be managed separately.

Caribou herds are conventionally defined on the basis of the cow's fidelity to a traditional calving ground. Satellite telemetry has revealed that cows that calve together also remain together during the rut, suggesting that caribou within a herd are breeding together. This means that for caribou, "herd" is equivalent to "population." Satellite telemetry has also revealed that a few cows occasionally switch calving grounds, usually on a temporary basis, and then return to the calving ground of their birth.

The definition of a herd is based on female behaviour. For part of the year, the two sexes are geographically segregated. Only during the insect harassment season and the rut are both sexes together. After the rut, the bulls tend to migrate south, especially the prime bulls. In spring, the bulls lag behind the often rapid migration of the cows to the calving ground. Apart from calving, at least part of the reason for this sexual segregation is response to predators — cows with calves are more likely move in order to reduce the predictability of their locations to predators and even to mobile parasites such as warble flies.

We know less about juvenile or male dispersal strategies than we do about those of cows. We also know relatively little about mate selection. A reasonable assumption is that the males will have fidelity to the females in any one herd, given their geographic proximity during summer and fall. In terms of evolutionary fitness, it makes sense to stay within reach of the females. In other members of the deer family, the whereabouts of the males before the rut is predicted by the females' whereabouts. And during the rut, females respond to the distribution of males that display in breeding territories that move as the caribou migrate.

Mass exchange of individuals between herds is rare. There have been a few documented instances of herds merging over the last 30 years, although not among migratory tundra caribou herds. Herds go through highs and lows in abundance, and their ranges expand and contract. Overlap on winter ranges is relatively common when the herds are large and increasing in size, but the herds separate during spring migration and the pregnant cows return to their own traditional calving grounds. If changes in the use of winter range shifted spring migration routes and the route crossed another herd's calving ground, the potential could exist for changes in fidelity and the formation of a new herd. However, this has not yet been recorded for migratory tundra caribou, despite widespread radio-collaring.

HABITAT

From a caribou's perspective, habitat is a mosaic of tundra plant communities and physical features such as eskers, where caribou can select habitats that allow for more efficient foraging while avoiding predation and parasites. These choices are made at different scales, ranging from mouthfuls of forage and patches of plants all the way to landscapes several thousand square kilometres in size. From a biologist's point of view, caribou habitats used to be classified on the basis of vegetation classes, as prostrate dwarf shrub tundra and erect shrub tundra. The shrubs are dwarf birch and several species of willow. Among the shrubs, grasses and sedges form swards and tussocks scattered across the tundra with many species of flowering plants, mosses, and lichens. Tundra is further characterized by being underlain with permafrost, which means that much of the area is wet in summer with myriads of lakes and ponds. Outcrops of rock with drier plant communities are common, where lichens are often the most typical plant cover. More recent computer modelling is allowing biologists to move beyond describing caribou habitat just as

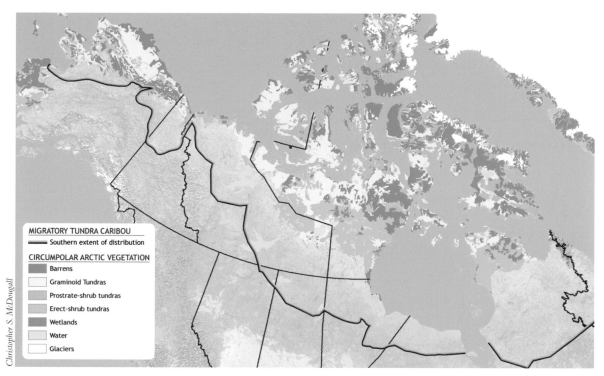

Christopher S. McDougall

Map 4.1.4. *Vegetation classes north of the tree line, showing an east-west trend across the mainland, with more wetlands in Alaska to large areas of erect shrub tundra in Nunavut. Likewise, across the arctic islands there is an east-west trend, with more barrens and less graminoid tundra in the east. Complexity is added by a north-south trend, with prostrate tundra being more plentiful on the arctic islands compared to erect shrub tundra.*

formal associations between plants and to build in features such as predator risk, elevation, or nature and intensity of the human footprint.

Caribou are generalist feeders and are not totally dependent on lichens. In times of environmental variation, and in particular situations (such as islands), caribou themselves may temporally limit adequate forage through their effects on plant availability. On the treed winter ranges, forest fires are part of boreal forest ecology and can change the vegetative characteristic of large areas for decades. Although lichens are slow to regrow, grasses, sedges, and shrubs recover relatively quickly and still provide forage for caribou, at least in early winter before the snow becomes too deep.

Through our eyes, there is no one conspicuous habitat characteristic that distinguishes calving grounds, other than their tendency to be located in the northern end of the annual range. Calving grounds in Alaska are on the coastal plains and have extensive sedge and shrub plant communities. In Canada, calving grounds are often at slightly higher elevations, with a diversity of habitats from lichens to sedges and shrubs. This gives the calving caribou a choice — if spring green-up is late, the cows can feed on lichens.

The fact is that caribou need space, in the sense of a patchwork of tundra habitats, rather than a particular habitat type. This allows them to maximize their options with respect to foraging and finding refuge from predation and parasites. We know from experience in Russia and Alaska that such space can be compromised by the cumulative effect of human activities.

CURRENT STATUS AND KEY THREATS

Caribou herds typically cycle from high to low numbers, which of course can leave the impression that when caribou numbers are low, the caribou will return as they always have. But as human influence grows (larger population, global warming, and industrial development), the past may no longer be a secure guide to the future. When caribou numbers are low, the caribou are less resilient to changes in their environment. Climate change and more hunting, for example, may make it more difficult for the caribou to recover. In northern Canada, most of the migratory tundra herds in the Northwest Territories and Nunavut have declined from the 1990s up to the present. Herds in Alaska are stable or declining, and in northern Quebec and Labrador, the Leaf River herd is increasing while the George River herd is declining.

A prevalent threat to the persistence of migratory tundra caribou is, quite simply, complacency. There is a frequently unspoken notion that the sheer number of caribou is an adequate hedge against threats. But this ignores a fundamental rule of conservation biology: it is the rate of decline, not the absolute population size, that determines persistence. There are many examples of gregarious migratory marine and terrestrial mammals bought almost to, or over, the edge of extinction by commercial harvesting or cumulative land use practices in a short period of time. The future of many large-bodied herbivores elsewhere in the world — animals that were migratory and gregarious like caribou — has been compromised by agriculture practices, sometimes with or without hunting. This includes the Saiga antelope, the Tibetan gazelle, and the wildebeest. Agricultural practices do not constitute a threat for North American migratory caribou. However, experience with oil and gas fields, especially in Russia, does raise the question of how much change to the land caribou can endure in the world's more remote landscapes.

Concerns about effects of industrial exploration and development on caribou date back to at least the 1970s and have triggered quite a few studies. Most research was designed to determine short-term behavioural responses by caribou to human activities. Perhaps unsurprisingly, we have learned that caribou respond to human activity as though such activity is an approaching predator. In other words, caribou become more alert and move away. Bulls and cows often differ in their responses, with the cows being more cautious and more likely to flee.

Recent analyses suggest that behavioural responses also occur at greater geographic scales. For example, biologists working on the range of the Bathurst herd in the Northwest Territories documented a shift in caribou distribution at distances of twenty to twenty-five kilometres from a large open-pit mine for post-calving and summer ranges. Those findings should inject a note of caution: we do not fully understand the effects of human activity on barren-ground caribou, and what we do know is not always encouraging.

Most studies have revealed short-term behavioural responses, partly because they are relatively easy to measure. However, we have not measured the cumulative effects of relatively minor reductions in foraging time, or avoidance of areas as a consequence of human disturbance. During the time on the calving, post-calving, and summer ranges, the cows are driven to forage to produce enough milk for their calf's growth and survival, as well as to rebuild their own body reserves to be able to sustain themselves and to conceive. Models have demonstrated that interruptions to forage amounting to 15 percent can reduce pregnancy rates in a herd, as cows need to have a certain level of body fat to conceive. While on calving grounds, caribou cows are especially vulnerable to disturbance, and all the cows of any one herd are gathered together in one place. Therefore, anything that affects the cows on their calving ground affects the future productivity of the herd.

Hunting is part of the ancient relationship between caribou and Aboriginal peoples. Caribou and Arctic peoples have a long relationship going back some forty thousand years in Russia, at least twenty-five thousand years in North America, and perhaps as long as two hundred thousand years in the Siberian sub-Arctic and Arctic. Those early people also hunted horses, steppe bison, and mammoths. But it was the caribou that survived the mega-faunal extinctions toward the end of the last glaciations about ten thousand years ago, probably thanks to their adaptability and migratory behaviour.

Hunting can be both a benefit and a threat to caribou. It's a benefit because as hunters and families kill and then butcher caribou, they are monitoring caribou condition. They of all people obviously have reason to care about the health and status of the herds that they rely on year after year for sustenance. It turns out that, although the words differ, there are similarities in how hunters and biologists rate body condition. Hunting becomes a threat, however, if it is responsible for additional deaths to a herd that is already in trouble.

Herds naturally fluctuate in size, and those fluctuations are regular enough to be considered cyclic. Information from Aboriginal elders and indications such as hoof scars on spruce roots attest to the long-term periodicity in caribou abundance over tens to hundreds of years. Evidence from Alaska and Canada also suggests that there is some regional synchrony in the highs and lows in caribou abundance, and perhaps even a relationship between caribou abundance and the decadal switches in weather patterns such as the Arctic Oscillation.

In fact, there is not one aspect of caribou ecology that is not linked to variability in weather. Sometimes caribou are affected directly by the weather, for example through the energetic costs of moving through snow or digging to forage. Sometimes they are affected indirectly, for example through forage quality, the intensity of warble fly harassment or the survival of eggs, or vulnerability to predators in deep snow. And decadal switches in weather mean there will be runs of favourable or unfavourable weather years. If a herd has had a run of good years, their numbers will have built up and they will be starting to affect the quality of their forage through overgrazing. The numbers of predators will have built up. And then a run of less favourable weather sets in. The caribou numbers, which had stabilized, then start to decline as pregnancy rates decrease, calf survival declines, and adult survival declines slightly. Under those conditions hunting can accentuate a decline.

Migratory tundra caribou have coexisted with people in North America for at least twenty-five thousand years (the age of the oldest artifacts showing human use of caribou). Throughout that time, people have depended on caribou and built their cultures around the seasonal flow of caribou migration. Hunting was part of people's existence and part of caribou ecology. The next chapter in the saga of people and migratory tundra caribou is to ensure their persistence by managing human activities to leave the caribou's annual and seasonal ranges functionally intact. Caribou are adaptable, but they need their vast ranges to find enough forage and to space themselves away from predators, including us.

SPECIAL NOTE ON PEARY CARIBOU

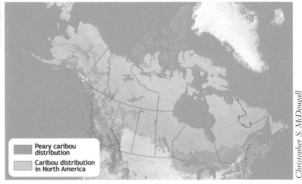

Map 4.1.5. *Present-day distribution of the Peary caribou subspecies.*

Peary caribou distribution

Caribou distribution in North America

Paul Nicklen

Christopher S. McDougall

WHAT IS A PEARY CARIBOU?

Peary caribou are found only on the Canadian High Arctic Islands. Their pelage (coat colour) is grey in summer and white in winter, which together with their small stature most distinguishes Peary caribou from all other caribou. Their faces and legs are relatively short. The hooves are large and broad relative to the size of the caribou. The summer coat is slate grey with a white belly, and the legs are white except for a narrow frontal stripe. Conspicuously absent is a dark bellyband, which is so obvious on migratory tundra and northern mountain caribou. Another striking difference is that Peary caribou have grey antler velvet, in contrast to the usually dark brown velvet of other caribou.

The smallest and whitest Peary caribou are found on the most northern High Arctic Islands, whereas farther south they tend to be a little larger and have a bit more brown on their backs and faces. But even these animals could never be mistaken for any other type of caribou. However, there are biologists who consider that only the Peary caribou on the northern islands (Queen Elizabeth Islands) should be called Peary caribou, while those on Banks, Victoria, Prince of Wales, and Somerset islands should be called Arctic Island caribou. J.A. Allen first described Peary caribou as a distinct species in 1902, from specimens collected on Ellesmere Island by Robert Peary, the American Arctic explorer. Since then, the gradient in their body size across the High Arctic Islands has led to arguments about whether Peary caribou should be a species, a subspecies, or one or two ecotypes. The current consensus, until such time as the caribou species undergoes a badly needed taxonomic revision, is to recognize them as a subspecies following the 1960s classification by Frank Banfield described in Section One. It is complicated, especially as on the Boothia Peninsula, Peary caribou and migratory tundra caribou both occur, although they do not seem to mix and have separate seasonal ranges.

Peary caribou live in a severe environment and therefore have been subject to extreme evolutionary selection. During the Wisconsin Glaciations, Peary caribou probably persisted in at least one glacial refugium in the High Arctic, as not all the islands were completely glaciated. The climate across the High Arctic Islands is strongly regionalized, with east-west and north-south gradients in snow depth and the number of days that plants can grow. Periodically, incursions of Pacific and/or Atlantic maritime air masses in the fall bring severe conditions, leading to caribou die-offs that leave only a few survivors. Evolutionary selection will likely be the most intense when survival of the caribou is reduced to just a handful of individuals. Analyses of genetic variation using nuclear DNA shows that Peary caribou are genetically differentiated between the High Arctic Islands, meaning that the populations have remained largely isolated from one another with little or no interbreeding. At the same time, they have low levels of genetic variation, with evidence that these small populations have recently gone through bottlenecks.

LIFE HISTORY AND ADAPTATIONS

By May, as the lengthening days bring more warmth and the snow melts, Peary caribou are feeding along ridges and slopes where the snow is shallow and bare patches of ground are revealed. Where the snow is deeper, the moisture from melting refreezes as an ice layer, which prevents the caribou from being able to feed. As the snow and ice retreat, some plants have already started their annual burst of growth, using the last of the snow as a mini-greenhouse to get a head start on the short season.

By late May, Peary caribou cows have begun their annual migration to calve. Since Peary caribou occur as island populations, they spend their annual cycle within one island or moving between two or more islands. For example, Peary caribou on Prince Patrick Island cross the sea ice and migrate along the coast to calve on eastern Melville Island.

Neither the migration nor the calving grounds approaches the spectacle typical of the large herds of migratory tundra caribou, because the scale is just so different. If migratory tundra caribou number from thousands to tens of thousands, Peary caribou herds number in the tens to hundreds. However, their natural constraints are similar, as access to adequate summer range is a key requirement for adult females. They need this for rebuilding their energy reserves to reach levels adequate for autumn/early winter conception, and for survival through often harsh conditions until the following summer. Similarly, bulls must regain body condition for the autumn/early winter rut and for winter survival.

The growing season for plants is short and varies regionally and annually across the High Arctic Islands. The long-term averages for the proportion of the year experiencing mean daily temperatures greater than 5°C range from only 4 percent on northern Ellesmere Island and at Resolute on Cornwallis Island to 10 percent at Sachs Harbour on Banks Island. The annual timing of the onset of plant growth is variable; generally speaking, only forty-five to eighty days separate the snowmelt from when the mean temperature is below freezing again. Thus, in some years, the timing of plant growth can be delayed at least two to three weeks in June, which can be critical for caribou food during the calving season.

The timing of calving is variable during June, even stretching into early July in the years when snow has been deep and had layers of ice, which combine to impede Peary caribou foraging. While calving, Peary caribou cows spread over the sparsely vegetated terrain, often drawn to nipping the flowers off purple saxifrage. Just as on the southern ranges on the continental mainland, the caribou track the plants as they flower and the leaf buds unfold. As summer moves through June into July, Peary caribou forage along the coast, then follow the flowering of the plants by moving inland to the uplands, where flowering takes place a week or two later. Flowering forbs such as saxifrage and Arctic poppies are sought along with willow leaves and sedges.

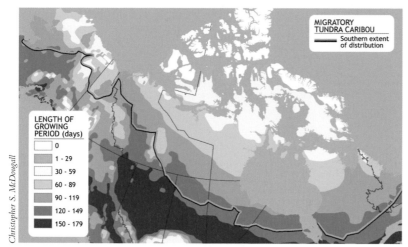

Christopher S. McDougall

Map 4.1.6. *Strong trends in a longer plant-growing season are evident in this map, which shows the sharp north and south reduction in the length of the plant-growing period.*

All too soon in August, the plants begin to die back, sending their nutrients into their roots while their above-ground parts become less and less nutritious for the foraging caribou. By September, the ground is usually already covered with snow, and the caribou drift to the coast on Melville, Bathurst, Banks, and southern Victoria islands, where they rut in October. As the sea ice forms in late October and early November, the caribou cross to their winter ranges. Although Peary caribou accumulate thick layers of fat in the fall, it provides only about a quarter of the energy needed for the long winter. The rest comes from foraging on the dried leaves of dwarf shrubs, sedges grasses, and mosses. Unlike on the mainland, lichens are uncommon and do not feature in their diet.

Peary caribou must contend with snow-covered forage for nine to ten months each year. When the snow is soft and relatively shallow, the caribou simply push the snow off the vegetation with their noses to feed. As the wind packs the snow and it becomes denser, Peary caribou use their large hooves to scrape out small individually scattered craters. As the snow becomes still harder and deeper, Peary caribou tend to seek wind-blown sites or places with only shallow fresh snow cover, and they avoid terrain with deeper snow, even if it is more vegetated. The caribou strike the snow with their hooves to break or crumble the hard-packed snow to reach the plants.

Apart from the seasonal patterns of movements and selection of foraging areas, not much is specifically known about Peary caribou adaptations to their taxing environment. Some features, such as their shorter faces and legs, are typical of island species in general, rather than specific to the Arctic. However, the relatively larger hooves are particularly useful for breaking up hard snow. The rumen of Peary caribou is proportionately larger than that of other caribou, which may be an adaptation to months of low-nutrition forage. Similar to boreal forest caribou, which are often known as "ghosts of the forests," Peary caribou are ghosts of the High Arctic — their white pelage leaves them almost invisible on the snow-covered islands.

DISTRIBUTION

Peary caribou occur on the Canadian Arctic Archipelago, which does not include Baffin Island or the islands in Hudson Bay. There are many islands (surprisingly, they total 2,123, although only eleven islands are larger than 10,000 square kilometres). Those small islands are important to Peary caribou, as they move freely between them both by walking over the sea ice and by swimming. The combined area of all the islands is just over 750,000 square kilometres, which is slightly larger than either Manitoba or Alberta.

On Banks Island, the caribou winter in the south, and many cows migrate to the northwest to calve. Other herds move between two or more islands (Prince of Wales and Somerset; Prince Patrick, Eglinton, and Melville). The exception to the Arctic Island distribution is that some Peary caribou who spend the summer on Prince of Wales Island calve and winter on Boothia Peninsula. Occasionally, Peary caribou do reach Greenland. And during exceptionally severe winters, caribou have left Banks Island, and crossed over to the mainland in search of favourable foraging conditions.

LOCAL POPULATIONS OR HERDS

Gaps in our understanding of seasonal movements — especially for the eastern High Arctic Islands — hamper our ability to identify local populations or herds. We do know that there are herds whose seasonal movements include calving and rutting areas within a single island (Banks, northwest Victoria, Bathurst). Larger islands, such as Banks, may have more than one herd. Peary caribou annual range is likely influenced by numbers: when their numbers are low, the caribou likely restrict their seasonal ranges and may not cross between islands between seasons.

HABITAT

Given the climate severity and restricted snow-free season, the High Arctic Islands are at the limit for plant growth. The combined factors of sheer size of the area, presence of permanent sea ice, and topographical diversity (ranging from high mountains and glaciers to coastal lowlands) render diversity in regional climates that in turn imposes complexity on the vegetation patterns. The climate is both dry and cold enough to restrict plant growth. Technically, the High Arctic Islands are largely polar desert, where large areas have less than 50 percent cover dominated by prostrate dwarf shrubs and forbs.

Peary caribou avoid the ice fields — bare ground and rock fields. They also do not select areas with the highest vegetation cover. Instead, the timing of flowering and leaf growth influences habitat selection during the snow-free season. At this time, coastal areas, river valley slopes, and plateaus with dwarf shrubs, forbs and sedges will attract foraging caribou. During the reminder of the year, snow cover influences habitat selection. Calving grounds have varied terrain that provides patches of snow-free or shallow snow-covered sites — at least shortly before and during calving — each year. Large river valleys and rugged coastal sites are typically calving areas.

Insects such as warble flies and mosquitoes are too infrequent and rare in these environs to drive caribou to seek habitats to reduce insect harassment, as is typical for migratory tundra caribou. And because Peary caribou spend their lives far above the tree line, some of the habitat selection strategies and behaviour seen in the boreal forest winter ranges for migratory tundra caribou — such as the selection of lakes for resting — are also absent in Peary caribou. We know almost nothing about how Peary caribou space themselves to reduce the chances of falling prey to the Arctic wolf. However, the little that we do know about Peary caribou use of range suggests that forage availability is the key factor that drives their choice of habitats. Peary caribou use relatively small areas in winter — five square kilometres in a winter with favourable snow conditions for foraging. During summer, as Peary caribou track the growth of plants, they use larger areas.

CURRENT STATUS AND KEY THREATS

Describing trends in Peary caribou numbers is hampered by lack of information. Except for north Victoria and Banks islands, information is either irregularly collected or out of date. The general picture is one of declines followed by some limited recoveries. But the recoveries have mostly not reached previous levels of abundance. Generalizations about Peary caribou status are difficult, given the regional differences in the timing and frequency of surveys to estimate abundance. Conservatively speaking, where there were at least thirty thousand Peary caribou in the early 1960s, there are now three to five thousand, as judged by the most recent surveys undertaken between 1997 and 2006. A disconcerting finding is that the once large population on Prince of Wales and Somerset islands and Boothia Peninsula (about five thousand caribou in 1980) has disappeared, not having been located in either the 1995 or 2004 surveys.

The first estimate of Peary caribou abundance was in 1961, when a low-coverage but extensive aerial survey of the Queen Elizabeth Islands put numbers at about twenty-six thousand animals. Most were then present on the western islands. By the next survey in 1972, they had declined by about 70 percent. Subsequent surveys were irregular; those undertaken from 1985 to 1987 placed the estimated number of Peary caribou on the western Queen Elizabeth Islands at only about 9 percent of the 1961 estimate. From 1988 to 1996, only Bathurst Island and its neighbouring islands were resurveyed, and by 1994, the number there had recovered to about 85 percent of the 1961 estimate. An aerial survey in 1997 revealed that the number of Peary caribou had declined once again since 1994 and had reached a low of only about 4 percent of the 1961 estimate. The eastern Queen Elizabeth Islands were covered by one range-wide aerial survey in 1961 and were not re-surveyed (except partially and sporadically) until a range-wide survey was completed in 2005 and 2006. The pattern appears to be local increases and decreases.

Inuvialuit elders recollect that Peary caribou on Banks and northwestern Victoria Island declined in the early 1950s and early 1960s. On Banks, the number increased to an estimated twelve thousand caribou in 1972, was relatively stable until 1982, then declined to an estimated one thousand caribou in 1992. Some recovery followed, but the recovery was then lost during a severe winter in 2003-04; in 2005, the number of caribou was only about nine hundred. On northwest Victoria Island, Peary caribou numbers declined from about three thousand to a low of about one hundred caribou in 1994. Some recovery occurred, but it was lost by 2005, likely a result of the 2002-03 and 2003-04 winters.

The Inuit report that Peary caribou on Prince of Wales and Somerset islands declined during the 1930s, were scarce in the mid-1940s, increased in the late 1950s, and were stable through the 1970s. In 1980, there were an estimated 5,100 caribou, which had almost completely disappeared by the time of the next survey in 1995. A follow-up survey in 2004 found no caribou.

The threats to Peary caribou are not well understood, and it has been difficult to reach agreement about what factors have driven declines. Among the reasons for these difficulties are: mistrust between hunters and biologists; lack of information on population trends; hunting; predation; and the rates, unpredictability, and widely scattered nature of rapid declines. Inuit knowledge speaks to a pattern of declines and recoveries, with weather, wolves, and forage playing key roles. Hunting has likely been a factor, and it is important to note that Inuit and Inuvialuit have themselves restricted their hunting when the caribou numbers are low. Restrictions in hunting have led to increases in Peary caribou, but then on at least Banks and northwest Victoria islands, the recoveries were lost during severe winters in 2002-03 and 2003-04 when a warmer Pacific maritime air mass brought freeze-thaw cycles in late fall. Thick layers of icing resulted, restricting access to the vegetation, so that both caribou and muskoxen died. On Bathurst Island, the snowfall during the four years with major winter/spring die-offs exceeded the early winter total (September to November) in each of those four years.

The pattern of caribou abundance since 1960s has been marked by declines and recoveries, embedded in an overall trend of decline across the southern and western islands. This pattern argues for a generalized threat of some kind. The most likely is climate, which shows strong regional differences in both weather patterns and recent climatic trends. For example, on southwestern Melville, southern Prince Patrick, and Banks islands, mean annual temperatures rose by about 0.25°C between 1961 and 1990, while there was no detectable warming trend on Prince of Wales Island, Somerset Island, and eastern Queen Elizabeth Islands. Precipitation increased between 1948 and 1992 in the west and central Arctic, but not in the eastern High Arctic. However, complexity is to be expected, as local and regional variation in weather is often high. A concern is that both maximum and minimum winter temperatures will rise more than summer temperatures. Temperature extremes of 0°C or above may occur in every month except March, which, although infrequent, could increase winter rain and consequent snow/icing events. While Peary caribou die-offs have certainly occurred before, the concern is that these events would increase in frequency, allowing less time for recovery in between.

The human footprint on the High Arctic Islands has been relatively light. There was a burst of oil and gas exploration in the 1970s that caused concerns. At that time, Inuit reported that seismic exploration caused caribou to move away from Bathurst and Ellesmere islands. Mining exploration and development have been limited by isolation and expense. However, oil and gas reserves exist, and exploration and development will likely resume. Many effects of human activities have been predicted, and Inuit and Inuvialuit communities frequently identify low flying aircraft as a possible problem, especially over calving grounds. Large-scale industrial activities could reduce use of or prevent access to different areas by caribou. There is also the potential for localized habitat disturbance or destruction from tracked vehicles; oil, fuel, or drilling mud spills; and road and aircraft landing strip construction. Extended season marine tanker shipping could disrupt or prevent inter-island migrations.

The declines and threats led COSEWIC in 1991 to officially list Peary caribou of the Queen Elizabeth Islands and Banks Island as endangered, and caribou residing in the Prince of Wales-Somerset, Boothia, and Dolphin and Union as threatened. The World Conservation Union assessed Peary caribou as endangered in 1996. In May 2004, COSEWIC reassessed Peary caribou separately from the Dolphin and Union population, and designated Peary caribou as endangered.

SPECIAL NOTE ON DOLPHIN AND UNION CARIBOU

Map 4.1.7. Present-day distribution of the Dolphin and Union caribou herd.

Caribou on Victoria Island are large — almost the same body weight as migratory tundra caribou, but very different in appearance. They look like large Peary caribou with shortened faces and short legs, and their light pelage and pale grey antler velvet add to this resemblance. Dolphin and Union caribou likely have a different origin, but their physical similarity to Peary caribou is probably the result of similar evolutionary selection. Peary caribou likely survived the most recent glaciations in a High Arctic refugium, while Dolphin and Union caribou may have reached Victoria Island from the south, following the retreating ice sheets, or from Banks Island.

One of the most significant genetic divisions among Canadian caribou is the distinctness of the Dolphin and Union caribou. Although genetically more related to the adjacent mainland migratory tundra caribou than the Peary caribou on northwest Victoria Island, Dolphin and Union caribou are more differentiated from any migratory tundra caribou than they are from each other. The distinctness of the Dolphin and Union caribou may be due to a severe population bottleneck that possibly occurred in the early 1900s or earlier, as well as to extreme evolutionary selection.

When they were first described in the 1960s, all that was available were some fifteen skulls and a few hides, as the herd was believed to be extinct by the 1920s. The size of the skulls, and the fact that the hides had some brown in them, nudged the description toward assuming a relationship with the mainland migratory tundra caribou, although the Dolphin and Union were clearly recognized as distinct.

Earlier accounts had suggested that perhaps as many as one hundred to two hundred thousand caribou had once summered on Victoria Island and migrated across the Dolphin and Union straits to the mainland for the winter. The migration stopped abruptly toward the end of the nineteenth century, coinciding with the introduction of rifles and coastal trading in caribou hides. However, also at about the same time, muskoxen on Banks Island disappeared in an ice storm, which raises the question of whether that storm played a role in the disappearance of the Dolphin and Union caribou herd as well.

Although the migration ended by the early 1920s between Victoria Island and the mainland coast, Inuit were aware of a very few caribou on Victoria Island. Sightings increased in number in the 1970s and 1980s, and by 1993 up to seven thousand caribou were once again migrating annually to the mainland. The skull measurements, pelage colour, and migratory behaviour of caribou on southern Victoria Island in the 1980s were so similar to those previously described that the caribou were assumed to be the Dolphin and Union herd.

The distinctive features of the Dolphin and Union herd are its seasonal pattern of movements, its appearance, and its genetic distinctiveness. The herd migrates from the mainland coastal range to Victoria Island in April to May. The cows usually return to areas where they previously

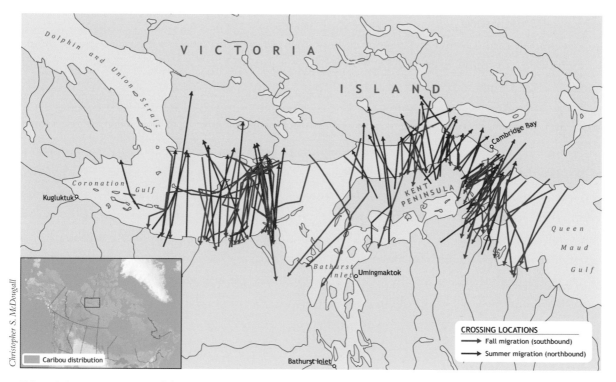

Map 4.1.8. *Movements of the Dolphin and Union caribou herd across the Dolphin-Union Strait.*

221

calved, but the calving is dispersed over almost two-thirds of Victoria Island. The caribou remain dispersed during the summer, feeding on dwarf shrubs, forbs, and grasses. By September, as the plants senesce, the caribou move rapidly and purposefully toward the south coast. They stage along the coast and rut there in late October. The caribou test the sea ice as it forms from the shoreline — occasionally with sad consequences if they break through and cannot extract themselves. From the air, it looks like long worm trails as the caribou struggle and keep breaking through. Sometimes they lever themselves out; sometimes they don't.

Once the sea ice is thick enough and not broken up by fall storms, the caribou reach the mainland coast, where they scatter to forage. Although the snow tends to be deeper than on Victoria Island, sheltered spots among the rocky uplands mean the wind does not pack the snow as hard, and foraging is less energy-intensive. There is also a greater quantity of vegetation and lichens compared to Victoria Island, even although the mainland coast is still far from the tree line. However, the Dolphin and Union herd may have traded the advantages of foraging on the mainland for the greater risk of predation and the risk of the journey across the sea ice. In some years, when freeze-up has been late, Inuit hunters have recorded that hundreds of caribou died after breaking through the ice. Like Peary caribou, this herd doesn't suffer severe summer insect harassment, so foraging time is not interrupted by the usual caribou drive to reduce their exposure to the insects.

Biologists take advantage of the breeding season along the coast to estimate the numbers of Dolphin and Union caribou. In 1997, the estimate was twenty-eight thousand. A subsequent count in 2007 suggested a decline, although poor weather hindered the efforts. The migration to the mainland brings the Dolphin and Union herd within reach of Inuit coastal communities. The caribou are preferred eating, as early in the winter they can be very fat.

In the early 1990s, the harvest of the Dolphin and Union herd was relatively high compared to the estimated size of the herd in 1997. The fall migration brings the herd close to Cambridge Bay and Holman, then migrating to the mainland brings them within reach of hunters from Kugluktuk, Umingmaktok, and Bathurst Inlet. There are also risks to the caribou as they cross the young sea ice, and those risks could be accentuated if the shipping season is extended. A warmer climate is reducing the extent of sea ice and delaying the timing of freeze-up. The level of harvest and the risks posed by crossing the sea ice were considerations when COSEWIC designated Dolphin and Union herd as "Of Special Concern" in 2004.

BOREAL FOREST CARIBOU

by James A. Schaefer

James A. Schaefer is Associate Professor of Biology at Trent University, where he teaches Conservation Biology, Mammalogy, and Ecology. Prior to his university appointment, he served as Senior Wildlife Biologist with the provincial Wildlife Division in Labrador. He has studied caribou for more than twenty years — in Manitoba, Ontario, Newfoundland, and Labrador — and has published several papers on the ecology and conservation of this species.

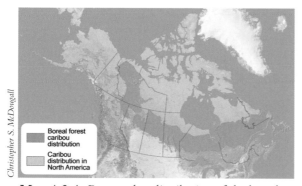

Christopher S. McDougall

Boreal forest caribou distribution

Caribou distribution in North America

Map 4.2.1. *Present-day distribution of the boreal forest caribou ecotype.*

John A. Nagy, GNWT

WHAT IS A BOREAL FOREST CARIBOU?

Shy and secretive creatures of northern forests, boreal forest caribou are one of the most widespread mammals in Canada. Yet even for people residing or travelling in boreal forest caribou range, an encounter with these animals — or a mere glimpse of them — is a rare and memorable event.

It's not just our inability to see the caribou for the trees. Boreal forest caribou assume a solitary existence for much of the year, and even at their most gregarious, seldom do they congregate in groups of more than a few dozen. Rareness and seclusion are some of their traits, perhaps even fundamental to their survival.

Less well known than their migratory tundra counterparts, boreal forest caribou are distinct genetically, demographically, behaviourally, and morphologically — and geographically too, because this ecotype lives year-round in the northern coniferous forests and peatlands that stretch, virtually unbroken, from Labrador to the Northwest Territories. Across most of the continent, boreal forest caribou represent the species at its southernmost point. Increasingly, this places them at the front line — a receding wilderness in the face of a broad northward advance of resource developments and roads.

The geographic and biological features of boreal forest caribou are more than academic curiosities. They are the basis for conservation. In the past few decades, in step with our growing scientific understanding of this ecotype has come the realization of the enormity of this task — keeping wild caribou in northern forests. This creature may be the single most formidable conservation challenge that we face in the North.

LIFE HISTORY AND ADAPTATIONS

Like caribou elsewhere, boreal forest caribou are superbly adapted to their northern environment — a forested, peaty, snowy, watery world. Unlike their migratory tundra counterparts, boreal forest caribou must contend year-round with high densities of predators, like wolves, which are often supported by alternate prey, like moose. Not surprisingly, these physical and biological stressors are reflected in boreal forest caribou morphology and behaviour.

Snow is a key feature of the boreal forest. For caribou, it represents a surcharge to the energy costs of winter travel and feeding; hence, snow has served as a strong evolutionary pressure that has literally shaped these animals. Their broad hooves, low footing loading, and relatively long legs are a reflection of their northern environment, typically blanketed in snow for more than half the year. Caribou also behave accordingly in winter. They seek habitats with thin and soft snow cover, adopt a more sedentary lifestyle, and travel in single file. They are chionophiles in Formovsov's lexicon — "lovers of snow."

Snow also appears to account for one of the most curious adaptations of the species: the possession of antlers by females, unique amongst deer. Antler possession is polymorphic; in other words, not all females have them. The proportion of antlered females varies from near 0 percent in some populations, like on the Avalon Peninsula of Newfoundland, to near 100 percent, as in the Red Wine Mountains of Labrador. The trait appears to have a genetic basis and so is predictable on a year-to-year basis within populations and individual females.

Why do some females allocate nutrients and energy each year to such expensive ornaments as antlers? Boreal forest caribou must dig for food through the snow cover, thus their feeding craters represent considerable energy investments, and they heighten the scope for competition amongst individuals. Under such conditions, antlered females have a distinct advantage. They are capable of displacing (intimidating, fending off, or chasing away) even larger, un-antlered males in contests for craters. Antlers on females are more common in populations where the depth and duration of snow cover are more severe, lending support to the idea that antlers are an adaptation by females to defend winter food resources.

But the chief limiting factor for boreal forest caribou is predation. Most mortalities occur during the first six weeks of life, and the greatest proportion of these deaths, as well as those of adults, is due to predators. Wolves, black bears, grizzly bears, and coyotes prey on fully grown animals; lynx and bald eagles may add to the mix of predators for calves. The primary response of caribou to this predation pressure is in their use of space, and this occurs on several spatial scales.

Spreading out is regarded as a strategy to minimize the risk of predation on calves. A caribou mother gives birth to its calf in seclusion, distant from other caribou. A typical density is one

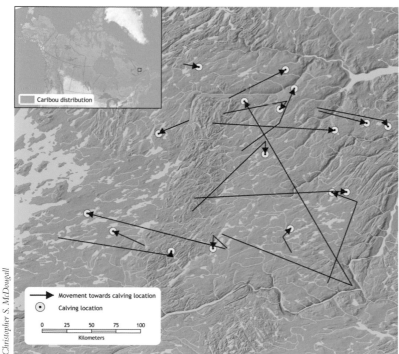

Christopher S. McDougall

Map 4.2.2*. Radio tracking reveals the movements and spacing-out behaviour of female caribou from the Red Wine Mountains herd in Labrador, spring 1983. Unlike migratory caribou, these forest-dwelling animals disperse at calving time; each female gives birth in solitude. By early June, the seventeen adult females were scattered across their entire range; they approached their calving locations (yellow points) from different directions (red lines). Such dispersion seems to be an anti-predator strategy — an attempt by females to make themselves and their calves rare, especially to wolves.*

animal per sixteen square kilometres. This scattered distribution of females — often across the whole range of the population — is a fundamental and defining trait that carries important implications: it is at this time of year when boreal forest caribou tend to occupy their range in its entirety. The need for space reaches its zenith.

Boreal forest caribou also distance themselves from predators by using relatively safe areas of intact habitat landscape refugia. In northwestern Ontario, for instance, the average distance of caribou from wolves during four winters was about fifteen kilometres. Although lichens, an important food source, and snow cover are typically more favourable in old forests, the risk of predation also may be lower in forests more than fifty years old. Boreal forest caribou rarely make use of younger forests. Such areas are risky, as they are often frequented by moose, deer, and their associated predators and parasites.

A YEAR IN THE LIFE

If movements are the most salient feature of caribou as a species, then for boreal forest caribou the most predictable portion of the annual cycle (at least for females) is calving in springtime. Research efforts have typically focussed on females, because of their importance in governing population growth; the movements of males are usually overlooked and are still not well known.

Typically in late May, pregnant females, often still carrying antlers, scatter across the landscape and settle down individually on islands in lakes and peatlands, secluded habitats that appear to provide ready escape from predators. A female will give birth to her single calf in solitude. Females may also remain faithful to these sites; some cows have given birth at the very same locale in consecutive years. Biologists suspect that the more success a female has in rearing a calf through this vulnerable life stage, the more likely she will return to this site in subsequent years.

Movement by the female just prior to calving is often swift and direct, a strategy that may enhance her chances of remaining undetected by predators. Once at the site, however, she typically becomes truly sedentary; she may become even more loyal to a particular place during the post-calving period in July and August. During this time, the cow may hide her calf while she ventures nearby to forage. Her diet is more varied than usual; it may include newly emerging and highly digestible sedges, grasses, forbs, and leaves of shrubs. There is a time and place for many plant species in the diet of caribou. Boreal forest caribou have more opportunities for feeding on the wide variety of foods in their midst than their more northern migratory counterparts.

Boreal forest caribou become more gregarious during autumn — a biological impera-tive for breeding. Males, attaining twice a female's weight, their semi-palmate antlers now

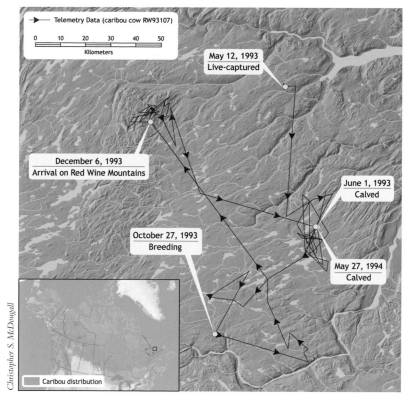

Telemetry Data (caribou cow RW93107)

0 10 20 30 40 50
Kilometers

May 12, 1993
Live-captured

December 6, 1993
Arrival on Red Wine Mountains

June 1, 1993
Calved

October 27, 1993
Breeding

May 27, 1994
Calved

Caribou distribution

Christopher S. McDougall

Map 4.2.3. A year in the life of a boreal forest caribou. This adult female, first captured in 1993, was tracked with satellite telemetry. She give birth that year, near a small, unnamed lake, and spent the summer with her calf in the peatlands and spruce forests in the heart of the caribou range. After breeding in autumn, she arrived on the windswept Red Wine Mountains, overwintering with dozens of others from her herd, where the snow cover was thinner and the feeding more favourable Then, in another swift movement but from a different direction, she returned to the same calving site. Once again, she gave birth to her calf in solitude. In all, she traversed more than eight hundred kilometres during the year.

resplendent and polished, attempt to monopolize matings with harems of perhaps a few dozen females. Like many other ungulates, the bulls' fat stores will become depleted during this exhausting rut, and their antlers — a key weapon for sparring in competition for females — will be cast shortly thereafter. Yearling males will tend to retain their antlers into the winter, as do females. Females exhibit some fidelity to breeding sites, although it is less pronounced than to their birthing locales.

Sociality spills over into winter, and snow cover may accentuate this, as animals coalesce in small groups in areas with favourable snow conditions. Boreal forest caribou seek areas with soft, thin snow cover. Lichens are the dominant food at this time of year, especially ground lichens like *Cladina stellaris*, *C. mitis*, and the appropriately named *C. rangiferina*. These are supplemented by the leaves of evergreen shrubs, by leafy lichens that cling to rocks (such as *Umbilicaria*), and by arboreal lichens that suspend from trees (like *Alectoria*) until snow cover in low-lying treed bogs makes foraging on uplands and windswept ridges more profitable. Boreal forest caribou continue to move at a pace typical of most of the rest of the year, about two kilometres per day, interspersed with alternating bouts of feeding and ruminating. Prior to ice breakup in late April or May, small bands of boreal forest caribou may be seen loafing on frozen lakes.

Springtime beckons. The boreal forest caribou's world becomes dominated once more by ice-free lakes. For females, this open water represents escape from predators; pregnant cows disperse, becoming solitary in anticipation of giving birth. And with the flush of new vegetation, males may begin rebuilding their fat stores.

In one year, a female caribou may traverse hundreds of kilometres, criss-crossing a home range that covers hundreds, perhaps thousands, of square kilometres. (It may rival the size of Prince Edward Island.) There is, however, immense variation in home range size for boreal forest caribou, and larger individual expanses seem to occur at the northernmost extent for the ecotype. The reasons for this variation are unknown although this is a general trend in mammals that may be related to latitudinal gradients in productivity.

DISTRIBUTION

As their name suggests, these caribou are permanent residents of the boreal forest, and their historic range is remarkably coincident with the extent of this biome. But it may not be forest, per se, that dictates the distribution of boreal forest caribou. As with other animals in the northern hemisphere, the limits of this species' range may be governed by physical factors to the north and by biological factors to the south.

In Quebec and Labrador, for instance, the northern extent of the sedentary ecotype occurs at about 54–55°N latitude. This coincides with the limits of ice-free lakes in early June, implying that open water — and the predator escape it provides — is crucial to a successful dispersed calving strategy. And to the south, high moose and deer densities encourage greater densities of wolves, leading to higher predation on caribou as well. There is also circumstantial evidence that brainworm, whose normal host is white-tailed deer in eastern North America, may be lethal to boreal forest caribou — a situation detrimental to caribou where these deer cousins also occur.

But there is geographic variation on this general theme. In some portions of their range, such as western Canada, boreal forest caribou calve in extensive peatlands, largely devoid of moose and deer — another form of refuge from predation. And at the extreme northern distribution of this ecotype in the Northwest Territories, calving habitat appears varied, perhaps reflecting drivers other than predation, such as insect harassment or early emergence of spring foods.

One of the central tenets of population ecology is that abundance and distribution of animals are linked. The southern limits of boreal forest caribou extent have changed dramatically, yet slowly, since the arrival of Europeans. In Ontario, for example, boreal forest caribou have been extirpated from half of their historic extent of occurrence — a northward recession of thirty-four kilometres per decade since the late nineteenth century. This is not a migration, as sometimes construed, but a systematic demise of populations — a long and disturbing diminuendo, still largely unheard. The cold fact is that the present-day southern limits of forest-dwelling caribou are coincident with the northern extent of human encroachment, like roads, forestry operations, and other forms of resource extraction.

Global warming has been linked to poleward distributional shifts of myriad other species, like birds and butterflies. Could it also be the reason behind caribou range recession? Although climate change cannot be entirely discounted, it is unlikely to account for these historic changes. The pace of caribou range loss is more than five times faster than range shifts by other poleward-moving species. In addition, caribou are longer lived and less mobile than birds or butterflies, and thus are less likely to respond as rapidly as these species to climate warming.

Elsewhere in North America, boreal forest caribou have disappeared entirely, from Vermont, Prince Edward Island, New Hampshire, Maine, Nova Scotia, Cape Breton, New Brunswick, Minnesota, Michigan, and Wisconsin. At the dawn of the twenty-first century, boreal forest caribou are found in less than half of their historic extent of occurrence on the continent.

Perhaps most disquieting, to paraphrase the late Jane Jacobs, is that even our memory of what has been lost is lost — a kind of mass amnesia that is deeply problematic. Such loss of collective memory leads to lowered conservation expectations. As noted by fisheries scientist Daniel Pauly, each generation accepts as its baseline the ecological circumstances that occurred at the beginning of their careers, producing ever-shrinking expectations of what constitutes species recovery.

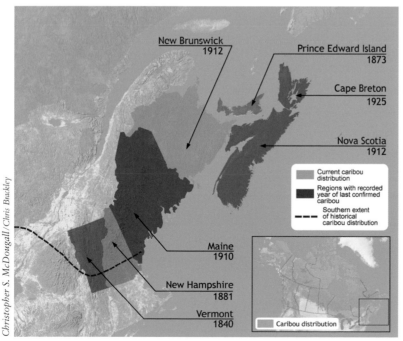

Christopher S. McDougall / Chris Brackley

New Brunswick
1912

Prince Edward Island
1873

Cape Breton
1925

Nova Scotia
1912

Current caribou distribution

Regions with recorded year of last confirmed caribou

Southern extent of historical caribou distribution

Maine
1910

New Hampshire
1881

Vermont
1840

Caribou distribution

Map 4.2.4. *Disappearance of boreal forest caribou from eastern North America. Forest-dwelling caribou once lived surprisingly far south, but have suffered local extinctions. Because of the difficulty in establishing the fate of the last caribou, the dates of disappearance are approximate. Caribou have also vanished from upper portions of Wisconsin (1850), Michigan (1931), and Minnesota (1942).*

The range collapse of forest-dwelling caribou provides a vivid picture that they are declining throughout much of their geographic distribution. It underscores the threatened status of the boreal forest caribou population, a designation reached by the Committee on the Status of Endangered Wildlife in Canada in 2000.

LOCAL POPULATIONS OR HERDS

Boreal forest caribou exemplify the conundrum for denoting populations in biology: Where to set the geographic bounds? In some instances, the one classic definition seems to apply — a population is simply what a population biologist chooses to study.

Whereas migratory tundra and some mountain caribou populations can be readily delineated by their traditional, discrete calving grounds, no such criterion is possible for boreal forest caribou. The spacing-out behaviour of females means that boreal forest caribou occur more or less as a continuum: a shotgun scatter of individuals across a region of favourable calving sites. Boreal forest caribou do aggregate in winter, but these small groups are not analogous to calving aggregations in other ecotypes. There appears to be fluidity to their membership, as well as little site fidelity during winter. Inescapably, for biologists, the bounds of boreal forest caribou populations are blurred throughout most of their extent of occurrence, so that group identity is often indistinct.

The exception is where the extent of caribou occurrence has been fragmented by human activities. In much of Alberta, as well as the southern distributional limits of Manitoba, Ontario, and Quebec, boreal forest caribou appear to be structured in discrete herds, with little or no interchange between neighbouring populations. Such isolation appears to be a consequence of habitat loss and fragmentation — the creation of inhospitable, human-dominated landscape between herds — rather than individuals adhering to strict population boundaries.

Population units are necessary for science and management. And many "herds" have been identified. Across North America, a typical population of sedentary caribou (as denoted by biologists, at least) encompasses nine thousand square kilometres and includes some six hundred animals — a median density of 0.066 animals per square kilometre. The outer limits of these population ranges are typically defined by the distribution of radio-collared females at calving.

Some have attempted to place a figure on the total number of boreal forest caribou in a given jurisdiction, or even the entire country — an exercise doomed to inexactness. Imprecision is inescapable when estimating the abundance of a secretive animal residing at low density across a massive area. Perhaps this is a good thing. We can remind ourselves of C.H.D. Clarke's wishful phrase, nearly seventy years ago: "It is to be hoped that there will never be so few caribou that it will be possible to count them."

HABITAT

Habitat is perhaps the most used, and most misunderstood, word in ecology. Frequently, it merely denotes dwelling space, little more than topography, rocks, and vegetation, presumably because these features can readily be quantified and mapped. But in its full sense, *habitat* encompasses the broader suite of resources and conditions that govern the survival, reproduction, and presence of a population. Ecologists already have a term for such drivers: "population limiting factors."

And for boreal forest caribou, a long list of potential population limiting factors has been assembled: snow, forages, weather, parasites, and predators. In some instances, heated debates have ensued, for instance whether lichens are preferred, or whether food or predators is the more important limiting factor. Such understanding is not merely academic; it is pivotal to management. One key to wildlife conservation is to identify which variables affect the rate of population growth of any species.

The other key is scale. In a landmark study in 2000, Jim Rettie and François Messier at the University of Saskatchewan hypothesized that the most important population limiting factors are revealed by the spatial scales at which animals select habitat — the broader the scale, the more significant the factor.

If their reasoning is correct, then what denotes habitat for boreal forest caribou becomes a little clearer. At the broadest scale, which is the most important for caribou survival and conservation, the chief limiting factor becomes apparent: predation. The very distribution of caribou — whole population ranges — appears to occur in refugia, away from high densities of wolves and their alternate prey. There is also strong selection at this broad scale away from human landscape disturbances like roads, rails, and clear-cuts. If caribou can find such refugia, then snow cover appears to act as a habitat selection factor at slightly finer scales, such as foraging areas with softer and thinner snow cover. Finally, selection for lichens occurs at even finer scales: feeding craters are chosen for their high lichen content.

Teasing out the two broadest limitations — predation and human changes to the landscape — is difficult, however, because forest disturbances are often associated with heightened densities of predators, such as black bears and wolves. And to complicate matters further, landscape changes are often multifaceted: one form of development often incites others in a piecemeal fashion, but not entirely unpredictable. When roads are constructed, for example, they may be followed by other changes to the landscape associated with recreation (such as a network of ATV trails off the main road to access fishing lakes) or resource extraction (such as forest operations or mines). In the boreal forest, the prevalence of water and wetlands makes road construction costly; once this access is secure, it literally paves the way for many other activities. The conclusion that predation is a key limiting factor is in keeping with population studies of caribou, often done by tracking the whereabouts and fate of individuals using radio telemetry. In general, grey wolves and black bears account for the majority of adult and juvenile deaths. At the same time, even for populations in steep decline, biologists typically find females in good condition, with high rates of pregnancy and birth. Such observations tend to discount the other common hypothesis for boreal forest caribou decline: food limitation.

Are humans responsible for the decline of boreal forest caribou? The geographic correlation between caribou disappearance and human-driven changes to the forest landscape — seismic lines, roads, cutovers, and the like — is stark evidence. While boreal forest caribou are sensitive to over-hunting, there is growing consensus that habitat loss, mediated by predation, is indeed the primary agent of extirpation of this particular caribou ecotype.

How can we know? The most compelling signals of human-caused impacts on wildlife are impairments to individual survival, to reproduction, and ultimately to persistence of the population. However, because of the long lives and mobile habits of boreal forest caribou, few studies have satisfactorily investigated population-level effects of industrial developments. Biologists, therefore, generally have relied on examining changes in distribution or movements. Given the importance of space in caribou biology, distribution and movement seem like reasonable indicators of human effects on these animals. Restriction of the movements or distribution of female boreal forest caribou as a result of development (such as a road, mine, or clear-cut) could conceivably compromise their "spacing out" strategy, leading to greater rates of predation.

Part of the response of caribou to habitat loss is behavioural. Animals (especially females, and most often those with calves) are inclined to avoid such areas and tend not to be found even in the adjacent undisturbed forest — an effect that is often measurable several kilometres beyond the precise footprint of development. This means that habitat is effectively lost to a surprising extent relative to the human footprint. It also means that small "parcel perceptions" of habitat, as we conventionally regard the boreal forest, are insufficient. Caribou view and respond to their world at remarkably broad spatial scales, outstripping our conventional, human-centred scales.

The response of caribou to habitat loss may also be demographic. For example, individual caribou may be at higher risk of dying from predation in the vicinity of disturbances. In Alberta, boreal forest caribou tend to avoid linear corridors, and deaths due to predation occur closer to corridors than expected. Wolves also appear to capitalize on corridors as travel routes, increasing access to caribou ranges that would otherwise be more remote.

Ultimately, the reaction of caribou at the population level to habitat loss will be either persistence or extirpation. The scale of this response also appears to be remarkably extensive. In Ontario, for instance, the southern limits of boreal forest caribou can be predicted on the basis of the distribution of disturbances — a 50 percent chance that populations will survive within thirteen kilometres of the nearest forestry cutover. Moreover, the relationship appears strongest between present-day caribou distribution and cutovers twenty years ago. This is evidence of an "extinction debt" — reflecting the lag between habitat loss and species disappearance. This means that the outcome of habitat loss may not be immediately apparent. In this case, two decades corresponds with the expected delay for successional changes in vegetation, resulting in increases in moose and deer after forest disturbance, bringing with them increased predation by wolves, which may lead to the extirpation of boreal forest caribou. The delay would be further accentuated if predation was especially heavy on calves, leading to a recruitment failure, an ever-aging population, and finally, diminished survival of adults.

CURRENT STATUS AND KEY THREATS

Boreal forest caribou are in trouble. In Canada, many investigations have reported dwindling populations, in keeping with the worldwide trend for forest-dwelling *Rangifer*. In Alberta, nine of eleven identified populations are declining, even those recently thought to be stable. In Ontario, the sole demographic study of boreal forest caribou documented an 11 percent-per-year decline — a population being halved every six to seven years.

Some recent studies have placed estimates on how long caribou populations can persist. If the current momentum is sustained, the outcomes are sobering. Boreal forest caribou may be virtually extirpated from Alberta in less than forty years and from Ontario before the end of the century, if the current pace of human-induced changes to their habitat continues. Only a few scattered populations might remain.

There is a clear negative relationship between caribou persistence and human encroachment. Across the land, the geography of human activity is the mirror image of boreal forest caribou persistence — two firmly fitting but mutually exclusive pieces of a jigsaw puzzle. This affords little doubt that humans are the root cause of the decline, although compelling evidence of the exact mechanism remains elusive.

There is a fine balance between gains and losses in caribou populations, a point emphasized years ago by Tom Bergerud. Boreal forest caribou are the classic *K*-selected species: females give birth to a single calf, but not in every year; typically, the mortality rate is high in the first few weeks of life, such that the rate of recruitment to the adult population tends to be low to moderate. To offset this limited capacity for increase, the survival of adult females is critical. Annual survivorship rates of at least 80 to 85 percent must be sustained for numerical stability. Heightened mortality of this critical segment of the population (due to predation or hunting, for example) tips the demographic balance and causes populations to dwindle, sometimes rapidly.

A growing number of studies has investigated the response of boreal forest caribou to development activities and infrastructure — low-level aircraft, energy and mineral extraction, timber harvesting, and roads.

To draw a reasonable conclusion of negative impacts, avoidance of an affected area need not be complete, nor are anecdotes of animals crossing a corridor or using a disturbed area compelling evidence of no effect. Detrimental effects can be inferred when use of an area is lower than expected, as documented from a study conducted before and after disturbance or by comparing disturbed and undisturbed areas. Simple observations, for example of caribou in the vicinity of a disturbance or of a change in caribou numbers coincident with development, are not an unequivocal signal of impact or its absence. This is a common error, even by experienced scientists. Ultimately, we must identify the agents *causing* caribou decline, not simply the factors associated with it.

Far and away, habitat loss is the most serious problem facing boreal forest caribou. Habitat fragmentation and over-hunting represent other important threats, sometimes coincident with habitat loss. But a parallel challenge resides in our thinking. To speak the language of caribou conservation, we need to grapple with not just a few acres or square kilometres, but with thousands of square kilometres (millions of hectares). We must break the bonds of everyday perception to view whole landscapes, rather than just forest stands, and to consider multiple decades, rather than just the immediate future.

Habitat Loss

Forest harvesting, road building and other disruptions do not obliterate boreal forest caribou outright. They appear to initiate a series of insidious, slow-motion changes to habitat: flushes of new vegetation that follow disturbance of the forest and spur increasing numbers of moose, which in turn support more predators, which ultimately leads to caribou demise. The disappearance of boreal forest caribou is thus a slow domino effect, occurring sometimes over the course of decades. And this delay implies that a caribou population may continue to dwindle inexorably, even once the activity has ceased.

In some instances, the extent of habitat loss may be massive enough in itself to lead to decline. Although never quantified directly, the inundation by the Smallwood Reservoir in Labrador (formerly Michikamau Lake) in the early 1970s likely contributed to the decline of the Lac Joseph population. The flooding covered most the northern portion of the calving range.

There are growing examples of habitat loss occurring well beyond the precise bounds of landscape alterations. This effective habitat loss may be a few hundred metres, such as with seismic lines associated with oil and gas exploration in Alberta and the Mackenzie Valley of the Northwest Territories. Or it may be at the scale of kilometres. For boreal forest caribou, avoidance thresholds between one and five kilometres have been documented, although such effective habitat loss may not be absolute. Differences in the avoidance zone may reflect the type and intensity of human activity, the greater sensitivity of females compared to males, and the time of year at which encounter occurs. What is clear is that basing evaluations on the exact physical footprint of industrial developments greatly underestimates the effective loss of caribou habitat.

Such loss of habitat is likely long-term, possibly permanent. To date, there are no examples of boreal forest caribou reoccupying their ranges once extirpated by habitat loss, despite attempted reintroductions to Cape Breton and Maine. (Both attempts failed — brainworm was the suspected culprit.) Perhaps these landscape changes are irreversible. Or perhaps we simply have not had sufficient opportunity to witness the full return of trees, other plants, and wildlife to disturbed landscapes, and their eventual reversion to caribou habitat. This distinction is crucial to how we manage the boreal forest for caribou, but because of the long time frames involved in successional change, it could be decades before we have an answer to this question.

Our understanding is far from complete, complicated by some intriguing exceptions to the general pattern. In Manitoba, the Owl-Flintstone population represents a remarkable case of resilience — a boreal forest caribou herd that has persisted, at the southern distributional limits of the species, in the midst of extensive logging for several decades. It is a noteworthy instance. Our ability to conserve this animal on managed landscapes will depend on capitalizing on such circumstances to develop knowledge that might be applied to populations elsewhere.

Habitat Fragmentation

Fragmentation — literally, the breaking apart of habitat parcels — often accompanies habitat loss. There is evidence that linear corridors, such as roads, may subdivide boreal forest caribou ranges by hindering travel and potentially isolating populations. In one study in Alberta, improved gravel roads with moderate vehicular traffic were found to act as a semi-permeable barrier to caribou movements; in late winter, when seasonal traffic volume was at its peak, crossings occurred at one-sixth of the expected rate. The response may depend on traffic volume, but the threshold appears to be low. Altered caribou behaviour has been detected from as few as twenty vehicles per day.

Linear corridors may also provide ready access for predators into caribou range, increasing travel and hunting efficiency, and reducing refuge areas. Similarly, recently harvested areas interspersed with caribou habitat can compromise the separation strategy employed by caribou to reduce overlap with alternate prey. Large-scale fragmentation of caribou ranges may be sufficient for population decline even when the apparent availability of habitat remains high. This is yet another example of the importance of scale in understanding the needs of boreal forest caribou.

Over-Hunting

In some regions, hunting has been implicated as a serious agent of decline. Like other species slow to recover from disturbance because of low inherent reproductive capability, boreal forest caribou appear prone to over-harvesting. Such an outcome is not unexpected, especially when prime-aged adult females are removed from the population.

Licensed harvest of boreal forest caribou is banned in most jurisdictions, so documentation is rare. Quantifying hunting mortality is profoundly difficult. Some circumstantial evidence comes from Labrador, where dwindling of the Mealy Mountains herd in the 1950s and 1960s, demise of the White Bear Lake herd in the 1960s, and decline of the Red Wine Mountains herd in recent years have all been attributed to over-hunting. The broad expanse of some herds, spanning jurisdictions, complicates the task of managing hunting mortality. The old adage — that wildlife management is based on the principle of common consent — is particularly apt for boreal forest caribou.

THE FUTURE

We continue to scrutinize the boreal forest for its resource potential, so it is certain that the pressures on boreal forest caribou will only increase in the foreseeable future. Striking the right balance will test our science, our skills at finding compromise, and our way of thinking. And for caribou habitat itself, perhaps our human expectations have been be too high. From these northern forests, we have desired it all: timber, hydroelectric power, hydrocarbons, minerals, recreation. Yet at the same time, we expect their continuing ecosystem services and the conservation of caribou.

It is unlikely that all these desires will be wholly satisfied, especially if we continue to insist on rapid, short-term exploitation. For a viable caribou future, tempering our expectations, perhaps by moderating the tempo of development, would be a good place to start.

In addition to direct pressures from resource development, this century is likely to usher in a hotter, less benign climate, as much as 4°C warmer. A major consequence will be changes to the fire regime, the primary agent of natural disturbance in the boreal forest. More severe and frequent fires are anticipated, and, indeed, the early signal of an altered fire regime is already here. For a creature that depends on old forests, this is not favourable news. Recent invasions by mountain pine beetles and white-tailed deer — the consequence of milder winters — may be a harbinger of what a hotter planet might entail for forest-dwelling caribou.

Many of the challenges to conserving boreal forest caribou can be traced to scale mismatches — discrepancies between the biology of this animal and our human institutions. Unfortunately, some of the species' attributes invite delay, sometimes even delusion. Boreal forest caribou are rarely seen; their declines are hard to detect; a population may persist for decades following habitat loss; and caribou conservation demands a vision that extends beyond individual careers, management units, sometimes even political jurisdictions.

The sensitivity of these caribou to human impact was one reason why the boreal forests of northwestern and eastern Canada were identified as two of twenty global hot spots for latent extinction risk, with high potential for future species loss. Here we find species, like boreal forest caribou, with biological traits that make them especially vulnerable to human-caused effects: a "slow" lifestyle, with limited reproductive capacity.

But boreal forest caribou also invite us to be optimistic. After all, if we succeed at conserving this animal, then we enhance the chances of persistence of other species and the healthy functioning of ecosystems. But our accomplishments may even be broader than biological. Because the greatest concerns of society are intertwined, we are also more likely to rise to a whole constellation of other challenges: social, economic, and environmental. Caribou give us reason to hope. They will be a genuine gauge of our success at a sustainable future.

SPECIAL NOTE ON NEWFOUNDLAND CARIBOU

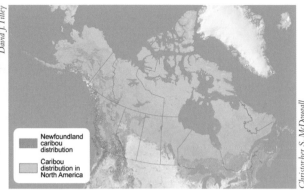

Map 4.2.5. *Present-day distributioin of Newfoundland caribou.*

Unique in form and often migratory in habit, caribou are Newfoundland's only native species of deer. While often assumed to be boreal forest caribou, their habitats and ecology resemble those of the migratory tundra ecotype. The Straits of Belle Isle may be a mere seventeen kilometres across, but a history of isolation, possibly over thousands of years, has resulted in a distinct caribou, distinguished by its pelage, large size, and woodland caribou–like antlers. They are "perhaps the handsomest of all the Caribou," declared naturalist Radclyffe Dugmore in the 1913 book *The Romance of the Newfoundland Caribou.*

Dugmore, who spent many seasons photographing and observing the ways of the caribou, was struck by their key trait: movement. "In no way is the Newfoundland Caribou so well known as by its peculiar and much discussed habit of migration," he wrote. Today, about a dozen herds are recognized on the basis of traditional calving grounds, the end-point of their annual spring migration. There they reside until the first snows of autumn, spurred to seek relatively greater amounts of forage for the winter.

But not all Newfoundland caribou are migratory. A substantial proportion of some herds fail to undertake the annual trek. One entire population, the Corner Brook Lakes herd, is non-migratory. Such versatility underscores the point that caribou are "both highly adapted and highly adaptable," in the words of Tom Bergerud, pioneer of scientific studies of caribou on this island.

In early 1900s, Dugmore was concerned about the demise of Newfoundland caribou in the wild, but the latter half of that century saw substantial growth in caribou numbers. Some herds increased a hundredfold in less than forty years. By 1996, the total island population had peaked at more than ninety thousand caribou — a trajectory that has since reversed dramatically. By

2008, caribou had declined by 60 percent, accompanied by decreases in body size, numbers of antler points, birth rates, and especially survival of young. At least one herd altered the timing of its migration, spending two months less on its calving and summer range than it had forty years earlier. Another herd may have virtually abandoned its calving grounds altogether. Such patterns suggest summer food has become limited.

But the ecological interplay may be more subtle and intricate. Newfoundland caribou are exposed to heavy predation from black bears; lynx and bald eagles also prey on calves. Wolves have been extinct since 1922 here, but coyotes arrived in the mid-1980s, traversing the Gulf of St. Lawrence on pack ice. Given their versatility, these canids are now likely permanent fixtures of the island's ecology, capable of preying on both adult and juvenile caribou.

With intense predation, during this most recent decline few calves have lived beyond fourteen weeks of age. Why has predation increased? One possibility is that female caribou, under nutritional stress, may be seeking foods in riskier habitats, where predators are more frequent.

And disease appears to have a role too. While some calves die directly from lynx predation, others may succumb to infection from *Pasteurella*, a bacterium transmitted during attack by fleas. Furthermore, the parasitic nematode *Elaphostrongylus rangiferi* can trigger neurological disease; it may have contributed to the decline of the Avalon herd on its arrival on that peninsula in about 1990. The nematode can be ultimately traced to the introduction, a century ago, of infected Norwegian reindeer — a reminder that by translocating animals, we may be introducing their parasites, too.

The dramatic changes in Newfoundland caribou are echoed by the land itself, carved by ice and time: "a frivolously sculptured masterpiece of mountains, plateaus, and fjords," in the words of biologist Shane Mahoney. It is a land of romance. Radclyffe Dugmore knew it well: "Not for anything would I give up the memories of my most fortunate days in the land of the Caribou."

MOUNTAIN CARIBOU

by Dale Seip and Bruce McLellan

Dale Seip is a wildlife ecologist with the British Columbia Ministry of Forests in Prince George, British Columbia. He has been involved in caribou research in British Columbia for twenty-five years, focusing on trying to understand the diversity of habitat use patterns exhibited by caribou in mountainous areas, as well as complex predator-prey interactions. He is a member of numerous scientific advisory teams and recovery groups working on caribou conservation and management.

Bruce McLellan has been a research ecologist with the British Columbia Ministry of Forests and Range Research Branch since 1977 and has worked primarily on the conservation of grizzly bears and mountain caribou. Bruce focused his research on the implications of human activities such as forestry, mining, oil and gas exploration, and recreation on the behaviour and population status of these relatively rare species and other members of their ecological community. He has spent much of the past thirty years on foot or on skis in mountainous terrain tracking and watching bears and caribou, but has also been deeply involved with land use planning and industries at the operational scale. Bruce is an adjunct professor at the University of British Columbia and currently co-chair of the World Conservation Union's Bear Specialist Group, which has 130 members from 54 different counties.

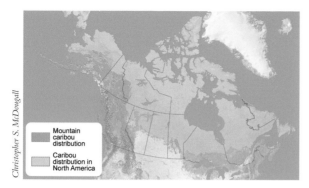

Christopher S. McDougall

Map 4.3.1 *Present-day distribution of the mountain caribou ecotype.*

Elena_Jones

WHAT IS A MOUNTAIN CARIBOU?

Mountain caribou are the ecotype of caribou that live in the mountains of western North America (the focus of this section), with a few populations also residing in eastern Canada. Pacific and continental air masses converging across the numerous high mountain ranges combine to create an enormous diversity of ecological communities. Habitats include towering forests of old-growth cedar and hemlock, vast tracts of pine, spruce, and fir forests, lush alpine meadows, barren alpine tundra, and glaciers. The caribou that occupy those mountains display a correspondingly broad diversity of habitat use patterns. By simply moving from valley bottom to mountaintop, mountain caribou can experience an ecological and climatic change equivalent to that experienced by migratory tundra caribou moving north or south during their long migrations.

The western mountains also contain a number of other species that create a web of ecological interactions. Mountain caribou exist in a predator-prey system that includes grizzly bears, black bears, wolves, coyotes, cougars, wolverines, lynx, and golden eagles as predators, with moose, white-tailed deer, mule deer, elk, mountain goats, bison, mountain sheep, and numerous smaller species as potential prey. This diversity makes the predator-prey system for many mountain caribou much more complex than that experienced by caribou in other parts of North America.

Two different subspecies of caribou are recognized in the mountains of western North America. Mountain caribou in Alberta, British Columbia, Idaho, and the southern Yukon are the woodland caribou subspecies (*Rangifer tarandus caribou*), the same as the caribou that occur throughout the boreal forest in Canada. The mountain caribou in northern Yukon and most of

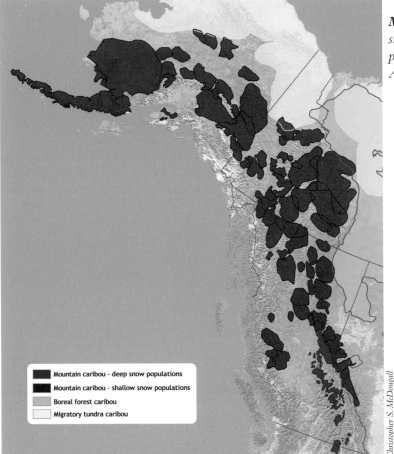

Map 4.3.2. *Deep snow and shallow snow mountain caribou populations in western North America.*

Christopher S. McDougall

Legend:
- Mountain caribou – deep snow populations
- Mountain caribou – shallow snow populations
- Boreal forest caribou
- Migratory tundra caribou

Alaska are Grant's caribou (*R.t. granti*). However, as discussed in Section One, the classification of caribou subspecies across North America is in flux, as DNA studies are beginning to question some of the previous designations.

Unfortunately, the term "mountain caribou" has been used inconsistently, and this has led to confusion. In some areas the term is used to describe any caribou population that spends all or part of the year living in mountains. Biologists in British Columbia reserve the term for a distinct ecotype of caribou that lives in the deep snow zone in the southeastern portion of the province. In this chapter, we use the term to refer to any caribou that live in mountainous habitat. We refer to the caribou in southeastern British Columbia as deep-snow caribou herds.

LIFE HISTORY AND ADAPTATIONS

Snow depth and firmness have a major effect on how and where caribou live during winter. Once snow begins to fall in the mountains in the late autumn and covers the low-growing plants, most mountain caribou migrate to lower elevations where snow is shallow enough for them to feed on terrestrial lichens. Although they will crater through more than a metre of light snow to feed, snow depth and hardness in open habitats soon becomes unsuitable for cratering, and the caribou remain mostly in the forest, where the canopy has intercepted some snow and there is less wind and sun-crusting. If excessively deep or crusted snow in the forest makes cratering too difficult, the caribou begin to make increasing use of arboreal (tree-borne) lichens or shrubs. Alternatively, mountain caribou may move to upper elevations to feed on either arboreal lichens in subalpine forests or terrestrial lichens on windswept ridges in the alpine. In other populations, the caribou do not migrate to low elevations in early winter, but remain in alpine zones throughout this time and feed on terrestrial lichens in windswept areas where snow is absent or very shallow.

A different pattern of winter habitat use is observed in the mountain caribou living in southeastern British Columbia and northern Idaho. Those caribou live in rugged, mountainous terrain where the snowpack often exceeds two metres in depth, which prevents them from cratering for terrestrial lichens. Here, the caribou rely almost exclusively on arboreal lichens for winter food. For three to six months each year, they walk on top of the deep snowpack to access lichen in the canopy of old trees within subalpine parkland habitats. There is, however, variation in the movements of these caribou, because the snowpack is often more than four metres deep in some areas and only about two metres in others. Arboreal lichen does not grow on conifers below the height that is covered by the winter snowpack. Consequently, in areas with very deep snow, there is no lichen within reach of the caribou early in the winter, and it does not become accessible until the snow has accumulated and become firm enough to provide some support. Alternatively, in areas where the snowpack is somewhat shallower, lichen may be found less than two metres above the ground, within the reach of the caribou.

In late autumn, when snow begins falling in the mountains and covers terrestrial foods, caribou in areas that typically have only two metres of snow or less can switch to eating arboreal lichen which is still within reach within high-elevation subalpine forests. However, in areas where the snowpack is sometimes more than four metres deep, the lichen is too high in the canopy for the caribou to reach. In these extremely deep snowfall areas, caribou descend to old-growth cedar and hemlock forests in the valley bottoms. The forest canopy of those stands (often many hundreds of years old) is quite effective at intercepting snow, so snow depth is generally lower than in surrounding areas. When snow is still shallow within those low-elevation forests, the caribou strip the small leaves from evergreen shrubs, especially false boxwood, and feed on any lichen they encounter. Because most arboreal lichens in these cedar-hemlock forests are high in the canopy and out of reach, they feed on lichen that has fallen from the canopy or on lichen on fallen trees and branches. As winter progresses, the caribou move to higher elevations, and by February they are found primarily near the tree line in their preferred winter habitat of open parkland forest. Those subalpine fir forests provide abundant arboreal lichens that are now within reach of caribou standing on the deep, consolidated snow. Mountain caribou prefer relatively gentle terrain within the subalpine, and in fact they are sometimes killed in avalanches when they venture onto steep slopes.

It is important to recognize this difference between mountain caribou that forage primarily on terrestrial lichen and those that feed almost exclusively on arboreal lichen, and even those that are forced into low cedar-hemlock forests, when discussing habitat selection patterns and planning for conservation of caribou in different areas.

The winter foraging pattern of mountain caribou is also an effective strategy for avoiding predators, and winter is often the period when caribou experience the lowest rate of mortality. Caribou that remain in the alpine or subalpine regions in the winter have limited exposure to predators. Bears are hibernating at this time, and wolves and cougars usually remain at lower elevations where they have access to a wider variety of prey such as moose, elk or deer. Wolverines are the only predator that caribou are likely to encounter in the alpine during the winter.

Caribou that use low-elevation forests in winter are more likely to encounter predators than caribou in the alpine, but the habitats they use may still provide some separation from predators. Forests that support abundant terrestrial lichens often constitute poor habitat for other prey species. Caribou feeding in forests with abundant terrestrial lichens may still be separated from predators that are concentrating on ungulate species that use more productive shrub or grassland habitats. Similarly, caribou that move to old-growth cedar-hemlock forests in valley bottoms are using habitats that support low numbers of other ungulate prey, and consequently low numbers of the predators associated with them.

During the spring and summer, the pattern of habitat use between caribou in deep-snow areas and shallow-snow areas is similar. In the spring, many caribou seek out areas where the snow melts first and new green vegetation is available. These areas typically include low elevation and south-facing openings such as avalanche chutes and meadows, but also include roadsides, power lines, and regenerating clear-cuts. Caribou that move down to feed on new spring growth have a higher quality diet than caribou that remain in the subalpine and alpine. Yet many caribou remain in high-elevation habitats through the spring. This is likely a strategy that serves to reduce their exposure to predators. Caribou that feed at low elevations in spring are much more likely to be killed by predators than caribou that remain at higher elevations. The sites that provide new spring growth to caribou are also sought out by bears, as well as by other herbivores such as sheep, deer, and elk. This abundance of ungulates attracts a variety of predators. The concentration of predators in areas that provide early green-up makes those areas a dangerous place for caribou.

Mountain caribou give birth to their calves in late May and the first half of June. Calving usually occurs at upper elevations in the alpine or adjacent subalpine forests. Some caribou calve in essentially the same area where they wintered, but others migrate one hundred kilometres or more to their calving/summer range. That migration is usually to areas of more rugged mountain habitat. Migration routes often go through low-elevation valleys where the caribou experience high levels of predation.

Adult females are usually solitary when they give birth, but within a few days females with calves begin to form into groups. Depending on the density of caribou, those aggregations may range from three or four cow-calf pairs to hundreds or even thousands of caribou. Some of the large mountain caribou herds in the north are not solitary at calving but instead utilize concentrated calving areas similar to those of migratory tundra caribou. At the time of calving, the quality of forage available in the alpine may still be poor, so again it appears that caribou will go to considerable lengths to reduce their exposure to predators, even at the expense of food quality.

Newborn calves experience a very high rate of mortality, and over half can die within the first few weeks following calving. Young calves die from a wide variety of causes, including birthing problems and accidents, but studies show that 60 to 95 percent of the deaths are caused by predators, including wolves, bears, wolverine, and golden eagles.

Within a few days or weeks of calving, green-up occurs at upper elevations, and the caribou are finally able to feed on more nutritious forage. This is important for the lactating females and their young calves. The caribou feed on a variety of grasses, forbs, and shrubs in alpine and subalpine habitats during the summer months.

Summer nutrition is not usually thought to be a limiting factor for mountain caribou, as the subalpine and alpine meadows have an abundance of caribou forage. However, the mortality rate of both adults and calves in summer can be substantial due to predation. In contrast to the winter months, a variety of ungulate species (as well as bears) utilize the abundant and nutritious plant forage in alpine and subalpine meadows during the summer. Predators follow the prey to higher elevations, leading to increased encounters with caribou. Those encounters are often deadly for caribou and their young calves.

Mountain caribou use snow patches in summer to avoid excessive heat and to seek insect relief. In the Yukon and Alaska, recent climatic warming has accelerated the melting of some permanent snow patches, exposing prehistoric hunting relics dating back more than four thousand years. Evidence suggests that the prehistoric hunters relied on predictable caribou use of these snow patches to help them kill caribou.

The rutting period of mountain caribou occurs in late September and October, and typically takes place in open alpine areas. In areas with large caribou populations and wide expanses of open alpine habitat, rutting groups can number in the thousands. Small caribou populations, and less expansive alpine habitat, lead to rutting groups that are often fewer than a dozen animals.

As winter approaches, caribou that use different winter and summer ranges migrate back to their winter range. However, as indicated previously, some caribou herds use the same ranges in winter and summer.

DISTRIBUTION AND STATUS

The abundance and status of mountain caribou populations generally improves from south to north. In the past, caribou distribution was contiguous within the mountains of southeastern British Columbia and extended into northern Idaho, Washington, and Montana. Those populations declined in number and distribution over the past century, with only small, isolated remnant populations in this region. At the southern extreme of their extent, the South Selkirk population straddles the border between British Columbia and Idaho. That herd numbers only about thirty-five animals, and their continued existence is in part due to transplants of more than one hundred caribou from other areas in past years. The extreme southeast portion of British Columbia contains ten other very small and isolated mountain caribou populations. Six of those populations currently contain fewer than twenty animals, and only one has more than a hundred. All of these small herds are at a very high risk of extirpation.

Moving slightly farther north into central British Columbia, there is greater overlap among populations, resulting in a more contiguous distribution. That includes caribou that live on the east side of the Rocky Mountains into Alberta, northern British Columbia, the Yukon, the Northwest Territories, and Alaska.

Many individual populations are recognized within the extent of occurrence of mountain caribou, based on evidence that there is limited range overlap. However, the longer these populations are studied, the more likely we are to see evidence of overlapping boundaries and exchange of individuals among populations. The boundaries and definitions of individual populations are continually being reviewed and updated. Currently, about forty mountain caribou populations are recognized in British Columbia, four in Alberta, twenty-two in the Yukon, two in the Northwest Territories, and twenty-five in Alaska. The ranges of many caribou populations cross jurisdictional borders, increasing the complexity of caribou conservation and land use planning

The number of mountain caribou also greatly increases going from south to north. There are an estimated 19,000 caribou in British Columbia, with 5,000 occurring in the southern

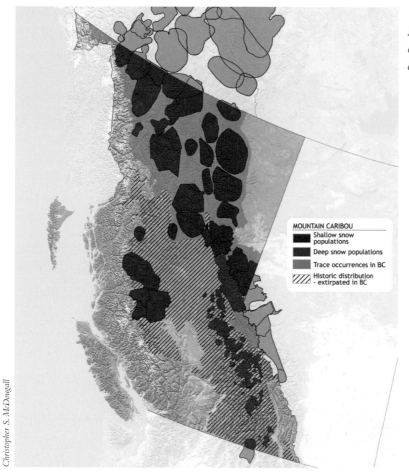

Map 4.3.3. *Current and historical extent of occurrence of mountain caribou in British Columbia.*

MOUNTAIN CARIBOU
- Shallow snow populations
- Deep snow populations
- Trace occurrences in BC
- Historic distribution - extirpated in BC

Christopher S. McDougall

half of the province and 14,000 in the north. Alberta has about 600 mountain caribou living on the eastern slopes of the Rocky Mountains in the west-central part of the province. The Yukon supports about 35,000 mountain caribou, including herds that extend into the Northwest Territories. Alaskan mountain caribou herds total about 150,000 animals, although the numbers vary dramatically over time as some of the large herds have exhibited major increases and declines. Overall, the total number of mountain caribou in western North America is about 200,000 animals, living in about ninety different populations.

The dramatic difference in the abundance of caribou going from south to north is reflected in their conservation status. The South Selkirk caribou population that extends into Idaho is listed as an endangered species in the United States. The mountain caribou populations in the southern two-thirds of British Columbia and the caribou in west-central Alberta are listed as threatened in Canada. The status of caribou living in the deep-snow zone of southeastern British Columbia is especially dire. Many of these populations have dramatically decreased in numbers over the past decades, and two have recently been extirpated. Those populations are red-listed (endangered) in British Columbia.

In contrast, populations are not considered to be at risk in Alaska, although populations from northern British Columbia and the Yukon are designated as of Special Concern in Canada. Individual populations have periodically decreased in response to factors such as over-hunting, severe weather, or excessive predation, but overall there is no widespread decrease evident in these populations. The northern populations are managed as a game species by wildlife agencies.

HABITAT

The two constants that drive all caribou are the need to obtain sufficient lichens for winter food and the need to avoid predation throughout the year. Mountain caribou employ a variety of habitat use strategies in different areas to achieve these necessities; conservation of caribou is based on maintaining suitable habitat for caribou to find food and avoid predators.

The key characteristic that differentiates caribou from other ungulate species is their strong dependence on lichens for winter food. Although they will occasionally graze on other plants in winter, lichens dominate their winter diet. In some areas caribou feed almost exclusively on arboreal lichens, but in most areas they feed primarily on terrestrial lichens in winter. Caribou are so reliant on lichen that understanding the ecology of lichens is fundamental to understanding the ecology of mountain caribou.

Arboreal lichens, particularly the genus *Bryoria* that is favoured by caribou, attach and grow best on dead or static bark and are found most abundantly on the dead branches and inner portions of living branches of older trees. *Bryoria* also grows best where there are either frequent changes in humidity or wetting and drying cycles. Consequently, arboreal lichens are most abundant in old, slow-growing, widely spaced forests. Caribou may feed on arboreal lichens in any forest type, but old-growth subalpine forests and black spruce bogs are often favoured by caribou because of their abundance of arboreal lichens.

Terrestrial lichens tend to grow in harsh environments that will not support other ground cover species. On sites with richer soils, mosses or vascular plants will typically displace terrestrial lichens. Terrestrial lichens tend to flourish on rocky outcrops and coarse-textured soils that contain sand and gravel, with little soil organic matter. In the mountains of western North America, caribou typically find abundant terrestrial lichens either on alpine ridges or in pine-lichen or black spruce-lichen forests on poor growing sites.

The destruction of old forests by fire or logging will reduce the amount of arboreal lichens available to caribou. Regenerating forests may take well over a hundred years before they provide large amounts of arboreal lichen. In areas where caribou rely heavily on arboreal lichens for winter forage, complete protection of old-growth forests, or selective cutting of these forests, is used to maintain caribou habitat.

Although wildfires in pine-lichen and spruce-lichen forests will also destroy the terrestrial lichen ground cover, terrestrial lichens will typically recover within a few decades — much faster than arboreal lichens — if the soil and moisture conditions are favourable. Peak abundance of terrestrial lichens occurs in 40- to 120-year-old forests, depending on the growing conditions. Lichen recovery can be faster on logged sites if the terrestrial lichen ground cover is not heavily disturbed. In some forests, terrestrial lichens will decline and virtually be eliminated if the forest becomes too old, because mosses and vascular plants begin to out-compete the terrestrial lichens in older stands. However, this is not always the case, as some forest stands growing on very poor growing sites will continue to provide terrestrial lichens for hundreds of years.

Consequently, some forest stands require periodic disturbance to re-initiate the pattern of forest succession that leads to abundant terrestrial lichen availability. In wilderness landscapes, the frequency and pattern of wildfires determine the amount and distribution of high-quality terrestrial lichens stands within a caribou range. Wildfire may temporarily reduce the availability of terrestrial lichens, but a long absence of fire may also lead to a loss of terrestrial lichens as mosses begin to take over on the forest floor.

In areas where commercial forestry is taking place, the rate and pattern of forest harvesting and fire management practices will determine the amount and distribution of terrestrial lichen habitat. It should be possible for land managers to adapt forest harvesting and fire management practices to ensure a perpetual supply of terrestrial lichen on caribou ranges. Foresters and wildlife biologists are working to develop forest management prescriptions that will do just that, and these plans are being implemented in some areas. However, it will be many years before we can be sure if these habitat management practices are successful at maintaining caribou habitat.

In addition to providing lichens for winter forage, caribou habitat must also be distributed across the landscape in order to provide a refuge from predators. Unlike other large herbivores that share their ranges, caribou are not powerful and dangerous like moose, nor attentive and fast like deer and elk, nor do they use rugged escape terrain like sheep or goats. Rather, they rely primarily on a strategy of minimizing encounters with predators.

Mountain caribou are vulnerable to a wide range of predators, including wolves, bears, cougars, and wolverines. Golden eagles can be a significant predator on young calves. None of these predator species rely on caribou as a sole food source, and caribou are usually only a minor component of their diet. In many areas, wolves are sustained primarily by moose, and caribou are a secondary prey. Cougars feed on deer as their primary prey but will also kill caribou if the opportunity arises. Bears feed primarily on plants, but they can kill caribou and other animals, particularly in the first few week of life when they are most vulnerable. Golden eagles mostly kill ground squirrels and marmots but will also kill caribou calves in summer. Hence, if caribou use habitats where other prey species are scarce, they are less likely to encounter the predators that are associated with those other prey species. Similarly, if they avoid productive growing sites for bear foods, they are less likely to encounter bears. The seasonal movements and habitat selection patterns of mountain caribou combine the need to obtain lichens for winter forage with the need to maintain spatial separation from predators throughout the year.

KEY THREATS

In Alaska, Yukon, and northern British Columbia, mountain caribou are quite abundant, and populations are currently not at risk. Those populations are managed as a game species through standard wildlife management techniques such as hunter-harvest management, predator management, and habitat management. Most of these herds are abundant enough to sustain hunting. Hunting is usually concentrated on males, but in some areas where caribou are very abundant there is also a season for females. Caribou hunting seasons are restricted or closed where caribou numbers are low.

Most of the caribou in the northern portion of mountain caribou distribution live in relatively pristine wilderness conditions. Forestry activities are encroaching on caribou habitat in some areas, but the extent is minor compared to the southern portions of mountain caribou extent of occurrence. However, one of the major habitat protection concerns in the northern region is the development of new roads, which can lead to improved human access and excessive human harvest of previously inaccessible caribou herds.

In southern areas, caribou and their habitat have not fared as well. Over the past century, mountain caribou have declined in or disappeared from many of the areas where they previously occurred. This decline was in part due to over-hunting that started following European settlement and continued until as recently as the 1970s. Another important factor was the increase in other ungulates, in particular moose. Moose were uncommon west of the Rocky Mountains in British Columbia prior to the 1900s. Starting in the early 1900s, moose began to colonize interior British Columbia, and by the 1930s they had spread over most caribou ranges. The cause of this colonization is unclear, but it may have been related to climatic warming following the end of the Little Ice Age. Reports of major declines in caribou corresponded with the arrival of moose from the north, and perhaps with an increase in deer from the south. Caribou disappeared from many of the lower elevation areas where they had previously occurred, with the remaining animals living in more mountainous areas and at higher elevations.

It is believed that the arrival of moose supported an increase in the wolf population, leading to increased predation and a decline in caribou numbers in central British Columbia. The decline was especially pronounced in lower elevation areas where caribou, wolves, and moose would have been in close proximity. Caribou living at higher elevations in the mountains were better able to survive because they could maintain more separation from the moose and wolves living in the valley bottoms. Similarly, the caribou decline in southern British Columbia, where moose are still not abundant, may have in part been due to increased deer and cougar numbers. Cougar are currently the major limiting factor in some of these southern herds.

Although the spatial separation between caribou and moose/wolves in the mountains increases the probability of caribou survival, it is not clear if it is effective enough to allow caribou to be self-sustaining over the long term. Most mountain caribou herds in southern British Columbia have continued to decline. However, the more recent declines are thought to be largely related to ongoing human-caused landscape changes that lead to increased rates of predation on caribou. It will not be possible to determine if caribou populations can become self-sustaining until the negative human-related impacts are reduced or eliminated.

Caribou living on the east side of the Rockies, in British Columbia and Alberta, have also declined over the past decades. Those declines cannot be attributed to moose colonization, because caribou and moose coexisted in those areas prior to European settlement. Consequently, it appears more likely that those declines are related to human activities. Human-caused habitat changes that increase the numbers and efficiency of predators are believed to be the primary cause of declining mountain caribou herds on the east side of the Rockies.

Forest harvesting and other land-clearing activities can affect both the lichen availability and the predation risk for caribou. Historically, caribou in the low snow zones were able to survive in a landscape where wildfires periodically disturbed the forests that provided terrestrial lichens. Some forests actually require periodic disturbance to perpetuate terrestrial lichens. On managed landscapes, forest harvesting is usually the primary disturbance agent on forested winter ranges. Maintaining caribou on managed landscapes requires that the rate and pattern of forest harvesting will provide a perpetual supply of forest stands containing terrestrial lichens. Fire management practices, such as prescribed burning or fire suppression, will also influence the availability of terrestrial lichens on caribou ranges.

In addition to the presence of terrestrial lichen, the pattern and distribution of habitat are also important. Caribou prefer large, contiguous habitats and will avoid fragmented patches created by clear-cuts. A forest landscape that is fragmented by numerous clear-cuts will also have a large number of active roads. Other industrial activities, such as oil and gas development and mining, can also fragment the landscape with roads and linear corridors. Caribou may avoid roads and linear corridors, thereby reducing the amount of usable habitat. More important, caribou have a higher mortality rate from predators when they live in a fragmented landscape. The creation of early succession shrub habitat in clear-cuts and along roads and linear corridors provides habitat for other ungulate species like moose, elk, and deer. The increase in those prey species can draw more predators into caribou habitat, leading to increased predation on caribou. Roads and linear corridors also provide improved access for predators and human hunters into caribou habitat.

Consequently, it is preferable for forest harvesting and other industrial development within caribou habitat to be concentrated into a portion of the range, rather than dispersed over the entire range. This allows other portions of the range to be retained as large, unfragmented patches where caribou can better avoid predators. In the future, when the harvested areas have grown back into suitable caribou habitat, it is hoped that they can effectively replace the previously retained habitat areas.

The management of pine-lichen caribou habitat in western Canada is being threatened by a massive epidemic of mountain pine beetle. The beetle outbreak started in central British Columbia in the 1990s and crossed the Rockies into Alberta in the early 2000s. Large-scale salvage logging is being conducted to recover the timber value from these dead stands. Many central British Columbia caribou herds have had their entire pine-lichen range killed by pine beetles, and caribou habitat east of the Rockies is now being attacked. Caribou continue to use beetle-killed stands for at least the first decade, although over time those stands are likely to deteriorate as the dead trees begin to fall. The management practice that is currently being undertaken is to retain large patches of dead pine to provide habitat for the caribou in the short term and hopefully to sustain the population until the salvaged areas grow back.

The low-elevation forested habitat for mountain caribou within the low snow zone of British Columbia and Alberta is a dynamic ecosystem, subject to large-scale natural disturbances. Human activities have become another significant source of landscape change on caribou ranges. These caribou are adapted to a changing landscape so long as they can always find large patches of suitable habitat within their range. The long-term survival of caribou within this area is dependent on developing and implementing forest and land management practices that provide a perpetual supply of suitable forested habitat.

Until recently, caribou that used windswept alpine ridges to feed on terrestrial lichens in winter faced few threats from human activities. Now, however, mountain caribou are being confronted by a barrage of industrial activities being developed or proposed on alpine winter ranges. These include gas exploration and development, mining (especially coal mining), and major wind farm developments. (The same windy conditions that caribou require to keep the alpine area free of snow for feeding are also attractive to wind farm companies.) Industrial activities in the alpine and subalpine areas can directly destroy habitat by removing the lichen layer, displacing caribou from their preferred habitat, and increasing access for predators. The explosion of interest in developing alpine and subalpine areas is challenging the ability of wildlife managers to adequately protect caribou habitat.

Caribou that live in deep snowfall areas provide a different suite of management issues, as they feed almost exclusively on arboreal lichens in old-growth forests during winter. Protecting those old-growth forests from harvesting and other industrial activities is the best way to maintain the habitat for caribou, and hundreds of thousands of hectares have been protected for caribou in British Columbia. Also, logging methods that remove some of the trees while maintaining others to provide arboreal lichens are used in some areas of caribou habitat. The concern with this approach is that although it provides lichens for the caribou, it may still increase the risk of predation by improving access and drawing other ungulates and predators into the area.

The subalpine forests that are preferred by caribou in winter are also very attractive for snowmobiling and heli-skiing. The popularity of these sports continues to grow, and improved snowmobile technology allows participants to travel to areas that were inaccessible just a decade ago. Unless they are gradually habituated to such disturbances, caribou run away from motorized vehicles or people that approach them too closely. If the level of disturbance becomes very high, the caribou will completely abandon those parts of their range. Thus, low levels of disturbance may disrupt feeding and increase energy expenditures for the caribou. High levels of disturbance can displace the caribou into inferior habitat, where they may experience higher energy costs, reduced nutrition, and/or an increased risk of predation and avalanches.

The tools to reduce disturbance of caribou by recreational users include closing areas to recreational traffic, restricting times of use, and educating users about how to minimize disturbance. However, actually implementing effective management is challenging because commercial and non-commercial recreational users are an influential group and a major economic contributor to many small communities.

Although large amounts of habitat have been protected, caribou populations in much of southeastern British Columbia have continued to decline. The major immediate cause of that decline is predation, related to high predator numbers. In some areas these are primarily wolves being sustained by moose; in other areas it is cougars being sustained by deer and elk. Deer, elk, and moose, unlike caribou, prefer early seral shrubland habitats that are created by logging, fires, and other land-clearing activities.

Historically, the forests in the wet belt of southeastern British Columbia had a very low rate of natural wildfires, resulting in a broad region that was naturally dominated by old-growth forests. Forest harvesting increases the amount of early seral habitat. Even if the entire core caribou habitat is protected, logging in adjacent areas can enhance moose, elk, and deer and thus support increased numbers of predators that will then travel into caribou habitat. Reducing the rate of forest harvesting in areas adjacent to caribou habitat could reduce populations of early seral ungulates and their associated predators, in order to benefit caribou.

The other approach is to directly manage the predator-prey system. Liberal hunting practices could be used to reduce the numbers of moose, elk, and deer, thereby reducing the food supply that supports high predator numbers. This approach is being tried in some areas but has not yet been shown to be effective. Although in some areas sport hunters have greatly reduced the number of early seral ungulates, they may be unable to do so in relatively inaccessible areas.

The most direct way to reduce predators is with a predator control program. A variety of predator management techniques have been used to reduce the rate of predation on mountain caribou herds. Predator management has usually been limited to populations where there is evidence that the caribou numbers have declined and recovery is being limited by predation. The most controversial method has involved shooting wolves from aircraft (primarily helicopters). Although this technique is efficient and can be effective in increasing caribou survival rates, public opposition limits its use. Reproductive control of wolves by conducting vasectomies on male wolves and tubal ligations on females has also been successfully used to reduce wolf numbers and allow caribou populations to increase. A recent approach has been to capture pregnant female caribou just prior to the calving season and hold them in a predator-proof enclosure called a maternity pen. The caribou give birth to their calves in the enclosure and are held there for several weeks to avoid the high level of predation that often occurs on young calves. The technique can increase calf survival, but is obviously very expensive and only a consideration for very small herds.

Relying on direct management of predators and prey, without addressing the early seral habitat on which these species thrive, creates a permanent commitment to ongoing predator-prey management. If the abundance of early seral habitat is not reduced, as soon as predator-prey management is stopped predators and prey will increase in response to the favourable habitat conditions, and the problem with excessive predation on caribou will return.

In some situations, however, habitat management alone may not be adequate. If a caribou range currently has an excessive amount of early seral habitat and/or roads, even if the decision is made to stop any further development, it could take several decades for the habitat to recover. In the meantime, directly reducing the number of predators may be necessary if the caribou herd is to be maintained. Some environmental organizations have accepted the need for temporary predator control to save critically endangered caribou herds, but only if it is used as an interim measure while habitat and the caribou are recovering.

As we look to the future, climate change will likely further compromise caribou recovery actions in the south and threaten the viability of herds farther to the north. Warmer temperatures, shorter winters, and more wildfires would create conditions favouring ungulates that prefer younger forests, at the expense of caribou. In areas where mountain caribou occur, the distribution of deer and elk has been expanding and may continue to expand northward. Eventually, changes to the predator-prey system may affect northern caribou herds, putting their current abundance and security at risk. If so, the need for more intensive conservation efforts to maintain caribou across their ranges will continue to grow.

Dave Gustine

APPENDIX A

Useful Links Relevant to Caribou Conservation, Research, and Management in North America

GOVERNMENT AGENCIES RESPONSIBLE FOR CARIBOU	WEBSITE ADDRESSES
Alaska Department of Fish and Game	http://www.adfg.state.ak.us
Alberta Sustainable Resource Development, Fish and Wildlife	http://srd.alberta.ca/fishwildlife/
British Columbia Ministry of Environment, Fish and Wildlife Branch	http://www.env.gov.bc.ca/fw
Committee on the Status of Endangered Wildlife in Canada (COSEWIC)	http://www.cosewic.gc.ca/
Canadian Wildlife Service (CWS)	http://www.cws-scf.ec.gc.ca/
Environment Saskatchewan– Wildlife Management Unit	http://www.environment.gov.sk.ca/
Indian and Northern Affairs Canada	http://www.ainc-inac.gc.ca/
Manitoba Conservation, Wildlife and Ecosystem Protection Branch	http://www.gov.mb.ca/conservation/wildlife/
Ministère des Ressources naturelles et de la Faune du Québec:	http://www.mrnf.gouv.qc.ca/
Newfoundland and Labrador Department of Environment and Conservation	http://www.env.gov.nl.ca/
Nunavut Avatiliqiyikkut (Department of Environment)	http://www.gov.nu.ca/env/
Northwest Territories Department of Environment and Natural Resources, Wildlife Division	http://www.nwtwildlife.com/

Ontario Ministry of Natural Resources	http://www.mnr.gov.on.ca/
Parks Canada	http://www.pc.gc.ca/
Species at Risk Public Registry (Government of Canada)	http://www.sararegistry.gc.ca/
U.S. Fish and Wildlife Service, Endangered Species Program	http://www.fws.gov/Endangered/wildlife.html
U.S. National Park Service	http://www.nps.gov/
U.S. Fish and Wildlife Service	http://www.fws.gov
U.S. National Wildlife Refuges	http://www.fws.gov/refuges
Yukon Department of Environment, Wildlife and Biodiversity	http://www.environmentyukon.gov.yk.ca/ wildlifebiodiversity

NORTH AMERICAN CARIBOU MANAGEMENT BOARDS

Beverly and Qamanirjuaq Caribou Management Board	http://www.arctic-caribou.com
Porcupine Caribou Management Board	http://www.taiga.net/pcmb/

ABORIGINAL ORGANIZATIONS WITHIN CARIBOU DISTRIBUTION

Akaitcho Treaty 8 First Nations:	http://www.akaitcho.info
Alaska Federation of Natives	http://www.nativefederation.org/
Assembly of Manitoba Chiefs	http://www.manitobachiefs.com/
Centre for Indigenous Environmental Resources	http://www.cier.ca/
Le Comité conjoint de chasse de pêche et de piégeage	http://www.cccpp-hftcc.com/
Dehcho First Nations	http://www.dehchofirstnations.com
Dene Nation	http://www.denenation.com
Grand Council of the Crees (Quebec)	http://www.gcc.ca/
Gwich'in First Nations	http://www.gwichin.org
Gwich'in Renewable Resources Board	http://www.grrb.nt.ca
Innu Nation	http://www.innu.ca
Inuvialuit Game Council	http://www.jointsecretariat.ca/gc
Inuvialuit Wildlife Management Advisory Council (NWT)	http://www.jointsecretariat.ca/wmacnwt
Kaska Dena Council	http://www.kaskadenacouncil.com/
National Aboriginal Forestry Association	http://www.nafaforestry.org/
Nishnawbe Aski Nation (NAN), James Bay Treaty 9	http://www.nan.on.ca/
Northern Nations Alliance	http://northernnations.ca/
North Slope Borough	http://www.north-slope.org

Nunatsiavut Government (Labrador Inuit Association) http://www.nunatsiavut.com/
Nunavut Planning Commission http://www.npc.nunavut.ca
Nunavut Tunngavik Incorporated http://www.tunngavik.com
Nunavut Wildlife Management Board http://www.nwmb.com
Sahtu First Nations http://www.sahtu.ca
Sahtu Renewable Resources Board http://www.srrb.net.ca
Teslin Tlingit Council http://www.ttc-teslin.com/
Tlicho First Nations http://www.tlicho.ca/
Treaty 8 First Nations of Alberta http://www.treaty8.ca/
Ukpequik Inupiat Corporation http://www.ukpik.com
Wabanong Nakaygum Okimawin (WNO) http://www.gov.mb.ca/conservation/wno/
Wek'èezhìi Renewable Resources Board http://www.wrrb.ca
Whitefeather Forest Initiative http://www.whitefeatherforest.com

NON-GOVERNMENT/RESEARCH ORGANIZATIONS WITH SOME FOCUS ON CARIBOU

Alaska Coalition http://www.alaskacoalition.org/
Alberta Wilderness Association http://www.albertawilderness.ca/
Canadian Boreal Initiative http://www.borealcanada.ca
Canadian Forest Network http://www.forest.ca
Canadian Wildlife Federation http://www.cwf-fcf.org/
Center for Biological Diversity http://www.biologicaldiversity.org/
CARC (Canadian Arctic Resources Committee) http://www.carc.org/
CPAWS (Canadian Parks and Wilderness Society) http://www.cpaws.org
    (with chapters in NWT, YK, BC, AB, SK,
    MB, ON, NF)
David Suzuki Foundation http://www.davidsuzuki.org/
Defenders of Wildlife (U.S. and Canada offices) http://www.defenders.org
Ducks Unlimited http://www.ducks.org
Ducks Unlimited Canada http://www.ducks.ca
Ecojustice Canada http://www.ecojustice.ca/
Ecotrust Canada http://www.ecotrust.ca/
Forest Ethics http://www.forestethics.org
Forest Stewardship Council of Canada http://www.fsccanada.org/
Global Forest Watch Canada http://www.globalforestwatch.ca/
Greenpeace Canada http://www.greenpeace.ca
Initiative for Responsible Mining Assurance http://www.responsiblemining.net/
International Boreal Conservation Campaign http://www.interboreal.org
Manitoba Wildlands http://manitobawildlands.org/

Mining Watch Canada	http://www.miningwatch.ca/
Mushkegowuk Environmental Research Centre	http://www.merc.ontera.net/
National Audubon Society	http://www.audubon.org/
National Council for Air and Stream Improvement, Inc.	http://www.ncasi.org/
Nature Canada	http://www.naturecanada.ca
Nature Conservancy of Canada	http://www.natureconservancy.ca
NRDC (Natural Resources Defense Council)	htpp://www.nrdc.org
Nature Québec	http://www.naturequebec.org/
Oil Sands Watch	http://www.oilsandswatch.org/
Ontario Nature	http://www.ontarionature.org/
Pembina Institute	http://www.pembina.org/
Réseau Québécois Groupes des Écologistes	http://www.rqge.koumbit.org/
Saskatchewan Environmental Society	http://www.environmentalsociety.ca/
Sierra Club of Canada	http://www.sierraclub.ca
Sierra Club U.S	http://www.sierraclub.org
The Nature Conservancy	http://www.nature.org
Trustees for Alaska	http://www.trustees.org
WCS (Wildlife Conservation Society)	http://www.wcs.org
WCS Canada	http://www.wcscanada.org
Wilderness Society	http://www.wilderness.org
WWF (World Wildlife Fund)	http://www.wwf.org
WWF-Canada	http://www.wwf.ca
WWF-US	http://www.worldwildlife.org
Yukon Conservation Society	http://www.yukonconservation.org/

NATIONAL INDUSTRY ASSOCIATIONS (CANADIAN) AND SOME COMPANIES OPERATING WITHIN CARIBOU DISTRIBUTION

Alberta-Pacific Forest Industries, Inc.	http://www.alpac.ca/
Areva Canada	http://www.arevacanada.ca
BHP Billiton Ekati Diamond Mine	http://www.ekati.bhpbilliton.com
BP America in Alaska	http://www.bp.com/alaska
Cameco Corporation:	http://www.cameco.com
Canadian Association of Petroleum Producers	http://www.capp.ca/
ConocoPhillips-Alaska	http://www.conocophillipsalaska.com/
DeBeers Canada	http://www.debeerscanada.com
Diavik Diamond Mine	http://www.diavik.ca
Domtar Inc:	http://www.domtar.com
Forest Products Association of Canada	http://www.fpac.ca/

Mining Association of Canada	http://www.mining.ca/www/
Prospectors and Developers Association of Canada	http://www.pdac.ca/
Suncor Energy Inc.	http://www.suncor.com
Tembec, Inc.	http://www.tembec.com

OTHER CARIBOU-RELATED PROJECTS

Being Caribou	http://www.beingcaribou.com
Boreal Caribou Research Program (Alberta)	http://www.deer.rr.ualberta.ca/caribou/bcrp.htm
Canadian BEACONs Project (University of Alberta)	http://www.ales2.ualberta.ca/rr/beacons/
Caribou Migration Animations for the NWT (8 herds)	http://www.mwtwildlife.com/nwtwildlife/caribou/animation.htm
Caribou Migration Animations for Nunavut (3 herds)	http://www.arctic-caribou.com/Journey/
CircumArctic Rangifer Monitoring and Assessment Network (CARMA)	http://www.rangifer.net/carma
Foothills Model Forest Woodland Caribou Program (Alberta)	http://www.fmf.ca/pa_WC.html
Human Role in Reindeer / Caribou Systems (University of Alaska-Fairbanks)	http://www.rangifer.net/rangifer/about.cfm
Manitoba Model Forest Woodland Caribou Research Initiative	http://www.manitobamodelforest.net/caribou.html
Sustainable Forest Management Network	http://www.sfmnetwork.ca/

APPENDIX B

Data Sources for Maps

MOST MAPS APPEARING in this volume contain the current caribou distribution in North America either as part of the map or in an inset map. Current caribou distribution is the summed distribution of three caribou ecotypes: migratory tundra, boreal forest, and mountain. The authors wish to make note of the fact that the distribution and individual population ranges of caribou depicted in these maps represent the most current information; these will undoubtedly undergo changes in the future as new and better information is collected and/or as caribou distribution and individual ranges themselves shift with time.

1) **Migratory tundra caribou distribution and ranges**: Shapefiles compiled from CircumArctic Rangifer Monitoring and Assessment Network (CARMA), Figure 2, in Abraham, K.F., Thompson, J.E. Defining the Pen Islands caribou herd of Southern Hudson Bay. *Rangifer Special Issue* 10: 33–40 (1998), and Figure 4 in Harris, A. *Report on the Status of Woodland Caribou in Ontario*. Report for the Committee on the Status of Species at Risk in Ontario, Ontario Ministry of Natural Resources, 1999. Ranges were modified with new information from Government of Northwest Territories, Government of Nunavut, Government of Quebec, and Manitoba Conservation.

2) **Boreal forest caribou distribution and ranges**: Shapefiles compiled by Canadian BEACONS Project, University of Alberta (April 2007, modified November 2007) from: National Boreal Caribou Technical Steering Committee – Environment Canada. 2006. National Recovery Strategy for Woodland Caribou (*Rangifer tarandus caribou*), Boreal Population. Draft for consultation intended for the Species at Risk Act Recovery Strategy Series. Ottawa: Environment Canada. Additional modifications from Government of Quebec and Government of Newfoundland and Labrador with further credit to Department of National Defence, Parks Canada, Institute for Environmental

Monitoring and Research, Newfoundland and Labrador Hydro, Government of Quebec.

3) **Mountain caribou distribution and ranges**: BC Ministry of Environment, Government of British Columbia; Alaska Department of Fish and Game, and Yukon Department of Environment, Fish and Wildlife Branch, Yukon Government.

The southern extent of historical (ca. 1880's) distribution of caribou in North America appears in Maps 1.3, 2.3, 2.4, 2.5, 2.11, 2.12, 3.1, 3.2, 4.2.4, and 4.3.3. This line is derived from the following source: Kelsall, J. P. *Status Report on the Woodland Caribou Rangifer tarandus dawsonii and Rangifer tarandus caribou*. Ottawa: Committee on the Status of Endangered Wildlife in Canada, 1984, and British Columbia Ministry of the Environment.

Additional information that is in maps appearing in this book is derived from the following sources:

The "Natural Earth" background image that appears in Maps 1.1, 1.3, 1.4, 1.5, 1.6, 1.7, 1.8, 1.9, 2.1, 2.2, 2.3, 2.4, 2.5, 2.8 (inset only), 2.9, 2.10, 2.11, 2.12, 4.1.1, 4.1.2, 4.1.3, 4.1.4, 4.1.5, 4.1.7, 4.1.8 (inset only), 4.2.1, 4.2.2 (inset only), 4.2.3 (inset only), 4.2.4, 4.2.5, 4.3.1, 4.3.2, 4.3.3 was created by Tom Patterson, US National Park Service.

MAP 1.1. Eurasian range from: *Family-Based Reindeer Herding and Hunting Economies, and the Status and Management of Wild Reindeer/Caribou Populations, A Report to the Sustainable Development Working Group of the Arctic Council*, edited by Birgitte Ulvevadet and Konstantin Klokov, Centre for Saami Studies, University of Tromsø, 2004.

MAP 1.2. Terrestrial Ecosystems of the World – Version 2.0, 2004 World Wildlife Fund – US.

MAP 1.5. M. Boulet, S. Couturier, S.D. Côté, R. D. Otto, and L. Bernatchez. Integrative use of spatial, genetic, and demographic analyses for investigating genetic connectivity between migratory, montane, and sedentary caribou herds. *Molecular Ecology* 16: 4223–4240 (2007); R. Courtois, J.P.Ouellet, L. Breton, A. Gingras, and C. Dussault. Effects of forest disturbance on density, space use, and mortality of woodland caribou. *EcoScience* 14:491–98 (2007).

MAP 1.7. Data analysis performed by Isabelle Schmelzer and Rebecca Jeffery, Wildlife Division, Department of Environment and Conservation, Government of Newfoundland and Labrador. Data ownership: Department of Environment and Conservation, Government of Newfoundland and Labrador; Department of National Defence, Goose Bay; Institute for Environmental Monitoring and Research, Goose Bay.

MAP 1.8. A.J. Magoun, K.F. Abraham, J.E. Thompson, J.C. Ray, M.E. Gauthier, G.S. Brown, G. Woolmer, C.J. Chenier, and F.N. Dawson. Distribution and relative abundance of caribou in the Hudson Plains Ecozone of Ontario, *Rangifer* Special Issue No. 16: 105–121 (2005).

MAP 1.9. J.C. Morrison, W. Sechrest, E. Dinerstein, D.S. Wilcove, and J.F. Lamoreux. Persistence of large mammal faunas as indicators of global human impacts. *Journal of Mammalogy*, 88: 1363–1380 (2007).

MAP 1.10. Compiled by James A. Schaefer.

MAP 2.1. Canadian fire data source from: Canada Large Fire Database, Canadian Forest Service (2005), and Alaska fire history from: Bureau of Land Management, Alaska Fire Service (2007).

MAP 2.2. Mountain Pine Beetle Data from: British Columbia Forest Service (2007).

MAP 2.3. Gray wolf, grizzly bear (Yellowstone region), and elk: A.S. Laliberte and W.J. Ripple: Range contractions of North American carnivores and ungulates, *BioScience*, Vol. 54 No. 2, 2004; Grizzly Bear (outside of Yellowstone): J. Kansas. *Status of the Grizzly Bear (Ursus arctos) in Alberta.* Wildlife Status Report No. 37, Edmonton: Alberta Sustainable Resource Development, Fish and Wildlife Division, and Alberta Conservation Association, 2002. Wolverine: current distribution: The Wolverine Foundation, Inc.; historical distribution: COSEWIC. *COSEWIC Assessment and Update Status Report on the Wolverine Gulo gulo in Canada.* Ottawa: Committee on the Status of Endangered Wildlife in Canada, 2003.

MAP 2.4. CANFI forest forest data from: J.J. Lowe; S.L Gray; K. Power. Canada's forest inventory 1991: the 1994 version. Canadian Forest Service, Pacific Forestry Centre Information Report BC-X-362E, 1996. Agricultural data from: Statistics Canada – Catalogue No. 92F0175GIE, Agricultural Ecumene Census Division Boundary File, 2001 Census of Agriculture.

MAP 2.5. CANFI forest data from: J.J. Lowe; S.L. Gray; K. Power. Canada's forest inventory 1991: the 1994 version. Canadian Forest Service, Pacific Forestry Centre Information Report BC-X-362E, 1996. Agricultural data from: Statistics Canada – Catalogue No. 92F0175GIE Agricultural Ecumene Census Division Boundary File, 2001 Census of Agriculture. Road data from: Global Forest Watch Canada using copyright data supplied by DMTI Spatial.

MAP 2.6. The Wilderness Society; Northern Alaska Environmental Center; Alaska Center for the Environment.

MAP 2.7. The Wilderness Society; Northern Alaska Environmental Center; Alaska Center for the Environment.

MAP 2.8. Original maps and analysis performed by Global Forest Watch Canada using copyright data supplied by DMTI Spatial (roads), IHS Energy (petroleum and natural gas wellsites) NTS 1:250,000 mapsheets (seismic). Additional road data from: National Road Network, AB version 4.0 -Government of Canada, Natural Resources Canada, Earth Sciences Sector, Mapping Services Branch, Centre for Topographic Information- Sherbrooke, 2007-06-20; Road Network File, Catalogue No. 92-500-

GIE, Statistics Canada, 2006. Human disturbance and intact forest landscape data from: Global Forest Watch Canada.

MAP 2.9. Indian and Northern Affairs Canada, 2008.

MAP 2.10. Indian and Northern Affairs Canada, 2008.

MAP 2.11. Committee on the Status of Endangered Wildlife in Canada, 2008; U.S. Fish and Wildlife Service, 2008.

MAP 3.1. World Wildlife Fund-Canada. The Nature Audit, Report No. 1. Toronto: World Wildlife Fund-Canada, 2003.

MAP 3.2. World Wildlife Fund-Canada. The Nature Audit, Report No. 1. Toronto: World Wildlife Fund-Canada, 2003.

MAP 4.1.2. Calving areas: CircumArctic Rangifer Monitoring and Assessment Network (CARMA), A. Gunn and B. Fournier. Identification and substantiation of caribou calving grounds on the NWT mainland and islands. Department of Resources, Wildlife and Economic Development, Government of the Northwest Territories, 2000, and A.J. Magoun, K.F. Abraham, J.E. Thompson, J.C. Ray, M.E. Gauthier, G.S. Brown, G. Woolmer, C.J. Chenier, and F.N. Dawson. Distribution and relative abundance of caribou in the Hudson Plains Ecozone of Ontario, *Rangifer Special Issue* No. 16: 105-121, 2005.

MAP 4.1.3. Department of Environment and Natural Resources, Government of Northwest Territories.

MAP 4.1.4. CAVM Team. *Circumpolar Arctic Vegetation Map.* Scale 1:7,500,000. Conservation of Arctic Flora and Fauna (CAFF) Map No. 1. Anchorage, Alaska: U.S. Fish and Wildlife Service, 2003.

MAP 4.1.7. Modified from the Length of Available Growing Period grid dataset, United Nations Environment Program (UNEP), 2002. Food and Agriculture Organization of the United Nations FAO SDRN Working Series Paper No. 10, 2002.

MAP 4.1.8. Telemetry data source: Brent Patterson and Mathieu Dumond – Nunavut.

MAP 4.2.2. W. Kent Brown.

MAP 4.2.3. Newfoundland and Labrador Wildlife Division.

MAP 4.2.4. J.P. Kelsall. *Status report on the woodland caribou Rangifer tarandus dawsonii and Rangifer tarandus caribou.* Ottawa: Committee on the Status of Endangered Wildlife in Canada, 1984.

REFERENCES

Below are listed the key sources that were consulted in the preparation of this manuscript, including those that were referred to directly. They are a sampling of the many books, articles, and reports that have been written on caribou and related topics in North America and Europe.

BOOKS AND BOOK CHAPTERS

Banfield, A.W.F. *The Mammals of Canada.* Toronto: University of Toronto Press, 1974.

Bergerud, A.T. "The role of the environment in the aggregation, movement, and disturbance behaviour of caribou." In *The Behaviour of Ungulates and its Relation to Management*, edited by V. Geist and F.R. Walther, 552–584. Morges: IUCN. 1974.

Bergerud, A.T. "Caribou." In *Ecology and Management of Large Mammals in North America*, edited by S. Demarais and P.R. Krausman, 658–693. Upper Saddle River: Prentice Hall, 2000.

Bergerud, A.T., Luttich, S.N. and Camps, L. *The Return of Caribou to Ungava*. Montreal and Kingston: McGill-Queen's University Press, 2008.

Bielawski, E. *Rogue Diamonds.* Vancouver: Douglas & McIntyre, 2003.

Calef, G.W. *Caribou and the Barren-lands*. Ottawa: Canadian Arctic Resources Committee; Toronto: Firefly Books, 1981.

Dugmore, A.R. *The Romance of the Newfoundland Caribou : An intimate account of the life of the reindeer of North America*. Philadelphia: J.B. Lippincott Co., 1913.

Formozov, A.N. "Snow cover as an integral factor of the environment and its importance in the ecology of mammals and birds." Edmonton: Boreal Institute for Northern Studies, 1964.

Hall, A. *Discovering Eden.* Toronto: Key Porter Books, 2003.

Heuer, K. *Being Caribou.* Seattle: The Mountaineers Books, 2005.

Kelsall, J.P. *The Caribou.* Ottawa: Queen's Printer, 1968.

Leopold, A.S. *A Sand County Almanac (1949) with Essays on Conservation from Round River (1953).* New York: Oxford University Press, 1966.

Leopold, A.S. and Darling, F.F. *Wildlife in Alaska.* New York: Ronald Press, 1953.

Loo, T. States of Nature: *Conserving Canada's Wildlife in the Twentieth Century.* Vancouver: UBC Press, 2006.

Madsen, K. *Under the Arctic Sun.* Englewood, Colorado: EarthTales Press, 2002.

Miller, F.L. "Caribou, *Rangifer tarandus.*" In *Wild Mammals of North America: Biology, Management, and Economics,* edited by J.A. Chapman and G.A. Feldhammer, 923–959. Baltimore: Johns Hopkins University, 1982.

Lytwyn, V.P. *Muskekowuck Athinuwick: Original People of the Great Swampy Land.* Winnipeg: University of Manitoba Press, 2002.

Murie, O.J. *Alaska-Yukon Caribou. North American Fauna.* Washington, DC: United States Department of Agriculture, 1935.

Ray, J.C., Redford, K.H., Steneck, R.S., and Berger, J. *Large Carnivores and the Conservation of Biodiversity.* Washington, D.C.: Island Press, 2005.

Sandlos, J. *Hunters at the Margin: Native People and Wildlife Conservation in the Northwest Territories.* Vancouver: UBC Press, 2007.

REPORTS

Alberta Woodland Caribou Recovery Team. *Alberta Woodland Caribou Plan 2004/05–2013/14.* Edmonton: Alberta Sustainable Resource Development, Fish and Wildlife Division, 2004.

Arctic Climate Impact Assessment (ACIA). *Arctic Climate Impact Assessment — Scientific Report.* Cambridge, UK: Cambridge University Press, 2005.

References

Arthur, S.M. and Del Vecchio, P.A. *Effects of Oil Field Development on Calf Production and Survival in the Central Arctic Herd.* Interim Research Technical Report. Juneau: Alaska Department of Fish and Game, 2007.

Beverly and Qamanirjuaq Caribou Management Board. *Economic Valuation and Socio-Cultural Perspectives of the Estimated Harvest of the Beverly and Qamanirjuaq Caribou Herds.* Stonewall, Manitoba, 2008.

Beverly and Qamanirjuaq Caribou Management Board. *Protecting Calving Grounds, Post-Calving Areas, and Other Important Habitats for Beverly and Qamanirjuaq Caribou; A Position Paper.* Stonewall, Manitoba, 2004.

Broadhead, J. "Haida Gwaii and the Extinction of Dawson Caribou." Unpublished. Toronto: WWF-Canada.

Carlson, M., Bayne, E., and Stelfox, B. *Seeking a Balance: Assessing the Future Impacts of Conservation and Development in the Mackenzie Watershed.* Ottawa: Canadian Boreal Initiative, 2007.

Clarke, C.H.D. "A biological investigation of the Thelon Game Sanctuary." Ottawa: National Museum of Canada, Biological Series no. 25, Bulletin no. 96, 1940.

COSEWIC. *COSEWIC Assessment and Update Status Report on the Peary Caribou Rangifer tarandus pearyi and the Barren-ground Rangifer tarandus groenlandicus (Dolphin and Union population) in Canada.* Ottawa: Committee on the Status of Endangered Wildlife in Canada, 2004.

COSEWIC. *COSEWIC Assessment and Update Status Report on the Woodland Caribou Rangifer tarandus caribou in Canada.* Ottawa: Committee on the Status of Endangered Wildlife in Canada, 2002.

Crichton, V., Whaley, K., Cross, D., Collins, G., Hedman, D., and Leavesley, K. *A Reference Document for Manitoba's Boreal Woodland Caribou (Rangifer tarandus caribou) Strategy.* Winnipeg: Manitoba Conservation, 2004.

Dzus, E. *Status of the Woodland Caribou (Rangifer tarandus caribou) in Alberta.* Wildlife Status Report No. 30. Edmonton: Alberta Environment, Fisheries and Wildlife Management Division, and Alberta Conservation Association, 2001.

Environment Canada. *The Identification of Critical Habitat for Woodland Caribou (Rangifer tarandus caribou), Boreal Population, in Canada.* Ottawa: Environment Canada, 2008.

Field, C.B., Mortsch, L.D., Brklacich, M., Forbes, D.L., Kovacs, P., Patz, J.A., Running, S.W., and Scott, M.J. "North America: Climate change impacts, adaptation and vulnerability." Contribution of Working Group II to the *Fourth Assessment Report of the Intergovernmental Panel on Climate Change*, edited by Parry, M.L., Canziani, O.F., Palutikof, J.P., van der Linden, P.J., and Hanson, C.E., 617–652. Cambridge, UK: Cambridge University Press, 2007.

Global Forest Watch Canada. *Recent Anthropogenic Changes within the Boreal Forests of Ontario and Their Potential Impacts on Woodland Caribou.* Edmonton: Global Forest Watch Canada, 2007.

Government of the Northwest Territories, Environment and Natural Resources. *Caribou Forever-Our Heritage, Our Responsibility: A Barren-ground Caribou Management Strategy for the Northwest Territories, 2006-2010.* Yellowknife: Government of the Northwest Territories, 2005.

Government of the Northwest Territories, Environment and Natural Resources. *NWT Barren-ground Caribou Summit Report.* Yellowknife: Government of the Northwest Territories, 2007.

Gray, T. "Woodland Caribou: The Politics of Conservation." Unpublished. Toronto: WWF-Canada.

Griffith, B., Douglas, D.C., Walsh, N.E., Young, D.D., McCabe, T.R., Russell, D.E., White, R.G., Cameron, R.D., and Whitten K. R. "The Porcupine caribou herd," edited by Douglas, D.C., Reynolds, P.E., and Rhode, F.B., 8–37. *Arctic Refuge Coastal Plain Terrestrial Wildlife Research Summaries*, USGS Biological Science Report, USGS/BRD/BSR-2002-0001, 2002.

Griffith, R. "Lutsel K'e Dene and Caribou." Unpublished. Toronto: WWF-Canada, 2007.

Gunn, A. and Fournier, B. *Identification and Substantiation of Caribou Calving Grounds on the NWT Mainland and Islands.* Department of Resources, Wildlife and Economic Development, Government of the Northwest Territories, 2000.

Hall, A. "The Great Herd." Unpublished. Toronto: WWF-Canada, 2007.

Hall, A. "The Value of Caribou." Unpublished. Toronto: WWF-Canada, 2007.

Harris, A. *Report on the Status of Woodland Caribou in Ontario.* Status Report prepared for Committee on the Status of Species at Risk in Ontario. Toronto: Ontario Ministry of Natural Resources, 1999.

Innes, L. "The Innu and Caribou." Unpublished. Toronto: 2007.

Kelsall, J. P. *Status Report on the Woodland Caribou Rangifer tarandus dawsonii and Rangifer tarandus caribou.* Committee on the Status of Endangered Wildlife in Canada, Ottawa, 1984.

Kofinas, G. and Russell, D.E., "North America," in *Family-Based Reindeer Herding and Hunting Economies, and the Status and Management of Wild Reindeer/Caribou Populations,* A Report to the Sustainable Development Working Group of the Arctic Council, edited by B. Ulvevadet and K. Klokov, 21–52. University of Tromsø: Centre for Saami Studies, 2004.

Manitoba Conservation. *Manitoba's Conservation and Recovery Strategy for Boreal Woodland Caribou,* Winnipeg: Manitoba Conservation, 2005.

Mountain Caribou Technical Advisory Committee. *A Strategy for the Recovery of Mountain Caribou in British Columbia.* Victoria: British Columbia Ministry of Water, Land and Air Protection, 2002.

National Council for Air and Stream Improvement, Inc. (NCASI). *Ecological interactions among caribou, moose, and wolves: Literature review.* Technical Bulletin No. 893. Research Triangle Park, N.C.: National Council for Air and Stream Improvement, Inc., 2004.

National Council for Air and Stream Improvement, Inc. (NCASI). *A review of ungulate nutrition and the role of top-down and bottom-up forces in woodland caribou population dynamics.* Technical Bulletin No. 934. Research Triangle Park, N.C.: National Council for Air and Stream Improvement, Inc., 2007.

Pelly, D. "Inuit and Caribou." Unpublished. Toronto: WWF–Canada, 2007.

Russell, D.E., Kofinas, G., and Griffith, B. *Barren-ground Caribou Calving Ground Workshop: Report of the Proceedings.* Technical Report Series Number 390. Ottawa: Canadian Wildlife Service, 2002.

Schmelzer, I., Brazil, J., Chubbs, J.T., French, S., Hearn, B., Jeffery, R., LeDrew, L., Martin, H., McNeill, A., Nuna, R., Otto, R., Phillips, F. , Mitchell, G., Pittman, G., Simon, N., and Yetman, G. *Recovery Strategy for Three Woodland Caribou Herds (Rangifer tarandus caribou; Boreal population) in Labrador.* Corner Brook: Department of Environment and Conservation, Government of Newfoundland and Labrador, 2004.

Spalding, D.J. *The early history of woodland caribou (Rangifer tarandus caribou) in British Columbia.* Victoria: British Columbia Ministry of Environment, Lands and Parks, 2000.

Stevenson, S.K., Armleder, H.M., Jull, M.J., King, D.G., McLellan, B.N., and Coxson, D.S. *Mountain caribou in managed forests: recommendations for managers, second edition.* Wildlife Report No. R-26. Victoria: Ministry of Environment, Lands and Parks, 2001.

Stewart, Andrew M. "Canadian Inuit Response to Changing Resource Availability on the Kazan River, Northwest Territories, Canada." Ph.D. thesis. Santa Barbara: University of California, 1993.

Tesar, C. "What Price the Caribou?" *Northern Perspectives,* Vol. 31, No. 1, Spring 2007. Ottawa: Canadian Arctic Resources Committee, 2007.

Weaver, J.L. *Big Animals and Small Parks: Implications of Wildlife Distribution and Movements for Expansion of Nahanni National Park Reserve.* Wildlife Conservation Society Canada Conservation Report No. 1. Toronto: WCS Canada, 2006.

Weaver, J.L. *Conserving Caribou Landscapes in the Nahanni-Trans-Border Region: Using Fidelity to Seasonal Ranges and Migration Routes.* Wildlife Conservation Society Canada Conservation Report No. 4. Toronto: WCS Canada, 2008.

Wenzel, G.W. "From TEK to IQ: Inuit Qaujimajatuqangit and Inuit Cultural Ecology." *Arctic Anthropology,* Vol 41, No 2. University of Wisconsin, 2004.

Whitefeather Forest Management Corporation (WFMC). *Keeping Woodland Caribou on the Land: Cross-cultural Research on the Whitefeather Forest.* Draft Report. Pikangikum, Ontario: WFMC, 2006.

WWF-Canada. *Canadian Living Planet Report 2007*. Toronto: WWF-Canada, 2007.

WWF-Canada. *The Nature Audit*. Report No. 1. Toronto: WWF-Canada, 2003.

JOURNAL ARTICLES

Adams L.G., Singer F.J., and Dale, B.W. Caribou calf mortality in Denali National Park, Alaska. *Journal of Wildlife Management* 59:584–594 (1995).

Apps, C.D., McLellan, B.N., Kinley, T.A., and Flaa, J.P. "Scale-dependent habitat selection by mountain caribou, Columbia Mountains, British Columbia." *Journal of Wildlife Management* 65: 65–77 (2001).

Armstrong, T., Racey, G., and Bookey, N. "Landscape-level considerations in the 1288 management of forest-dwelling woodland caribou (*Rangifer tarandus caribou*) in northwestern Ontario." *Rangifer* 12: 187–189 (2000).

Banfield, A.W.F. "Preliminary investigation of the barren ground caribou. Part I. Former and present distribution, migrations, and status." *Canadian Wildlife Service Wildlife Management Bulletin* Series 1, no. 10A (1954).

Banfield, A.W.F. "A revision of the reindeer and caribou genus *Rangifer*." *National Museum Of Canada Bulletin* No. 177 (1961).

Berger, J. "The last mile: how to sustain long distance migration in mammals." *Conservation Biology* 18: 320–331 (2004).

Bergerud, A.T. "The population dynamics of Newfoundland caribou." *Wildlife Monographs* 25: 1–55 (1971).

Bergerud, A.T. "Decline of caribou in North America following settlement." *Journal of Wildlife Management* 38: 757–770 (1974).

Bergerud, A.T. "Caribou, wolves, and man." *Trends in Ecology and Evolution* 3: 68–72 (1988).

Bergerud, A.T. "Evolving perspectives on caribou population dynamics: Have we got it right yet?" *Rangifer* 9: 95–116 (1996).

Bergerud, A.T., Jakimchuk, R.D., and Carruthers, D.R. "The buffalo of the north: caribou (*Rangifer tarandus*) and human developments." *Arctic* 37: 7–22 (1984).

Bergerud, A.T. and Elliot, J.P. "Dynamics of caribou and wolves in northern British Columbia." *Canadian Journal of Zoology* 64: 1515–1529 (1986).

References

Bergerud, A.T. and Mercer, W.E. "Caribou introductions in eastern North America." *Wildlife Society Bulletin* 17: 111–120 (1989).

Bergerud A.T. and Page, R.E. "Displacement and dispersion of parturient caribou at calving as an antipredator tactic." *Canadian Journal of Zoology* 65:1597–1606 (1987).

Boertje, R., Valkenburg, P., and McNay, M.E. "Increase in moose, caribou and wolves following wolf control in Alaska." *Journal of Wildlife Management* 60: 474–489 (1996).

Boudreau, S., Payette, S., Morneau, C., and Couturier, S. "Recent decline of the George River herd as revealed by tree-ring analysis." *Arctic, Antarctic, and Alpine Research* 35: 187–195 (2003).

Boulet, M., Couturier, S., Côté, S.D., Otto, R.D., and Bernatchez, L. "Integrative use of spatial, genetic, and demographic analyses for investigating genetic connectivity between migratory, montane, and sedentary caribou herds." *Molecular Ecology* 16: 4223–4240 (2007).

Cameron, R.D., Smith, W.T., White, R.G., and Griffith, B. "Central arctic caribou and petroleum development: distributional, nutritional, and reproductive implications." *Arctic* 58: 1–9 (2005).

Cardillo, M., Mace, G.M., Gittleman, J.L., and Purvis, A. "Latent extinction risk and the future battlegrounds of mammal conservation." *Proceedings of the National Academy of Sciences* 103: 4157–4161 (2006).

Courtois, R., Ouellet, J.P., Gringas, A., Dussault, C., Breton, L., and Maltais, J. "Historical changes and current distribution of caribou, *Rangifer tarandus*, in Québec." *Canadian Field Naturalist* 117: 399–414 (2003).

Courtois, R., Ouellet, J.P., Breton, L., Gingras, A., and Dussault, C. "Effects of forest disturbance on density, space use, and mortality of woodland caribou." *Ecoscience* 14: 491–498 (2007).

Couturier, S., Brunelle, J., Vandal, D., and St. Martin, G. "Changes in the population dynamics of the George River caribou herd 1976-87." *Arctic* 43: 9–20 (1990).

Darby, W.R. and Pruitt, W.O. "Habitat use, movements and grouping behaviour of woodland caribou, *Rangifer tarandus caribou*, in southeastern Manitoba." *Canadian Field Naturalist* 98: 184–190 (1984).

Duchesne, M., Côté, S.D., and Barrette, C. "Responses of woodland caribou to winter ecotourism in the Charlevoix Biosphere Reserve, Canada." *Biological Conservation* 96: 311–317 (2000).

Dunford, J. S., McLoughlin, P. D., Dalerum, F., and Boutin, S. "Lichen abundance in the peatlands of northern Alberta: implications for boreal caribou." *Écoscience* 13: 469–474 (2006).

Dyer, S.J., O'Neil, J.P., Wasel, S.M., and Boutin, S. "Avoidance of industrial development by woodland caribou." *Journal of Wildlife Management* 65: 531–542 (2001).

Edmonds, E.J. "Population status, distribution, and movements of woodland caribou in west-central Alberta." *Canadian Journal of Zoology* 66:817–826 (1988).

Ferguson, S.H. and Elkie, P.C. "Habitat requirements of boreal forest caribou during the travel seasons." *Basic and Applied Ecology* 5: 465–474 (2004).

Ferguson, S.H. and Elkie, P.C. "Seasonal movement patterns of woodland caribou (*Rangifer tarandus caribou*)." *Journal of Zoology*, London 262: 125–134 (2004).

Ferguson, S.H. and Elkie, P.C. "Use of lake areas in winter by woodland caribou." *Northeastern Naturalist* 12: 45–66 (2005).

Fuller, T.K. and Keith, L.B. "Woodland Caribou Population Dynamics in Northeastern Alberta." *Journal of Wildlife Management* 45: 197–213 (1981).

Gunn, A. "Voles, lemmings and caribou — population cycles revisited?" *Rangifer* Special Issue 14: 105–112 (2003).

Gunn, A., Miller F.L., and Thomas, D.C. "The current status and future of Peary caribou Rangifer tarandus pearyi on the arctic islands of Canada." *Biological Conservation* 19: 283–296 (1980).

Gunn, A. and Miller, F.L. "Traditional behaviour and fidelity to calving grounds b barren-ground caribou." *Rangifer*, Special Issue 1: 151–158 (1986).

Harrington, F.H. and Veitch, A.M. "Short-term impacts of low-level jet fighter training on caribou in Labrador." *Arctic* 44: 318–327 (1992).

Hayes, R.D., Farnell, R., Ward, R.M.P., Carey, J., Den, M., Kuzyk, G.W., Baer, A.M., Gardner, G.L., and O'Donoghue, M. "Experimental reduction of wolves in the Yukon: ungulate responses and management implications." *Wildlife Monographs* No. 152 (2003).

Heard, D.C. and Vagt, K.L. "Caribou in British Columbia: a 1996 status report." *Rangifer* Special Issue 10:177–123 (1998).

Hinzman, L.D., Bettez, N.D., Bolton, W. R., Chapin, F. S., Dyurgerov, M. B., Fastie, C. L., Griffith, B., Hollister, R.D., Hope, A., Huntington, H. P., Jensen, A. M., Jia, G.J., Jorgenson, T., Kane, D.L., Klein, D.R., Kofinas, G., Lynch, A.H., Lloyd, A.H., McGuire, A.D., Nelson, F.E., Nolan, M., Oechel, W.C., Osterkamp, T.E., Racine, C.H., Romanovsky, V.E., Stone, R.S., Stow, D.A., Sturm, M., Tweedie, C.E., Vourlitis, G.L., Walker, M.D., Walker, D.A., Webber, P.J., Welker, J., Winker, K.S., and Yoshikawa, K. "Evidence and implications of recent climate change in northern Alaska and other arctic regions." *Climatic Change* 72: 251–298 (2005).

James, A.R.C., Boutin, S., Hebert, D.M., and Rippin, A.B. "Spatial segregation of caribou from moose and its relation to predation by wolves." *Journal of Wildlife Management* 68: 799–809 (2004).

References

Johnson C.J., Parker K.L., Heard, D.C. "Foraging across a variable landscape: behavioral decisions made by woodland caribou at multiple spatial scales." *Oecologia* 127: 590–602 (2004).

Johnson C.J., Seip, D.R., and Boyce, M.S. "A quantitative approach to conservation planning: using resource selection functions to map the distribution of mountain caribou at multiple spatial scales." *Journal of Applied Ecology* 41: 238–251 (2004).

Johnson, C.J., Boyce, M.S., Case, R.L., Cluff, H.D., Gau, R.J., Gunn, A., Mulders, R. "Cumulative effects of human developments on arctic wildlife." *Wildlife Monographs* 160: 1–36 (2005).

Joly K., Nellemann, C., Vistnes, I. "A re-evaluation of caribou distribution near an oilfield road on Alaska's north slope." *Wildlife Society Bulletin* 34: 866–869 (2006).

Kinley, T.A. and Apps, C.D. "Mortality patterns in a subpopulation of endangered mountain caribou." *Wildlife Society Bulletin* 29:158-164 (2001).

Kinley, T.A., Bergenske, J., Davies, J., and Quinn D. "Characteristics of early-winter caribou, *Rangifer tarandus caribou*, feeding sites in the southern Purcell Mountains, British Columbia." *Canadian Field Naturalist* 117:352–359 (2003).

Laliberte, A.S. and Ripple, W.J. "Range contractions of North American carnivores and ungulates." *BioScience* 54: 123–138 (2004).

Lenton, T.M., Held, H., Kriegler, E., Hall, J.W., Lucht, W., Rahmstorf, S., and Schellnhuber, J. "Tipping elements in the earth's climate system." *Proceedings of the National Academy of Sciences* 105: 1786–1793 (2008).

Leroux, S.J., Schmiegelow, F.K.A., and Nagy, J.A. "Potential spatial overlap of heritage sites and protected areas in a boreal region of northern Canada." *Conservation Biology* 21: 376–386 (2007).

Magoun, A.J., Abraham, K.F., Thompson, J.E., Ray, J.C., Gauthier, M.E., Brown, G.S., Woolmer, G., Chenier, C.J., and Dawson, F.N. "Distribution and relative abundance of caribou in the Hudson Plains Ecozone of Ontario." *Rangifer* 16: 105–121 (2005).

Mahoney, S.P. and Schaefer, J.A. "Long-term changes in demography and migration of Newfoundland caribou." *Journal of Mammalogy* 83: 957–963 (2002).

Maier, J.A.K., Murphy, S.M., White, R.G., and Smith, M.D. "Responses of caribou to overflights by low-altitude jetcraft." *Journal of Wildlife Management* 62: 752–766 (1998).

Manseau, M., Huot, J., and Crête, M. "Effects of summer grazing by caribou on composition and productivity of vegetation: community and landscape level." *Journal of Ecology* 84: 503–513 (1996).

Martin, R.A. and Sneed, J.M. "Late Pleistocene records of caribou and elk from Georgia and Alabama." *Georgia Journal of Science* 47: 117–122 (1989).

McLoughlin, P.D., Dzus, E., Wynes, B., and Boutin, S. "Declines in populations of woodland caribou." *Journal of Wildlife Management* 67: 755–761 (2003).

Messier, F., Hout, J., Le Hénaff, D., and Luttich, S. "Demography of the George River caribou herd: evidence of population regulation by forage exploitation and range expansion." *Arctic* 41: 279–287 (1988).

Miller, F.L., Russell, R.H., and Gunn, A. "Inter-island movements of Peary caribou (*Rangifer tarandus pearyi*) on western Queen Elizabeth Islands, Arctic Canada." *Canadian Journal of Zoology* 55: 1029–37 (1977).

Morneau, C. and Payette, S. "Long-term fluctuations of caribou populations revealed by tree-ring data." *Canadian Journal of Zoology* 78: 1784–1790 (2000).

Morrison, J.C., Sechrest W., Dinerstein, E., Wilcove, D.S., and Lamoreux, F.J. "Persistence of large mammal faunas as indicators of global human impacts." *Journal of Mammalogy*, 88: 1363–1380 (2007).

Musiani, M., Leonard, J.A., Cluff, H.D., Gates, C.G., Mariani, S., Paquet, P.C., Vilá, C., and Wayne, R.K. "Differentiation of tundra/taiga and boreal coniferous forest wolves: genetics, coat colour and association with migratory caribou." *Molecular Ecology* 16: 4149–4170 (2007).

O'Flaherty, R.M., Davidson-Hunt, I.J., and Manseau, M. "Indigenous knowledge and values in planning for sustainable forestry: Pikangikum First Nation and the Whitefeather Forest Initiative." *Ecology and Society* 13: 6 [online] (2008).

Peterson A.T., Martinez-Meyer, E., Gonzalez-Salazar, C., and Hall, P.W. "Modeled climate change effects on distributions of Canadian butterfly species." *Canadian Journal of Zoology* 82: 851–858 (2004).

Post, E. and Forchhammer, M.C. "Climate change reduces reproductive success of an Arctic herbivore through trophic mismatch." *Philosophical Transactions of the Royal Society of London B (Biological Sciences)* 363: 2369–75 (2008).

Racey, G.D. "Climate change and woodland caribou in northwestern Ontario: a risk analysis." *Rangifer* Special Issue 16: 123–136 (2005).

Racey, G.D. and Armstrong, T. "Woodland caribou range occupancy in northwest Ontario: past and present." *Rangifer* Special Issue 12: 173–184 (2000).

Rettie, W.J. and Messier, F. "Dynamics of woodland caribou populations at the southern limit of their range." *Canadian Journal of Zoology* 76: 251–259 (1998).

Rettie, W.J., and Messier, F. "Hierarchical habitat selection by woodland caribou: its relationships to limiting factors." *Ecography* 23: 466–478 (2000).

Ritchie, J., Slade, B., and Wagner, F.H. "Management of small populations -concepts affecting the recovery of endangered species." *Wildlife Society Bulletin* 22: 307–316 (1994).

Rominger, E.M. and Oldemeyer, J.L. "Early-winter habitat of woodland caribou, Selkirk Mountains, British Columbia." *Journal of Wildlife Management* 53, 238–243 (1989).

Rominger, E.M., Robbins, C.T., Evans, M.A., and Pierce, D.J. "Autumn foraging dynamics of woodland caribou in experimentally manipulated habitats, northeastern Washington." *Journal of Wildlife Management* 64, 160–167 (2000).

Schaefer, J.A. "Long-term range recession and the persistence of caribou in the taiga." *Conservation Biology* 17: 1435–1439 (2003).

Schaefer, J.A. and Pruitt, W.O. "Fire and woodland caribou in southeastern Manitoba." *Wildlife Monographs* 116: 1–39 (1991).

Schaefer, J.A., Veitch, A.M., Harrington, F.H., Brown, W.K., Theberge, J.B., and Luttich, S.N. "Demography of decline of the Red Wine Mountains caribou herd." *Journal of Wildlife Management* 63: 580–587 (1999).

Schaefer, J.A., Bergman, C.M., and Luttich, S.N. "Site fidelity of female caribou at multiple spatial scales." *Landscape Ecology* 15: 731–739 (2000).

Schaefer, J.A., and Mahoney, S.P. "Effects of progressive clearcut logging on Newfoundland Caribou." *Journal of Wildlife Management* 71: 1753–1757 (2007).

Seip, D. R. "Factors limiting woodland caribou populations and their interrelationships with wolves and moose in southeastern British Columbia." *Canadian Journal of Zoology* 20: 1494–1503 (1992).

Seip, D.R., Johnson, C.J., and Watts, G.S. "Displacement of mountain caribou from winter habitat by snowmobiles." *Journal of Wildlife Management* 71: 1539–1544 (2007).

Serrouya, R., McLellan, B.N., and Flaa, J.P. "Scale-dependent microhabitat selection by threatened mountain caribou (*Rangifer tarandus caribou*) in cedar-hemlock forests during winter." *Canadian Journal of Forest Research* 37:1082–1092 (2000).

Smith, K.G., Ficht, E.J., Hobson, D., Sorenson, T.C., and Hervieux, D. "Winter distribution of woodland caribou in relation to clear-cut logging in west-central Alberta." *Canadian Journal of Zoology* 78: 1433–1440 (2000).

Sorensen, T., McLoughlin, P.D., Hervieux, D., Dzus, E., Nolan, J., Wynes, B., and Boutin, S. "Determining sustainable levels of cumulative effects for Boreal caribou." *Journal of Wildlife Management* 72: 900–905 (2008).

Stuart-Smith, A.K., Bradshaw, C.J.A., Boutin, S., Hebert, D.M., and Rippin, A.B. "Woodland caribou relative to landscape patterns in Northeastern Alberta." *Journal of Wildlife Management* 61: 622–633 (1997).

Terry, E.L., McLellan, B.N., and Watts, G.S. "Winter habitat ecology of mountain caribou in relation to forest management." *Journal of Applied Ecology* 37:589–602 (2000).

Thuiller, W. "Climate change and the ecologist." *Nature* 448: 550–552 (2007).

Valkenburg, P. "Stumbling towards enlightenment: understanding caribou dynamics." *Alces* 37: 457–474 (2001).

Vistnes, I. and Nellemann, C. "The matter of spatial and temporal scales: a review of reindeer and caribou response to human activity." *Polar Biology* 31: 399–407 (2008).

Vors, L.S., Schaefer, J.A., Pond, B.A., Rodgers, A.R., and Patterson, B.R. "Woodland caribou extirpation and anthropogenic landscape disturbance in Ontario." *Journal of Wildlife Management*. 71: 1249–1256 (2007).

Walsh, N.E., Fancy, S.G., McCabe, T.R., and Pank, L.F. "Habitat use by the porcupine caribou herd during predicted insect harassment." *Journal of Wildlife Management*. 56: 465–473 (1992).

Warren, J.M., Peeks, J.M., Servheen, G.L., and Zager, P. "Habitat use and movement of two ecotypes of translocated caribou in Idaho and British Columbia." *Conservation Biology* 10: 547–553 (1996).

Wenzel, G.W. "From TEK to IQ: Inuit Qaujimajatuqangit and Inuit cultural ecology." *Arctic Anthropology* 41: 238–250 (2004).

Wittmer, H.U., Sinclair, A.R., and McLellan, B.N. "The role of predation in the decline and extirpation of woodland caribou." *Oecologia* 114: 257–267 (2005).

Wittmer, H.U., McLellan, B.N., Seip, D.R., Young, J.A., McKinley, T.A., Watts, G.S., and Hamilton, D. "Population dynamics of the endangered mountain ecotype of woodland caribou (*Rangifer tarandus caribou*) in British Columbia, Canada." *Canadian Journal of Zoology* 83: 407–418 (2005).

Wittmer, H.U., McLellan, B.N., Serrouya, R., and Apps, C.D. "Changes in landscape composition influence the decline of a threatened woodland caribou population." *Journal of Animal Ecology* 76: 568–579 (2007).

LIST OF CONTRIBUTING
PHOTOGRAPHERS

PHOTOGRAPHER/WEBSITE   **PAGE NO**

Elena Jones   pp. 31, 119, 124, 241

Alex Kammer   p. 39
    Alex Kammer Photography
    http://www.alexkammerphotography.com/

Michael A. Lookman   pp. 94, 158

Clinton D. Long   p. 54
    The Wolverine Foundation
    http://www.wolverinefoundation.org/

Andrew Leith Macrae   pp. 76, 95, 135
    Advent Media
    http://www.adventmedia.net/

Tessa McIntosh   pp. 60, 64
    Tessa McIntosh Photography
    flickr.com/photos/tmacfoto

John A. Nagy   pp. 56, 103, 123, 125, 146, 223
    Government of Northwest Territories

Paul Nicklen   pp. 97, 212
    Paul Nicklen Photography
    http://www.paulnicklen.com/

Katherine Parker   p. 34
    University of Northern British Columbia

Jay and Carolyn Pritchett   pp. 34, 40, 91

Justina C. Ray   pp. 74, 187
    WCS Canada

Jiri Rezac   p.116(2)
    WWF/Polaris

Andrew J. Silver   pp. 2, 3

ACKNOWLEDGEMENTS

FIRST, WE THANK Anna Porter for her sage advice and guidance in the conceptual stages of this book, and Kirk Howard at Dundurn Press for his warm reception of our project when we first approached him.

We are indebted to Robert Redford and Stephen Kakfwi for providing such fine Forewords, and for their personal efforts on behalf of caribou. Both of these men go well beyond the label of "celebrity," to making bona fide contributions for caribou conservation. Similarly, Robert Bateman, who puts his art to work for the wildlife he portrays, created his wonderful "caribou quartet" of sketches for the special purpose of introducing each of the four major sections of this book. He also generously donated the originals to WWF/WCS as fundraisers for caribou.

We thank Anne Gunn, James Schaefer, Dale Seip, and Bruce McLellan for their excellent caribou ecotype profiles found in Section Four, and Fiona Schmiegelow who joined them in providing wise counsel on the structure and organization of this key section. Each of these individuals has spent a lifetime studying caribou; some even had books of their own in mind, but instead threw their lot in with us, which is much appreciated.

Chris McDougall worked tirelessly to help us chase data and create beautiful maps with diligence and enduring patience. James Snider produced several maps himself; he and Gillian Woolmer provided additional critical assistance with this monumental task. Chris Brackley from As the Crow Flies cARTography offered important cartographic advice and played a critical role in getting the maps ready for press. Peter Lee of Global Forest Watch Canada made himself generously available at a moment's notice to incorporate key advice and data for the map-making enterprise. Marilyn Katsabas provided general support in manuscript preparation, in particular with organizing photographs. And Patricia Buckley patiently assisted with obtaining photo images and permissions.

Ray Griffith, David Pelly, Larry Innes, and Alex Hall all contributed written reflections regarding the importance of caribou to people, and Norma Kassi kindly consented to an interview on the same subject, all of whom we heavily quoted in Chapter Four. We also appreciate permission from the elders of Pikangikum to include their perspectives from northwestern Ontario.

We thank Tim Gray for his hard-won thoughts on policy matters related to boreal forest caribou, and John Broadhead for sleuthing out the fate of the Dawson caribou on Haida Gwaii (Queen Charlotte Islands). Ken Whitten and David Klein took the time to provide additional insights regarding caribou in Alaska.

We are indebted to the many photographers who contributed their work that helped bring the accompanying text alive. Steven Barger's gorgeous photo of caribou in Denali National Park, Alaska, graces the cover. He contributed additional images, as did the following individuals: Ken Abraham, Roy Andresen, Rock Arssenault, Suzanne Barger, Kim Bennett, Lonnie Brock, George Calef, Sarah Couchie, Serge Couturier, Vince Crichton, Adele Curtis, Mathieu Dumond, Tyler Garnham, Glen and Rebecca Grambo, Dave Gustine, Alex Hall, Jeremy Harrison, Elena Jones, Alex Kammer, Michael Lookman, Clinton Long, Andrew Leith Macrae, Tessa McIntosh, John Nagy, Paul Nicklen, Katherine Parker, Jay and Carolyn Pritchett, Andrew Silver, David Tilley, Liv Vors, Julie Yamaguchi, and Paul Zakora. Thank you all. We hope your fine photographs, and the patient hours and days it took to obtain them, will now be put to work to help conserve what you have captured so well. Sean Kollee, Joan Kuyek, Jenni McDermid, Robert Powell, and Kimberley Tremblay provided additional help in leading us to just the right images.

We extend our appreciation to all the individuals and their agencies who provided supporting information and files: Jan Adamczewski, Alan Baldivieso, Mitch Campbell, Jeff Copeland, Rehaume Courtois, Serge Couturier, Vince Crichton, Brad Cundiff, Mathieu Dumond, Katherine Egli, Pete Ewins, Susan Fleck, Anne Gunn, Matt Hanneman, Eleanor Huffines, Larry Innes, Deborah Johnson, Evangelos (Van) Kirizopoulos, Peter Lee, Kim Lisgo, Judy and Clint Long, Gillian McEachern, Bruce McLellan, Alexis Morgan, Tom Paragi, Aran O'Carroll, Rachel Plotkin, Don Reid, Don Russell, James Schaefer, Isabelle Schmelzer, Fiona Schmiegelow, Wes Sechrest, Dale Seip, James Snider, Pat Valkenburg, Leslie Wakelyn, and Adrian Walton. Each of you provided valuable assistance in chasing down information to help maximize the accuracy of the maps that appear in our book.

We thank Biz Agnew, Anne Gunn, Leslie Wakelyn, Alex Hall, James Schaefer, Fiona Schmiegelow, and Steve Zack for reviewing all or portions of the manuscript, which collectively improved the quality of the final product.

At Dundurn Press, Beth Bruder provided enthusiastic leadership in the development of our book, Barry Jowett steadfast counsel on editorial matters, and Jennifer Scott did a masterful job on the design and layout.

Thanks are due to our families, who endured the personal fallout of having one member sealed away, working on "the book." A special thanks from Monte to Sherry Pettigrew who made up for what he does not know about computers, which is considerable. Justina extends her love and appreciation to Jay and Kai Malcolm at home, and to the staff of WCS Canada in Toronto for tolerating and supporting the intense pace of the last six months.

We have tried to do justice to an iconic and fascinating animal that will test society's resolve to maintain large natural areas right across northern North America. In undertaking this challenging task, we take full responsibility for any errors, or any emphasis that betrays our personal backgrounds and work experience.

MONTE HUMMEL AND JUSTINA C. RAY

INDEX